THE CHRYSOSTOM BIBLE
A Commentary Series for Preaching and Teaching
2 Corinthians: A Commentary

THE CHRYSOSTOM BIBLE
A Commentary Series for Preaching and Teaching

2 Corinthians: A Commentary

Paul Nadim Tarazi

OCABS PRESS
ST PAUL, MINNESOTA 55124
2013

THE CHRYSOSTOM BIBLE
2 CORINTHIANS: A COMMENTARY

Copyright © 2013 by
Paul Nadim Tarazi

ISBN 1-60191-021-5

All rights reserved.

PRINTED IN THE UNITED STATES OF AMERICA

Other Books by the Author

I Thessalonians: A Commentary

Galatians: A Commentary

The Old Testament: An Introduction
Volume 1: Historical Traditions, revised edition
Volume 2: Prophetic Traditions
Volume 3: Psalms and Wisdom

The New Testament: An Introduction
Volume 1: Paul and Mark
Volume 2: Luke and Acts
Volume 3: Johannine Writings
Volume 4: Matthew and the Canon

The Chrysostom Bible
Genesis: A Commentary
Philippians: A Commentary
Romans: A Commentary
Colossians & Philemon: A Commentary
1 Corinthians: A Commentary
Ezekiel: A Commentary
Joshua: A Commentary

Land and Covenant

The Chrysostom Bible
2 Corinthians: A Commentary

Copyright © 2013 by Paul Nadim Tarazi
All rights reserved.

ISBN 1-60191-021-5

Published by OCABS Press, St. Paul, Minnesota.
Printed in the United States of America.

Books are available through OCABS Press at special discounts for bulk purchases in the United States by academic institutions, churches, and other organizations. For more information please email OCABS Press at press@ocabs.org.

Abbreviations

Books by the Author

1 Thess	*I Thessalonians: A Commentary,* Crestwood, NY: St. Vladimir's Seminary Press, 1982
Gal	*Galatians: A Commentary,* Crestwood, NY: St. Vladimir's Seminary Press, 1994
OTI₁	*The Old Testament: An Introduction, Volume 1: Historical Traditions,* revised edition, Crestwood, NY: St. Vladimir's Seminary Press, 2003
OTI₂	*The Old Testament: An Introduction, Volume 2: Prophetic Traditions,* Crestwood, NY: St. Vladimir's Seminary Press, 1994
OTI₃	*The Old Testament: An Introduction, Volume 3: Psalms and Wisdom,* Crestwood, NY: St. Vladimir's Seminary Press, 1996
NTI₁	*The New Testament: An Introduction, Volume 1: Paul and Mark,* Crestwood, NY: St. Vladimir's Seminary Press, 1999
NTI₂	*The New Testament: An Introduction, Volume 2: Luke and Acts,* Crestwood, NY: St. Vladimir's Seminary Press, 2001
NTI₃	*The New Testament: An Introduction, Volume 3: Johannine Writings,* Crestwood, NY: St. Vladimir's Seminary Press, 2004
NTI₄	*The New Testament: An Introduction, Volume 4: Matthew and the Canon,* St. Paul, MN: OCABS Press, 2009
C-Gen	*Genesis: A Commentary.* The Chrysostom Bible. St. Paul, MN: OCABS Press, 2009
C-Phil	*Philippians: A Commentary.* The Chrysostom Bible. St. Paul, MN: OCABS Press, 2009
C-Rom	*Romans: A Commentary.* The Chrysostom Bible. St. Paul, MN: OCABS Press, 2010
C-Col	*Colossians & Philemon: A Commentary.* The Chrysostom Bible. St. Paul, MN: OCABS Press, 2010
C-1Cor	*1 Corinthians: A Commentary.* The Chrysostom Bible. St. Paul, MN: OCABS Press, 2011
C-Ezek	*Ezekiel: A Commentary.* The Chrysostom Bible. St. Paul, MN: OCABS Press, 2012
C-Josh	*Joshua: A Commentary.* The Chrysostom Bible. St. Paul, MN: OCABS Press, 2013
LAC	*Land and Covenant,* St. Paul, MN: OCABS Press, 2009

Abbreviations

Books of the Old Testament*

Gen	Genesis	Job	Job	Hab		Habakkuk
Ex	Exodus	Ps	Psalms	Zeph		Zephaniah
Lev	Leviticus	Prov	Proverbs	Hag		Haggai
Num	Numbers	Eccl	Ecclesiastes	Zech		Zechariah
Deut	Deuteronomy	Song	Song of Solomon	Mal		Malachi
Josh	Joshua	Is	Isaiah	Tob		Tobit
Judg	Judges	Jer	Jeremiah	Jdt		Judith
Ruth	Ruth	Lam	Lamentations	Wis		Wisdom
1 Sam	1 Samuel	Ezek	Ezekiel	Sir	Sirach	(Ecclesiasticus)
2 Sam	2 Samuel	Dan	Daniel	Bar		Baruch
1 Kg	1 Kings	Hos	Hosea	1 Esd		1 Esdras
2 Kg	2 Kings	Joel	Joel	2 Esd		2 Esdras
1 Chr	1 Chronicles	Am	Amos	1 Macc		1 Maccabees
2 Chr	2 Chronicles	Ob	Obadiah	2 Macc		2 Maccabees
Ezra	Ezra	Jon	Jonah	3 Macc		3 Maccabees
Neh	Nehemiah	Mic	Micah	4 Macc		4 Maccabees
Esth	Esther	Nah	Nahum			

Books of the New Testament

Mt	Matthew	Eph	Ephesians	Heb	Hebrews
Mk	Mark	Phil	Philippians	Jas	James
Lk	Luke	Col	Colossians	1 Pet	1 Peter
Jn	John	1 Thess	1 Thessalonians	2 Pet	2 Peter
Acts	Acts	2 Thess	2 Thessalonians	1 Jn	1 John
Rom	Romans	1 Tim	1 Timothy	2 Jn	2 John
1 Cor	1 Corinthians	2 Tim	2 Timothy	3 Jn	3 John
2 Cor	2 Corinthians	Titus	Titus	Jude	Jude
Gal	Galatians	Philem	Philemon	Rev	Revelation

*Following the larger canon known as the Septuagint.

Contents

Preface	*15*
Introduction	*19*
Chapter 1	*21*
Vv. 1-11	21
Vv. 12-22	37
Chapter 2	*57*
1:23-24	57
2:1-11	57
Vv. 12-17	63
Chapter 3	*69*
Vv. 1-3	69
Vv. 4-11	73
Vv. 12-18	86
Chapter 4	*99*
Vv. 1-6	99
Vv. 7-15	110
Chapter 5	*121*
4:16-18	121
5:1-5	128
Vv. 6-10	132
Vv. 11-21	134
Chapter 6	*143*
Vv. 1-2	143
Vv. 4-10	144
Vv. 11-13	146
Vv. 14-18	148

7:1	*148*
Chapter 7	***153***
Vv. 2-16	*153*
Chapter 8	***161***
Vv. 1-4	*161*
Vv. 6-7	*164*
Vv. 8-15	*168*
Vv. 16-24	*170*
Chapter 9	***175***
Vv. 1-15	*175*
Chapter 10	***181***
Vv. 1-6	*181*
Vv. 7-11	*185*
Vv. 12-18	*188*
Chapter 11	***193***
Vv. 1-15	*193*
Vv. 16-20	*201*
Vv. 21-33	*205*
Chapter 12	***211***
Vv. 1-6	*211*
Vv. 7-10	*213*
Vv. 11-21	*216*
Chapter 13	***223***
Vv. 1-10	*223*
Vv. 11-14	*227*
Further Reading	***231***
COMMENTARIES AND STUDIES	*231*
ARTICLES	*232*

Preface

The present Bible Commentary Series is not so much in honor of John Chrysostom as it is to continue and promote his legacy as an interpreter of the biblical texts for preaching and teaching God's congregation, in order to prod its members to proceed on the way they started when they accepted God's calling. Chrysostom's virtual uniqueness is that he did not subscribe to any hermeneutic or methodology, since this would amount to introducing an extra-textual authority over the biblical texts. For him, scripture is its own interpreter. Listening to the texts time and again allowed him to realize that "call" and "read (aloud)" are not interconnected realities; rather, they are one reality since they both are renditions of the same Hebrew verb *qara'*. Given that words read aloud are words of instruction for one "to do them," the only valid reaction would be to hear, listen, obey, and abide by these words. All these connotations are subsumed in the same Hebrew verb *šama'*. On the other hand, these scriptural "words of life" are presented as readily understandable utterances of a father to his children (Isaiah 1:2-3). The recipients are never asked to engage in an intellectual debate with their divine instructor, or even among themselves, to fathom what he is saying. The Apostle to the Gentiles followed in the footsteps of the Prophets to Israel by handing down to them the Gospel, that is, the Law of God's Spirit through his Christ (Romans 8:2; Galatians 6:2) as fatherly instruction (1 Corinthians 4:15). He in turn wrote readily understandable letters to be read aloud. It is in these same footsteps that Chrysostom followed, having learned from both the Prophets and Paul that the same "words of life" carry also the sentence of death at the hand of the scriptural God, Judge of all

(Deuteronomy 28; Joshua 8:32-35; Psalm 82; Matthew 3:4-12; Romans 2:12-16; 1 Corinthians 10:1-11; Revelation 20:11-15).

While theological debates and hermeneutical theories come and go after having fed their proponents and their fans with passing human glory, the Golden Mouth's expository homilies, through the centuries, fed and still feed myriads of believers in so many traditions and countries. Virtually banned from dogmatic treatises, he survives in the hearts of "those who have ears to hear." His success is due to his commitment to exegesis rather than to futile hermeneutics. The latter behaves as someone who dictates on a living organism what it is supposed to be, whereas exegesis submits to that organism and endeavors to decipher it through trial and error. There is as much a far cry between the text and the theories about it as there is between a living organism and the theories about it. The biblical texts are the reality of God imparted through their being read aloud in the midst of the congregation, disregarding the value of the sermon that follows. The sermon, much less a theological treatise, is at best an invitation to hear and obey the text. Assessing the shape of an invitation card has no value whatsoever when it comes to the dinner itself; the guests are fed by the dinner, not by the invitation or its phrasing (Luke 14:16-24; Matthew 22:1-14).

This commentary series does not intend to promote Chrysostom's ideas as a public relation manager would do, but rather to follow in the footsteps of his approach as true children and heirs are expected to do. He used all the contemporary tools at his disposal to communicate God's written instruction to his hearers, as a doctor would with his patients, without spending unnecessary energy on peripheral debates requiring the use of professional jargon incomprehensible to the commoner. The writers of this series will try to do the same: muster to the best of their ability all necessary contemporary knowledge to communicate to the general readers the biblical message without burdening them with data unnecessary for that purpose. Whenever it will be deemed necessary or even helpful to do so, and in order to curtail burdensome and lengthy technical asides within the commentaries, specialized monographs related either to specific topics or to the scriptural background—literary, socio-political, or archeological—will be issued as companions to the series.

Paul Nadim Tarazi
Editor

Introduction

The study of 2 Corinthians has been plagued with the unwarranted premise that the Corinthian correspondence contains different letters sent out on different occasions. The premise sounds convincing because several times one hears reference to Paul having written to the Corinthians (1 Cor 5:9; 2 Cor 2:2-3; 7:12), if not outright to "letters" (1 Cor 5:9; 2 Cor 7:8; 10:9-11). The extent to which this theory took a tight hold on New Testament scholarship is most evident in the 1985 publication of Hans Dieter Betz, *2 Corinthians 8 and 9: Commentary on Two Administrative Letters of the Apostle Paul* in one of the most prestigious Bible Commentary series, Hermeneia. However, when one deals with the New Testament books as *literature*, then one will realize that reference to something "written" is a mere literary stratagem to draw the hearer's attention to the importance of what is being "said." The breaking up of the intended canonical "division" of the New Testament into books results in the destruction of the intended canonical "oneness" of that literary corpus. After all, why not consider, as some do, that one lengthy letter to the Corinthians was split into two due to its size? On the other hand, even such a stand is a surmise since it cannot account for 1 and 2 Thessalonians, 1 and 2 Timothy, 1 and 2 Peter, and—even more à propos—1, 2, and 3 John.

A closer hearing of the Thessalonian correspondence will readily reveal that the second letter is dedicated to the judgment at Christ's coming (ch.1), which coming did not take place but still lies ahead (ch.2); in the meantime the Thessalonians are to continue working in order to earn their living (3:6-15). Such is clearly a more detailed re-visitation of the last parts of the first letter (4:11-5:11). A similar scheme can be detected in the Corinthian correspondence. The first letter is an appeal to unity around the Pauline teaching that is shared with all present during the common meal. In the last chapter (16) Paul reminds the Corinthians that the oneness is to be all inclusive, encompassing Jew as well as Gentile. Although the Jewish Jerusalemite leadership is opposed to such, nevertheless the Gentiles are still bound by their apostle's commitment at the Jerusalem meeting to "remember the poor, which very thing I was eager to do" (Gal 2:10) through a weekly collection whose proceeds he would carry to those leaders. The second letter revisits that topic in a very lengthy manner detailing the reality of the matter: Paul's "ministry" (*diakonia*) in which the Corinthians share is one of "fellowship" (*koinōnia*) around "the Lord" he is "imparting" among the Gentiles the way one imparts bread (1 Cor 11:23-26), unto the life of "all": "There is neither Jew nor Greek, there is neither slave nor free, there is neither male nor female;[1] for you are all one in Christ Jesus. And if you are Christ's, then you are Abraham's offspring, heirs according to promise." (Gal 3:28-29).

In this commentary series, I have included both Greek and English texts for each verse. The English is the RSV translation, which I have been using in my writings. In my comments, however, I often defer to the Greek with my own translation in order to render the meaning as close as possible to the original text.

---

[1] The original has "there is no male and female."

Chapter 1

Vv. 1-11 ¹Παῦλος ἀπόστολος Χριστοῦ Ἰησοῦ διὰ θελήματος θεοῦ καὶ Τιμόθεος ὁ ἀδελφὸς τῇ ἐκκλησίᾳ τοῦ θεοῦ τῇ οὔσῃ ἐν Κορίνθῳ σὺν τοῖς ἁγίοις πᾶσιν τοῖς οὖσιν ἐν ὅλῃ τῇ Ἀχαΐᾳ, ²χάρις ὑμῖν καὶ εἰρήνη ἀπὸ θεοῦ πατρὸς ἡμῶν καὶ κυρίου Ἰησοῦ Χριστοῦ. ³ Εὐλογητὸς ὁ θεὸς καὶ πατὴρ τοῦ κυρίου ἡμῶν Ἰησοῦ Χριστοῦ, ὁ πατὴρ τῶν οἰκτιρμῶν καὶ θεὸς πάσης παρακλήσεως, ⁴ ὁ παρακαλῶν ἡμᾶς ἐπὶ πάσῃ τῇ θλίψει ἡμῶν εἰς τὸ δύνασθαι ἡμᾶς παρακαλεῖν τοὺς ἐν πάσῃ θλίψει διὰ τῆς παρακλήσεως ἧς παρακαλούμεθα αὐτοὶ ὑπὸ τοῦ θεοῦ. ⁵ ὅτι καθὼς περισσεύει τὰ παθήματα τοῦ Χριστοῦ εἰς ἡμᾶς, οὕτως διὰ τοῦ Χριστοῦ περισσεύει καὶ ἡ παράκλησις ἡμῶν. ⁶ εἴτε δὲ θλιβόμεθα, ὑπὲρ τῆς ὑμῶν παρακλήσεως καὶ σωτηρίας· εἴτε παρακαλούμεθα, ὑπὲρ τῆς ὑμῶν παρακλήσεως τῆς ἐνεργουμένης ἐν ὑπομονῇ τῶν αὐτῶν παθημάτων ὧν καὶ ἡμεῖς πάσχομεν. ⁷ καὶ ἡ ἐλπὶς ἡμῶν βεβαία ὑπὲρ ὑμῶν εἰδότες ὅτι ὡς κοινωνοί ἐστε τῶν παθημάτων, οὕτως καὶ τῆς παρακλήσεως. ⁸ Οὐ γὰρ θέλομεν ὑμᾶς ἀγνοεῖν, ἀδελφοί, ὑπὲρ τῆς θλίψεως ἡμῶν τῆς γενομένης ἐν τῇ Ἀσίᾳ, ὅτι καθ' ὑπερβολὴν ὑπὲρ δύναμιν ἐβαρήθημεν ὥστε ἐξαπορηθῆναι ἡμᾶς καὶ τοῦ ζῆν· ⁹ ἀλλὰ αὐτοὶ ἐν ἑαυτοῖς τὸ ἀπόκριμα τοῦ θανάτου ἐσχήκαμεν, ἵνα μὴ πεποιθότες ὦμεν ἐφ' ἑαυτοῖς ἀλλ' ἐπὶ τῷ θεῷ τῷ ἐγείροντι τοὺς νεκρούς· ¹⁰ ὃς ἐκ τηλικούτου θανάτου ἐρρύσατο ἡμᾶς καὶ ῥύσεται, εἰς ὃν ἠλπίκαμεν [ὅτι] καὶ ἔτι ῥύσεται, ¹¹ συνυπουργούντων καὶ ὑμῶν ὑπὲρ ἡμῶν τῇ δεήσει, ἵνα ἐκ πολλῶν προσώπων τὸ εἰς ἡμᾶς χάρισμα διὰ πολλῶν εὐχαριστηθῇ ὑπὲρ ἡμῶν.

¹Paul, an apostle of Christ Jesus by the will of God, and Timothy our brother. To the church of God which is at Corinth, with all the saints who are in the whole of Achaia: ²Grace to you and peace from God our Father and the Lord Jesus Christ. ³Blessed be the God and Father of our Lord Jesus Christ, the Father of mercies and God of all comfort, ⁴who comforts us in all our affliction, so that we may be able to comfort those who are in any affliction, with the comfort with which we ourselves are comforted by God. ⁵For as we share abundantly in Christ's sufferings, so through Christ we share abundantly in comfort too. ⁶If we are afflicted, it is for your comfort and salvation; and if we are comforted, it is for your comfort, which you experience when you patiently endure the same sufferings that we suffer. ⁷Our hope for you is unshaken; for we know that as you share in our sufferings, you will also share in our comfort. ⁸For we do not want you to be ignorant, brethren, of the affliction we experienced in Asia; for we were so utterly, unbearably crushed that we despaired of life itself. ⁹Why, we felt that we had received the sentence of death; but that was to make us rely not on ourselves but on God who raises the dead; ¹⁰he delivered us from so deadly a peril, and he will deliver us; on him we have set our hope that he will deliver us again. ¹¹You also must help us by prayer, so that many will give thanks on our behalf for the blessing granted us in answer to many prayers.

2 Corinthians 1:1 is a shortened rendition of the more elaborate 1 Corinthians 1:1-2 with two exceptions.[1] The first, "the whole of Achaia," confirms that "every place" (2 Cor 1:2) is not to be taken literally as though it referred to the entire orb or the entire Roman empire. It is meant to reference the cities and villages of the Roman province Achaia, whose capital was Corinth.[2] The second difference is that the brother here is Timothy rather than Sosthenes (1 Cor 1:1). Since Sosthenes is a

---

[1] Paul, called by the will of God to be an apostle of Christ Jesus, and our brother Sosthenes, To the church of God which is at Corinth, to those sanctified in Christ Jesus, called to be saints together with all those who in every place call on the name of our Lord Jesus Christ, both their Lord and ours: Grace to you and peace from God our Father and the Lord Jesus Christ. (1 Cor 1:1-2)

[2] See further *NTI₄* 74.

generic reference to a Jew who endorsed Paul's gospel,[3] here we have a narrowing of the matter to the person of Paul's main helper, Timothy, whom the Apostle had circumcised (Acts 16:1-3). Such narrowing was prepared for in 1 Corinthians 16 where Timothy was introduced as the main heir of the next generation of leaders after Paul's demise. This is a direct indication that 2 Corinthians was intended as a continuation of 1 Corinthians and that both letters are meant to be heard in tandem. This conclusion is buttressed, as we shall see, by many statements in the second letter which follow and build on features and topics extant in the first letter.

It is only here and in Galatians that Paul omits the usual thanksgiving to God in behalf of his addressees—something that he included in all his other letters addressed to communities. In Galatians the reason is obvious: he had no cause to do so since he was unhappy with the Galatians' readiness to betray the gospel he had preached for another so-called gospel (Gal 1:6-7). In 2 Corinthians the motive is altogether different. The Apostle had just experienced an extreme affliction in Asia[4] to the extent that "we were so utterly, unbearably crushed that we despaired of life itself. Why, we felt that we had received the sentence of death (*apokrima tou thanatou*)" (1:8b-9a). Such wording is understandable in view of what he wrote in his earlier letter regarding the same event: "Why am I in peril every hour? I protest, brethren, by my pride in you which I have in Christ Jesus our Lord, I die every day! What do I gain if, humanly speaking, I fought with beasts at Ephesus?"[5] (1 Cor 15:30-32a) The reference is to his having been cast into a Roman arena

---

[3] See *C-1Cor* 22-23.
[4] Asia refers to the Roman province that lay in Asia Minor, on the shores of the Aegean Sea.
[5] Ephesus was the capital of the Roman province Asia.

where gladiators fought against wild beasts as well as among themselves. Luke describes that experience of near-death in Acts 19:21-40:

> So the city was filled with the confusion; and they rushed together into the theater (*theatron*), dragging with them Gaius and Aristarchus, Macedonians who were Paul's companions in travel. Paul wished to go in among the crowd, but the disciples would not let him; some of the Asiarchs also, who were friends of his, sent to him and begged him not to venture into the theater (*theatron*)." (vv.29-31)

In the Greco-Roman world, the *theatron* (theater) was an arena that was enclosed to protect the viewers from harm. The *amphitheatron* (amphitheater) was a semi-circle theater where plays and music performances were held. The close connection between the theater arena and near-death experience is corroborated in what Paul writes in describing the perils of the apostolic mission: "For I think that God has exhibited us apostles as last of all, like *men sentenced to death* (*epithanatious*; from the root *thanatos* [death]); because we have become a *spectacle* (*theatron*) to the world, to angels and to men." (1 Cor 4:9)

It is this escape from the clutches of death that prompted Paul to forego his usual thanksgiving to God for his addressees in order to offer praise to the Almighty who just saved him from being thrown into the arena. The highest expression of praise is to declare that God is "blessed."[6] At face value this passive participle is, to say the least, very strange since blessing, like honor and praise, is bestowed by a senior on a junior. In our contemporary Western society, we are not attuned to this reality;

---

[6] See Rom 1:25; 9:5; 2 Cor 1:3; 11:31; Eph 1:3; Tim 1:11; 6:15; 1 Pet 1:3.

we are used to saying that juniors throw a party in "honor" of their senior, at which occasion they "praise" that senior for his accomplishments. And yet, in addressing the senior, the speakers repeatedly use the phrase: "You honor us with your presence today." Conversely, in his speech, the senior often "praises" his hearers for their endeavors and accomplishments. So the inescapable bottom line question is, "Who is honoring whom?" The case in which the "honoree" is a bishop, it is he who blesses the audience, not vice-versa, in spite of the fact that some of the speakers, in addressing him, may use the phrase "Blessed are you!" In order to understand this linguistic phenomenon, one is to consider that, sometimes, the passive participle "blessed" *functions* differently when said of a senior than when used to speak of a junior. In the latter case, it bears the meaning that "so and so is blessed (assumedly by a senior)." However, in the former case, it connotes that the senior is "full" *of endless blessing*, just as a mountain source is "full" *of endless water*. Thus the senior can repeatedly *bestow* blessings on many without ever being depleted. The junior, on the other hand, *receives* the blessing and becomes "filled" *with it* just as the one who drinks from the source is "filled" *with water*.

The phrase "the God and Father of our (the) Lord Jesus Christ" is found several times in the New Testament epistles (Rom 15:6; 2 Cor 1:3; 11:31; Eph 1:3;[7] 1 Pet 1:3), which bespeaks of it being an established formula. In scripture, however, the only and exclusive source of blessing is the scriptural God who is introduced here as both the God and Father of the Lord Jesus Christ (2 Cor 1:3a). This "clarification"

---

[7] The fact that this formula occurs at the beginning of a Pauline letter besides 2 Corinthians only in that addressed to the Ephesians seals in its own way my earlier conclusion concerning Paul's "Ephesian" near-death experience.

to the immediately preceding "God our Father and the Lord Jesus Christ" is very important as it underscores that the *one* source of "grace and peace"[8] is God, who is the Father of the Lord Jesus Christ as he is ours, and also the God of the same Lord Jesus Christ as he is ours.[9] One can find an unequivocal basis for this conclusion when comparing the three "captivity letters."[10]

> ***Ephesians***: "Grace to you and peace from God our Father and the Lord Jesus Christ. Blessed be the God and Father of our Lord Jesus Christ ..." (1:2-3a)
>
> ***Philippians***: "Grace to you and peace from God our Father and the Lord Jesus Christ. I thank my God in all my remembrance of you ..." (1:2-3)
>
> ***Colossians***: "Grace to you and peace from God our Father. We always thank God, the Father of our Lord Jesus Christ when we pray for you ..." (1:2b-3).

Consequently, one should not assume that Jesus Christ is as much a source of grace, peace, and blessing as God. Such, unfortunately, is often the understanding among Christians who have been formatted by classical theology concerning the "Trinity." Not only is God the one to whom Paul addresses his prayer as high priest of his churches,[11] but in Ephesians God is introduced as the sole source of blessing, and in Colossians as the

---

[8] Notice the one preposition "from" before the two names.
[9] Notice the one definite article "the" that introduces both "God" *and* "Father" simultaneously. The Greek has *ho Theos kai patēr* and not *ho Theos kai ho patēr*.
[10] Ephesians, Philippians, and Colossians are usually known as such because Paul either introduces himself as *desmios* (chained, prisoner; Eph 3:1; 4:1) or refers to his "chains" (Phil 1;7, 13, 14, 17; Col 4:18).
[11] See especially Rom 15:15-16 and Phil 2:17; 4:18; see my comments on these verses in *C-Rom* and *C-Phil*.

sole source of grace and peace. Such being the case, the question that remains is, "What is the position and function of the Lord Jesus Christ?"

The answer to this question is found in a central passage from Galatians, the earliest Pauline letter that functions as a blueprint not only of the Pauline corpus, but actually of the entire New Testament:

> And if you are Christ's, then you are Abraham's offspring, heirs according to promise … I mean that the heir, as long as he is a child, is no better than a slave, though he is the owner of all the estate; but he is under guardians and trustees until the date set by the father. So with us; when we were children, we were slaves to the elemental spirits of the universe. But when the time had fully come, God sent forth his Son, born of woman, born under the law, to redeem those who were under the law, so that we might receive *adoption as sons* (*hyiothesia*; sonship). And because you are sons, God has sent the Spirit of his Son into our hearts, crying, "Abba! Father!" So through God you are no longer a slave but a son, and if a son then an heir. (Gal 3:29-4:7)

The Apostle's metaphoric language when dealing with relationships is based on the Roman household and not on the Greek philosophical mindset and vocabulary that pervaded later Christian literature. Notice how, upon concluding his discussion of the scriptural Law (3:19-28) with scriptural terminology (3:29), Paul moves immediately to explain that conclusion in terms of Roman law (4:1-7). The reason is that, according to Roman law, even the biological progeny of a paterfamilias are not legally his children unless they are officially adopted by him, thus becoming his genuine children.[12] Adoption is a fatherly prerogative of the paterfamilias, and so is the decision as to who would be his heir. The actual date of becoming the housemaster is indicated in the father's will or testament. Until that time the potential heir "is no better than a slave, though he is *the owner of all the estate* (*kyrios pantōn*; lord of all/everything in the household); he is under guardians and trustees until the date set by the father" (vv.1b-2). It is precisely such a rule that gives the believers hope that they would be "adopted" (v.5) and even assigned as "heirs" *through God*, that is to say through his will (v.7). Having firmly established this hope in the minds of his hearers who are privy to Roman law, Paul reverts to scripture—which for him is the ultimate authority—by appealing to the case of Isaac, as prototype for all believers (v.28a), in that he was "born" by God's will through a promise (v.23b, 28b) rather than by the will of (human) flesh (v.23a). The full similarity between the medium of Jesus' sonship and that of the believers to the one God who is the Father of all is corroborated in that (1) all children are invited to pray the Lord Jesus' prayer "Abba! Father!" (v.6; see also Rom 8:15), and (2) "and if children, then *heirs, heirs* of God and *fellow heirs* with Christ, provided we suffer with him in order that we may also be glorified with him" (v.17). The only difference is that Jesus retains the primacy as the "first-born Son" (v.29); that is why in sharing in *his* prayer we have the hope of sharing in *his* inheritance as *co-heirs* should we accept all that the Father's "will be done" entails, including suffering, as Jesus Christ did, due to such obedience. The primacy of Christ finds corroboration in that, although Paul is speaking of his own tribulation in Asia in 2 Corinthians 1:3-12,

---

[12] The term "genuine" is originally more legal than meets the eye. Unless and until a child was held by his father on the latter's knee (Latin *genu*)—or lap or bosom—the child was not considered genuinely the father's child.

he unexpectedly introduces the sufferings of Christ as a prototype for his own: "*For* as we share abundantly in Christ's sufferings, so through Christ we share abundantly in comfort too." (v.5)

In turn, all the preceding explains why Paul elaborates on "God and Father" as "the Father of mercies and God of all comfort" (v.3).[13] The two divine facets of "mercies" and "comfort" are linked in scripture to God's intervention at the exodus from Egypt and at the new exodus from Babylon when, through his unwarranted "mercy," he redeemed an undeserving people for no apparent reason except to give them another chance for life in obedience to his will.[14] Indeed the root *oiktirm—* is encountered for the first time in Exodus in conjunction with a second chance given to the people after they broke the first covenant (chs.32-33):

> The Lord said to Moses, "Cut two tables of stone like the first; and I will write upon the tables the words that were on the first tables, which you broke." ... So Moses cut two tables of stone like the first; and he rose early in the morning and went up on Mount Sinai, as the Lord had commanded him, and took in his hand two tables of stone. And the Lord descended in the cloud and stood with him there, and proclaimed the name of the Lord. The Lord passed before him, and proclaimed, "The Lord, the Lord, a God merciful (*oiktirmōn*) and gracious (*eleēmōn*, from the same root as *eleos* [mercy]), slow to anger, and abounding in steadfast love and faithfulness, keeping steadfast love for thousands, forgiving iniquity and transgression and sin, but who will by no means clear the guilty, visiting the iniquity of the fathers upon the children

---

[13] The intended link between the two phrases of v.3 is underscored through the use of the literary device *inclusio* ABB'A': "God and Father, Father and God."
[14] See Ezek 11:16-21; 36:24-27.

and the children's children, to the third and the fourth generation." (Ex 34:1, 4-7)

As for the root *parakal*— it is found at the outset of Isaiah 40 where the prophet announces the release of the sinful people from Babylon where they were sent for their disregard of God's commandments:

> Comfort (*parakaleite*), comfort (*parakaleite*) my people, says your God. Speak tenderly to Jerusalem, and cry to her that her warfare is ended, that her iniquity is pardoned, that she has received from the Lord's hand double for all her sins. (40:1-2)

That Isaiah 40-66 was definitely on Paul's mind is sealed through the addition of the otherwise unexpected "salvation" after "comfort" in 2 Corinthians 1:6a: "If we are afflicted, it is for your comfort and salvation."[15] The second part of Isaiah is studded with references to "salvation" and "redemption" and is the main reason for the name given to that prophetic book; the Hebrew *yeša'yahu* (Isaiah) means "the Lord shall save" or "May the Lord save!"

Although Paul starts with the element "mercies," it is the element "comfort" that steals the scene in 2 Corinthians 1:3-7. Linked to this concentration of "comfort" is Jesus Christ, the prototype child of God (v.3a) in the matter of suffering for the latter's cause (v.5). In Paul's letters, Jesus and his mission are a depiction of the figure of the Suffering Servant in Isaiah 53. Since all four passages concerning that personality are found in Isaiah 40-66, which is known as the Book of Consolation (Comfort) due to its opening statement (40:1), it stands to reason that the figure of the Suffering Servant would loom

---

[15] The following occurrence of "salvation" is found much later in 2 Cor 6:2.

behind the scenes in a passage woven around "comfort" (2 Cor 1:3-7). This becomes more à propos when it is the sufferings of Christ that are introduced as the reason for the Apostle's comfort in his tribulation: "For as we share abundantly in Christ's sufferings, so *through Christ* we share abundantly in comfort too." (v.5) This is precisely the thesis of Isaiah 53:

> But he was wounded for our transgressions, he was bruised for our iniquities; upon him was the chastisement that made us whole, and with his stripes we are healed ... and the Lord has laid on him the iniquity of us all ... and as for his generation, who considered that he was cut off out of the land of the living, stricken for the transgression of my people? ... he shall see the fruit of the travail of his soul and be satisfied; by his knowledge shall the righteous one, my servant, make many to be accounted righteous; and he shall bear their iniquities ... because he poured out his soul to death, and was numbered with the transgressors; yet he bore the sin of many, and made intercession for the transgressors. (vv.5, 6b, 8b, 11, 12b)

Although he refers to Jesus Christ as the ultimate channel of divine comfort for the Corinthians as well as for himself (2 Cor 1:5), Paul describes himself—not Christ—as the de facto medium of that same divine comfort for the Corinthians:

> Blessed be the God and Father of our Lord Jesus Christ, the Father of mercies and God of all comfort, who comforts us in all our affliction, so that we may be able to comfort those who are in any affliction, with the comfort with which we ourselves are comforted by God. For as we share abundantly in Christ's sufferings, so through Christ we share abundantly in comfort too. If we are afflicted, it is for your comfort and salvation; and if we are comforted, it is for your comfort, which you experience when you patiently endure the same sufferings that we suffer. Our hope

for you is unshaken; for we know that as you share in our sufferings, you will also share in our comfort. (vv.3-7)

The swift mention of Christ as the Isaianic suffering servant is "surrounded" by a lengthy and repetitive[16] reference to Paul's personal experience as the factual bridge through which the divine consolation reaches the Corinthians. But then where does the difference between Jesus Christ and Paul lie? The answer can be gleaned from Philippians where we encounter the same approach: before Jesus Christ is given as the prime example of the obedient slave (2:7) for the Philippians to follow (vv.1-5), Paul introduces himself as "slave" (1:1) and thus the tangible prototype whose example they are to follow.[17] This is confirmed in that, immediately before 2:1-11, we hear: "For it has been granted to you that for the sake of Christ you should not only believe in him but also suffer for his sake, *engaged in the same conflict which you saw and now hear to be mine.*" (1:29-30) Later Paul iterates this summons: "Brethren, join in imitating me (*symmimētai mou ginesthe*), and mark those who so live as you have an example in us." (3:17) In the Corinthian correspondence, Paul actually uses the same formula to present himself as the bridge between his addressees and Christ on the level of comportment: "Be imitators of me (*mimētai mou ginesthe*), *as I am of Christ.*" (1 Cor 11:1) The reason for this is that the Corinthians and the Philippians know Paul, but they do not know Christ except through Paul or, more specifically, through the gospel he—and only he—preached to them (1 Cor 9:1-2; 2 Cor 3:1-3; 11:1-4). Put otherwise, rather than Jesus Christ, it is Paul, in both his person and his preaching, who is the primary reference for them. Had it not been for Paul the

---

[16] Repetitiveness in a text is an aural underscoring device meant to reach the hearers.
[17] See my comments in *C-Phil* 57-8.

Corinthians and Philippians would have been as much "without Christ"[18] as the Ephesians (Eph 2:12); in other words, "without Paul" there would not have been any Christ at all![19]

This understanding is readily detectable in the original Greek. The noun *paraklēsis* (comfort; consolation) is from the verb *parakalō* (ask; summon; ordain) which is an expansion of *kalō* (call). God is also eminently known in the New Testament, especially in Paul's letters, as "the caller" (*ho kalōn*, the one who calls; Gal 5:8; 1 Thess 2:12; 5:24) or "the one who called" (*ho kalesas*; Gal 1:6, 15; 2 Tim 1:9; 1 Pet 1:15; 2:9; 5:10; 2 Pet 1:3); hence God's *klēsis* (calling; Rom 11:29; 1 Cor 1:26; 7:20; Eph 1:18; 4:1, 4; Phil 3:14; 2 Thess 1:11; [2 Tim 1:9]; Heb 3:1; 2 Pet 1:10), whence *paraklēsis*. Thus Paul's repeated use of both verb and noun connoting consolation whose ultimate facet is salvation (2 Cor 1:6) underscores that God is not only its sole source but also, and more importantly, its originator and promoter. Everything starts with God's calling the Corinthians through the message of Paul who, himself, has been "called" into that mission by one and the same God: "But when he who had set me apart before I was born, and *had called* (kalesas) *me*

---

[18] As in KJV and JB.
[19] The original Greek *khōris Khristou* (without Christ) is weakly rendered as "separated from Christ" in RSV. This translation assumes that there is a Christ "out there" independent from Paul and who would still be a valid Christ. However, such would be an invalid Christ according to Paul: "But I am afraid that as the serpent deceived Eve by his cunning, your thoughts will be led astray from a sincere and pure devotion to *the Christ* (*ton Khriston*). For if some one comes and preaches *another* (*allon*) Jesus than the one we preached, or if you receive a *different* (*heteron*) spirit from the one you received, or if you accept a *different* (*heteron*) gospel from the one you accepted, you submit to it readily enough" (2 Cor 11:3-4); "I am astonished that you are so quickly deserting him who called you in the grace of Christ and turning to a *different* (*heteron*) gospel—not that there is *another* (*allo*) gospel, but there are some who trouble you and want to pervert the gospel of *the Christ* (*tou Khristou*)." (Gal 1:6-8) In both cases RSV has "Christ" without the definite article.

through his grace, was pleased to reveal his Son to me, in order that I might preach him among the Gentiles, I did not confer with flesh and blood, nor did I go up to Jerusalem to those who were apostles before me, but I went away into Arabia; and again I returned to Damascus." (Gal 1:15-17) It is then only understandable that the afflictions and sufferings from which God consoles us are also part of his calling us (2 Cor 1:4-6) as Paul clearly states elsewhere: "For it has been granted to you that for the sake of Christ you should not only believe in him but also *suffer* for his sake, engaged in the same *conflict* (*agōna*; exhausting effort) which you saw and now hear to be mine." (Phil 1:29-30)

In writing that, whether in affliction or in comfort, the Apostle is providing comfort to the Corinthians (2 Cor 1:6a) Paul is making more palatable his request that they share in his sufferings (v.6b) and ultimately in Christ's sufferings (v.5a). Unless the Corinthians undergo a similar experience of suffering, they will not be privy to comfort (v.7b). One should thus desist from the teaching of "vicarious" suffering, whether on the part of Christ or the Apostle, *on behalf* of us. Their suffering is a prototype and, consequently, an *invitation* for us to follow suit; we are to "imitate the Apostle as he imitates Christ" (1 Cor 11:1) and thus "share in" *their* sufferings (2 Cor 1:7b). Unless we do so, we shall not "share in" the comfort that is provided by the God of mercies. God's mercy unto us lies in his having offered us two prototypes, his Christ and his Apostle, to convince us of the possibility for all to endure the difficult task of abiding by his commands at any cost: "No temptation has overtaken you that is not common to man. God is faithful, and he will not let you be tempted beyond your strength, but with the temptation will also provide the way of escape, that you may be able to endure it." (1 Cor 10:13) This is confirmed in that the Corinthians' ultimate and final comfort lies ahead of them. That is why, on the one hand, Paul is requiring them to proceed "in patience" (*en hypomonēs*; with forbearance, 2 Cor 1:6b)[20] and, on the other hand, he expresses "hope" that they would attain their share in his comfort (v.7). And, in order to further prod them on that path, he tells them that *his* hope is unshaken (*bebaia*; assured, v.7a). The view expressed here is not just a passing thought but a consistent teaching. We hear the same at two occasions in Romans:

> Therefore, since we are justified by faith, we have peace with God through our Lord Jesus Christ. Through him we have obtained access to this grace in which we stand, and we rejoice in our hope of sharing the glory of God. More than that, we rejoice in our sufferings, knowing that suffering produces endurance, and endurance produces character, and character produces hope, and hope does not disappoint us, because God's love has been poured into our hearts through the Holy Spirit which has been given to us. (5:1-5)

> For you did not receive the spirit of slavery to fall back into fear, but you have received the spirit of sonship. When we cry, "Abba! Father!" it is the Spirit himself bearing witness with our spirit that we are children of God, and if children, then heirs, heirs of God and fellow heirs with Christ, provided we suffer with him in order that we may also be glorified with him. I consider that the sufferings of this present time are not worth comparing with the glory that is to be revealed to us. For the creation waits with eager longing for the revealing of the sons of God; for the creation was subjected to futility, not of its own will but by the will of him who subjected it in hope; because the creation itself will be set free from its bondage to decay and obtain the glorious liberty of the children of God. We know that the whole creation has been groaning in travail together until now; and not only the creation,

---

[20] RSV has "patiently."

but we ourselves, who have the first fruits of the Spirit, groan inwardly as we wait for adoption as sons, the redemption of our bodies. For in this hope we were saved. Now hope that is seen is not hope. For who hopes for what he sees? But if we hope for what we do not see, we wait for it with patience. (8:15-25)

In describing the affliction he underwent in Asia (2 Cor 1:8a) Paul speaks repeatedly in terms of a near death experience (vv.8b, 9, 10) to the extent that he mentions his trust in "God who raises the dead" (v.9b).[21] However, in the present context, this is clearly metaphorical given that in v.10 Paul speaks of being delivered from "so great deaths" (*tēlikountōn thanatōn*) in the plural,[22] from which God both delivered him and would be delivering him in the future. This view will be corroborated later in 11:23 where, in speaking of his apostolic record, Paul writes: "Are they[23] servants of Christ? I am a better one—I am talking like a madman—with far greater labors, far more imprisonments, with countless beatings, and often *near death* (*en thanatois*; in deaths)." In other words, he is conveying to his addressees that he could have died and thus have been unable to write to them. If they are hearing his "voice" through this letter, they are to consider it as a gift (*kharisma*)[24] from God for which "thanks"[25] (1:11) to God ought to be raised by them and many

---

[21] His approach here harks back to what he did in 1 Cor 15 where, in discussing the raising of the dead, he makes a reference to his fight with the wild beasts in Ephesus (v.32).

[22] This reading is the *lectio difficilior* and thus is to be preferred as the original over the singular *tilikoutou thanatou* (so great death).

[23] He has dubbed his opponents as "false apostles, deceitful workmen" (2 Cor 11:13) and "servants (*diakonoi*; ministers) of Satan" (vv.14-15).

[24] RSV translates as "blessing."

[25] In the original there is wordplay on the "gift" and "thanks be raised" since they are from the same root *kharis* (grace): "You also must help (*synypourgountōn*; co-minister with) us by prayer, so that thanks be raised (*evkharistēthē*; acknowledge the grace) on our behalf by many persons (*ek pollōn prosōpōn*) for the gift (*charisma*; expression of

others; the many others are obviously the residents of the province Achaia referred to in v.1. Indeed, the God of mercies grants only "gifts (of mercy)" for which he is to be thanked by all: Paul was granted to live "through and beyond death" in order to continue his apostolic mission by writing to them. The Corinthians and all Achaians were granted to hear once more the Apostle's life-securing words *in this epistle,* as is clear from what he says to the Philippians:

> For I know that through your prayers and the help of the Spirit of Jesus Christ this will turn out for my deliverance, as it is my eager expectation and hope that I shall not be at all ashamed, but that with full courage now as always Christ will be honored in my body, whether by life or by death. For to me to live is Christ, and to die is gain. If it is to be life in the flesh, that means fruitful labor for me. Yet which I shall choose I cannot tell. I am hard pressed between the two. My desire is to depart and be with Christ, for that is far better. But to remain in the flesh is more necessary on your account. Convinced of this, I know that I shall remain and continue with you all, for your progress and joy in the faith, so that in me you may have ample cause to glory in Christ Jesus, because of my coming to you again. (Phil 1:19-26)

Vv. 12-22 ¹² Ἡ γὰρ καύχησις ἡμῶν αὕτη ἐστίν, τὸ μαρτύριον τῆς συνειδήσεως ἡμῶν, ὅτι ἐν ἁπλότητι καὶ εἰλικρινείᾳ τοῦ θεοῦ, [καὶ] οὐκ ἐν σοφίᾳ σαρκικῇ ἀλλ' ἐν χάριτι θεοῦ, ἀνεστράφημεν ἐν τῷ κόσμῳ, περισσοτέρως δὲ πρὸς ὑμᾶς. ¹³ οὐ γὰρ ἄλλα γράφομεν ὑμῖν ἀλλ' ἢ ἃ ἀναγινώσκετε ἢ καὶ ἐπιγινώσκετε· ἐλπίζω δὲ ὅτι ἕως τέλους ἐπιγνώσεσθε, ¹⁴ καθὼς καὶ ἐπέγνωτε ἡμᾶς ἀπὸ μέρους, ὅτι καύχημα ὑμῶν ἐσμεν καθάπερ καὶ ὑμεῖς ἡμῶν ἐν τῇ ἡμέρᾳ τοῦ κυρίου [ἡμῶν] Ἰησοῦ. ¹⁵ Καὶ ταύτῃ τῇ πεποιθήσει ἐβουλόμην πρότερον πρὸς ὑμᾶς ἐλθεῖν, ἵνα δευτέραν χάριν

---

grace) granted us in so many different ways (*dia pollōn*; in spite of so many near death experiences)." (2 Cor 1:11)

σχῆτε, ¹⁶ καὶ δι' ὑμῶν διελθεῖν εἰς Μακεδονίαν καὶ πάλιν ἀπὸ Μακεδονίας ἐλθεῖν πρὸς ὑμᾶς καὶ ὑφ' ὑμῶν προπεμφθῆναι εἰς τὴν Ἰουδαίαν. ¹⁷ τοῦτο οὖν βουλόμενος μήτι ἄρα τῇ ἐλαφρίᾳ ἐχρησάμην; ἢ ἃ βουλεύομαι κατὰ σάρκα βουλεύομαι, ἵνα ᾖ παρ' ἐμοὶ τὸ ναὶ ναὶ καὶ τὸ οὒ οὔ; ¹⁸ πιστὸς δὲ ὁ θεὸς ὅτι ὁ λόγος ἡμῶν ὁ πρὸς ὑμᾶς οὐκ ἔστιν ναὶ καὶ οὔ. ¹⁹ ὁ τοῦ θεοῦ γὰρ υἱὸς Ἰησοῦς Χριστὸς ὁ ἐν ὑμῖν δι' ἡμῶν κηρυχθείς, δι' ἐμοῦ καὶ Σιλουανοῦ καὶ Τιμοθέου, οὐκ ἐγένετο ναὶ καὶ οὒ ἀλλὰ ναὶ ἐν αὐτῷ γέγονεν. ²⁰ ὅσαι γὰρ ἐπαγγελίαι θεοῦ, ἐν αὐτῷ τὸ ναί· διὸ καὶ δι' αὐτοῦ τὸ ἀμὴν τῷ θεῷ πρὸς δόξαν δι' ἡμῶν. ²¹ ὁ δὲ βεβαιῶν ἡμᾶς σὺν ὑμῖν εἰς Χριστὸν καὶ χρίσας ἡμᾶς θεός, ²² ὁ καὶ σφραγισάμενος ἡμᾶς καὶ δοὺς τὸν ἀρραβῶνα τοῦ πνεύματος ἐν ταῖς καρδίαις ἡμῶν.

¹²For our boast is this, the testimony of our conscience that we have behaved in the world, and still more toward you, with holiness and godly sincerity, not by earthly wisdom but by the grace of God. ¹³For we write you nothing but what you can read and understand; I hope you will understand fully, ¹⁴as you have understood in part, that you can be proud of us as we can be of you, on the day of the Lord Jesus. ¹⁵Because I was sure of this, I wanted to come to you first, so that you might have a double pleasure; ¹⁶I wanted to visit you on my way to Macedonia, and to come back to you from Macedonia and have you send me on my way to Judea. ¹⁷Was I vacillating when I wanted to do this? Do I make my plans like a worldly man, ready to say Yes and No at once? ¹⁸As surely as God is faithful, our word to you has not been Yes and No. ¹⁹For the Son of God, Jesus Christ, whom we preached among you, Silvanus and Timothy and I, was not Yes and No; but in him it is always Yes. ²⁰For all the promises of God find their Yes in him. That is why we utter the Amen through him, to the glory of God. ²¹But it is God who establishes us with you in Christ, and has commissioned us; ²²he has put his seal upon us and given us his Spirit in our hearts as a guarantee.

At this point Paul reprises in extensive detail a matter he glossed over in 1 Corinthians 16:5, that is, his having visited Macedonia before coming to Corinth. What seems to complicate the matter is that he at first decided to come to Corinth, then go to Macedonia, then again to Achaia before heading to Judaea (2 Cor 1:15-16) with the contributions of the Gentile churches (1 Cor 16:1-4). The question is, "Why did Paul change his plans, and then, uncharacteristically, appear to apologize to the Corinthians for doing so?"

It would behoove us to start our research with Troas, which is mentioned in conjunction with Paul's "apology" (2 Cor 2:12a), especially since Paul writes that in Troas "a door was opened for me in the Lord" (v.12b). This recalls "a wide door for effective work has opened to me" (1 Cor 16:9) that was used earlier when Paul spoke of delaying his visit to Corinth until after his journey to Macedonia. In Acts, the mention of Troas brackets Paul's missionary activity among the Hellenes: in Macedonia, the land of Alexander and in Achaia, the land of the Greeks (16:8-20:6). The importance given that city is detectable in its double mention both at the beginning (16:8, 11) and at the end (20:5, 6). The sealing corroboration for such preeminence is found in 2 Timothy, Paul's final "testament," where Troas is honored as the city of the Apostle's "library": "When you come, bring the cloak that I left with Carpus at Troas, also the books, and above all the parchments." (4:13)

The symbolic importance of Troas (Troy) lies in that it is the site of a most impressive victory of the ancient Greeks which was eternalized in the Iliad, their most famous epic, which was the catalyst for the unification of the independent cities into one entity. So, upon embarking on his mission to Macedonia and Achaia, Paul has already firmly planted the gospel seed of the new life in Troas, a place left devastated by the Greeks. In other words, instead of the shield of Achilles, there is now the shield of righteousness and thus peace through the sword of the Spirit instead of death by the sword:

> Therefore take the whole armor of God, that you may be able to withstand in the evil day, and having done all, to stand. Stand therefore, having girded your loins with truth, and having put on the breastplate of righteousness, and having shod your feet with the equipment of the gospel of peace; besides all these, taking the shield of faith, with which you can quench all the flaming darts of the evil one. And take the helmet of salvation, and the sword of the Spirit, which is the word of God. (Eph 6:13-17)

That the mention of Troas in Acts 16:11 is a pointer to victory is corroborated by the immediately following reference to Samothrace, which is unique in the New Testament and thus intentional. The most important landmark of the otherwise insignificant small island of Samothrace, in the Northern Aeagean Sea between Troas and Philippi, was the marble statue of Nike (*nikē*; victory) nowadays known as the "Winged Victory of Samothrace." The first city of Macedonia visited by Paul was not its capital, Thessalonica,[26] but rather Philippi,[27] the site of

---

[26] The city was founded by King Cassander of Macedon around 315 B.C. near the site of the ancient town of Therma. He named it after his wife Thessalonike, who was a half-sister of Alexander the Great and the daughter of Philip II. Since she was born on the same day that the armies of Macedon and Thessaly won a major battle in Thessaly, King Philip is said to have named his daughter in commemoration of that victory: "Let her be called victory in Thessaly." Her name is made up of two words, Thessaly and Nike, which translate into "Thessalian Victory."

[27] The city of Philippi in eastern Macedonia was established by Philip II in 356 B.C. It reappears in sources during the Roman civil war that followed the assassination of

the victory of Mark Antony and Octavian over Julius Caesar's assassins, Brutus and Cassius, in 42 B.C., which led the way toward the establishment of the Roman empire under Octavian (Augustus Ceasar) who became its sole master after his defeating Mark Antony at the naval battle of Actium in 31 B.C. Finally, that the ultimate reference in Luke's mind is the planting of the gospel seed is evident in the mention—unwarranted at face value—of the "New City" between Troas and Samothrace, on the one hand, and Philippi, on the other hand: "Setting sail therefore from Troas, we made a direct voyage to Samothrace, and the following day to Neapolis (*Nean Polin*; New City), and from there to Philippi, which is the leading city of the district of Macedonia, and a Roman colony. We remained in this city some days." (vv.11-12) The "New City," just as unnecessary as Samothrace,[28] is an oblique reference to the Heavenly Jerusalem (Rev 21:2) whence originates the "gospel word" Paul was preaching (Eph 3:1-7) and ended "scripturalized" as "books" and "parchments" in his "library" at Troas (2 Tim 4:13).[29]

Against that background one can understand why both the Pauline corpus and Acts, which is a story-like rendering of the content of the Pauline letters,[30] reflect that Paul's gospel reached Macedonia before it did Achaia. The reason is to "belittle," in

---

Julius Caesar. Mark Antony and Octavian, Caesar's heirs, confronted the assassins Marcus Junius Brutus and Cassius at the Battle of Philippi in 42 B.C. Antony and Octavian were victorious and released some of their soldiers who colonized the city which was re-founded as *Colonia Victrix Philippensium*. When Octavian became Roman emperor in 30 B.C. he reorganized the colony and renamed it *Colonia Iulia Philippensis*. It was renamed *Colonia Augusta Iulia Philippensis* in 27 B.C. when Octavian received the title Augustus from the Roman Senate.

[28] Both are unique instances in the New Testament.
[29] Similar to the "Presidential Libraries" in the USA, which host the "official papers" of each corresponding president.
[30] See *NTI₂* 3-21.

one strike, both Athens and Rome by making them submit to the "power of God" *in the gospel* "for salvation to every one who has faith, to the Jew first and also to the Greek (Hellene)" (Rom 1:16-17) and even before reaching them! After having firmly planted the gospel in Troas, the city of Greece's victory eternalized for the ages, he had to do the same in Philippi, the city of Octavian's victory that paved the way for his becoming the master of the empire he conceived on the soil where Alexander of Macedon's Greek was the *lingua franca*. That Paul was aiming at Rome is corroborated by the fact that the four cities first visited by him in European territory, Neapolis (Acts 16:11), Philippi (v.12), Amphipolis, and Thessalonica (17:1), were located on the Via Egnatia in the direction of Rome. The Via Egnatia is one of the most famous Roman roads linking the Eastern and Western parts of the empire, stretching from Dyrrachium on the Adriatic Sea and Byzantium, later Constantinople; on the other hand, across the Adriatic Sea from Dyrrachium, lay Brundisium (actual Brindisi), on the southwestern coast of Italy, which was connected to Rome by the Via Appia. Paul's intention is further reflected in what he writes in Romans before embarking on his way to visit Rome:

> For I will not venture to speak of anything except what Christ has wrought through me to win obedience from the Gentiles, by word and deed, by the power of signs and wonders, by the power of the Holy Spirit, so that from Jerusalem and as far round as Illyricum[31] I have fully preached the gospel of Christ ... But now, since I no longer have any room for work in these regions, and since I have longed for many years to come to you, I hope to see you in passing as I go to Spain, and to be sped on my journey there by you, once I have enjoyed your company for a little. (Rom 15:18-19, 23-24)

---

[31] This major Roman province lay a little north of Dyrrachium.

The close link between this passage, on the one hand, and what we read in Acts and the Corinthian correspondence, on the other hand, concerning his plans to go to Jerusalem after his farewell visit to Macedonia and Achaia, is evident in what Paul writes immediately thereafter: "At present, however, I am going to Jerusalem with aid for the saints. For Macedonia and Achaia have been pleased to make some contribution for the poor among the saints at Jerusalem." (v.25-26)

So, in spite of all appearances, Paul is not relegating Achaia to a second position behind Macedonia. Rather, first all starts in and leads to Troas before his ascent to Jerusalem and, from there, to Rome. Secondly, upon his arrival in Corinth, Paul is bringing along the news that Macedonia, the land of Alexander who subdued Greece, has been itself "chained" into obedience to the gospel. Thirdly, Corinth, the capital of Achaia, the actual land of the *Hellenes*, is purposely made the last stop in the East before Paul embarks on his journey to Rome and the West, and thus is a test for the Apostle's success there; Paul needed to have fresh on his mind his experience in Achaia, the intellectual "mother" of Rome, in order not to be intimidated by the patricians of the imperial city and to be able to address them with the "power" of the gospel to which *Hellas* has submitted.[32] Fourthly, and most importantly, with a masterful adulatory stroke Paul tells the Corinthians that his confidence in them is so

---

[32] Luke seems to reflect that intention in the way he refers to Achaia in Acts 20: "After the uproar ceased, Paul sent for the disciples and having exhorted them took leave of them and departed for Macedonia. When he had gone through these parts and had given them much encouragement, he came to Greece (*tēn Hellada*) ... These [the brethren aforementioned in v.4] went on and were waiting for us at Troas." (vv.1-2, 5) This is the sole instance of *Hellas* (Greece) in the entire New Testament and thus its use is evidently intentional. It is only at this juncture that Luke calls Achaia by the official name of the Ancient Greece of the Iliad, granting that Roman province full honor in comparison with Macedonia.

great (2 Cor 7:4, 16) that he does not need to come himself at first to them as he did with the Macedonians; it is enough that he would send them his "brother, partner and fellow worker" Titus (2:13; 8:23). This reading explains the otherwise strange high incidence of reference in 2 Corinthians to Titus (2:13; 7:6, 13, 14; 8:6, 16, 23; 12:18) who appears elsewhere in the New Testament only in Galatians 2:1, 3; 2 Timothy 4:10; and Titus 1:4. Still sending them Titus is in no way demeaning to them since Titus was "showcased" by Paul before the pillars at the Jerusalem meeting where he promised to "remember the poor" (Gal 2:10), which he is precisely trying to accomplish in Corinth through Titus (2 Cor 8:1-6).

However, the bone of contention here (1:12-2:4) is that Paul seems to be reneging on his promise regarding his second visit to them, namely, that he would come to Corinth before going to Macedonia and even come back to see them again on his way to Judea (1:16). Instead he is sending them a letter explaining his change of plans; for the second time round he is going first to Macedonia and, given the tone of the letter, he might not come to Corinth at all. He begins with a preemptive strike against the Hellenes and their "wisdom" which is "earthly" (*sarkikē*: fleshly; [2 Cor 1:12]), a topic he developed in 1 Corinthians 1-2. His reference is rather "the grace of God" that is enacted in the gospel he is preaching (Gal 1:6-7). In other words, it is not human "logic," but rather the ministry of the gospel, that controls his behavior toward them and the world in general (2 Cor 1:12). It is along those lines that he will explain to the Corinthians what looks like a change of mind on his part, when actually he is following the dictates of the ministry assigned to him. In hope, he is inviting them to understand what he all along taught them in his writings, namely, that the ultimate accountability for them as well as for himself will be on the Day of the Lord (vv.13-14; see 1 Cor 4:1-5).

It would be worth our while to linger on what is said in 2 Corinthians 1:13-14: "For we write you nothing but what you can read (*anaginōskete*; read aloud) and understand (*epiginōskete*); I hope you will understand fully, as you have understood in part, that you can be proud of us as we can be of you, on the day of the Lord Jesus." Classical theology, under the influence of philosophy that stresses elitist comprehension of the so-called "intellectual truths," gives the impression that what is "revealed" in scripture is so profound a "mystery" that one needs a high level intellectual acumen and years of deep study in order to understand the content of scripture. Such a view is oxymoronic especially when it comes to letters that are intended to be clearly understood *immediately* by the addressees gathered together to hear them read aloud, as is evident from the openings of Philippians (Paul and Timothy, servants of Christ Jesus, To all the saints in Christ Jesus who are at Philippi, with the bishops and deacons; 1:1) and Revelation (Blessed is he who *reads aloud* [*anaginōskōn*] the words of the prophecy, and blessed are those who *hear*, and who keep what is written therein; for the time is near; 1:3). If the time is near, then it was definitely not in the writer's purview that his letter be studied by the elite over years at seminaries or schools of higher education. Consequently, Paul's hope that the Corinthians would understand fully what they understood in part is linked not to their "spiritual" ability since such has been shown to be inadequate (1 Cor 3). Rather, his hope lies in that they would listen more carefully while this second letter, with further information, is read aloud to them; put otherwise, his hope lies in that the Corinthians, this time round, would open their ears—not their intellect that is still the same—to "hear" what is being read aloud and abide by it.

Indeed, a few verses later, he will be asking them to do his bidding (2 Cor 2:6-11) regarding a matter he had discussed in the previous letter (1 Cor 5:1-5).

Since he is writing on hope, his assuredness does not lie in the Corinthians themselves, but rather is rooted in the gospel as the expression of God's grace. This is confirmed in the phraseology he uses to speak of his planned visit: "Because I was sure of this, I wanted to come to you first, so that you might have a double (*devteran*; second) pleasure (*kharin*; grace); I wanted to visit you on my way to Macedonia, and to come back to you from Macedonia and have you send me on my way to Judea." (2 Cor 1:15-16) His visit *as apostle* is an expression of divine grace to the Corinthians and, consequently, his second visit would be a "second grace." Furthermore, should his visit to Corinth not materialize, this letter itself would function as a literary visitation by him just as his letter to the Romans would function as his apostolic presence among them. And since this is his "second" letter to the church in Corinth and in it he discusses in detail his ministry to that community, then the letter itself is already the "second grace" he is speaking of. Among the Pauline letters, 2 Corinthians has by far the highest incidence of the root *diakon*— that denotes table fellowship ministry, table fellowship being the heart of Paul's gospel regarding which he would not compromise "even for a moment" (Gal 2:5) as is evident from the hard stand he takes at Antioch (vv.11-14), a stand that will reverberate later in 2 Corinthians (11:1-15).

In order to prove that he was never vacillating in his decisions, Paul appeals to his missionary visit. Although he preached in Macedonia before Achaia, it was the same gospel that resounded in both provinces. To make his point more tangible, he appeals to the fact that the Corinthians were evangelized by the same threesome that brought the message to Thessalonica: himself, Silvanus, and Timothy (1:19; see 1 Thess 1:1; 2 Thess 1:1).[33] Chronologically the Corinthians came second to the Macedonians, yet they heard the same gospel to the Gentiles—the promises of God found their "Yes," that is to say, their realization, in the Son of God, Jesus Christ—which is one and the same teaching that Paul was carrying throughout the Roman empire since his call and without second thoughts even during the showdown with the pillars in Jerusalem and in Antioch. Notice the closeness in vocabulary between 2 Corinthians and Galatians:

> For the Son of God, Jesus Christ, whom we preached among you, Silvanus and Timothy and I, was not Yes and No; but in him it is always Yes. For all the promises of God find their Yes in him. That is why we utter the Amen through him, to the glory of God. But it is God who establishes us with you in Christ, and has commissioned us; he has put his seal upon us and given us his Spirit in our hearts as a guarantee. (2 Cor 1:19-22)

> For I would have you know, brethren, that the gospel which was preached by me is not man's gospel. For I did not receive it from man, nor was I taught it, but it came through a revelation of Jesus Christ ... But when he who had set me apart before I was born, and had called me through his grace, was pleased to reveal his Son to me, in order that I might preach him among the Gentiles, I did not confer with flesh and blood ... And they glorified God because of me. (Gal 1:11-12, 15-16, 24)

> ... that in Christ Jesus the blessing of Abraham might come upon the Gentiles, that we might receive the promise of the Spirit through faith ... Is the law then against the promises of God?

---

[33] The importance given this point is evident in that it is put in relief in Acts (17:14-15; 18:5) where we are told that Paul gave the express command that Silas (Silvanus) and Timothy join him in Achaia "as soon as possible" (17:15).

Certainly not; for if a law had been given which could make alive, then righteousness would indeed be by the law. But the scripture consigned all things to sin, that what was promised to faith in Jesus Christ might be given to those who believe. (Gal 3:14, 21-22)

And because you are sons, God has sent the Spirit of his Son into our hearts, crying, "Abba! Father!" (Gal 4:6)

Since the divine "Yes" realized through Jesus Christ reached Achaia as well as Macedonia through Paul and his colleagues, how could the Corinthians even think of accusing him of tergiversating? Paul's response to the faithful (*pistos*) God's "Yes" through Jesus Christ (2 Cor 1:18, 20a) was an "Amen," a fully trusting (*pistos*) "Yes" (v.20b).[34] It is thus the Apostle's response to God's invitation, and the way he accomplishes it, that is the avenue through which God's promises reach the Corinthians, and not through any intrinsic value of theirs, let alone any worthiness on their part. Put otherwise, Paul's presence through his words of teaching *is* Christ's presence among the Corinthians; functionally, Paul in Corinth *is* tantamount to Christ in Corinth. This tradition established by the Pauline school has permeated all Christian churches in that it is the literary product of that school, the Codex of the New Testament writings, which is *Christ among the gathered believers*.[35]

---

[34] The Hebrew *'amin* is from the root *'aman* (trust; express full acceptance) whose Greek counterpart is *pistevō* whence *pistos*. A similar situation where *amēn* (indeed so) occurs as a response to a divine *nai* (yes) is found at the end of Revelation: "He who testifies to these things says, 'Surely (*nai* ; yes) I am coming soon.' Amen (*amēn*), come, Lord Jesus!" (22:20)

[35] One of the most striking expressions of this reality is witnessed at every Christian Orthodox liturgy when at the "entrance" the believers "bow down and worship" Christ *as the Gospel Book*.

Chapter 1 49

Paul viewed himself as the high priest of the Gentiles (Rom 15:16; Philippians 2:17; 4:18) before the divine throne in the Jerusalem above (Gal 4:26). This explains his customary thanksgiving for his addressees during his constant prayers for them at the beginning of his letters.[36] That the same thought was on Paul's mind here in 2 Corinthians is evident in that, a few verses down, he speaks of fragrance (*osmē*; 2:14, 16) and aroma (*evōdia*; v.15) that occur in combination in Ephesians and Philippians in a liturgical setting in both cases: "And walk in love, as Christ loved us and gave himself up for us, a fragrant (*osmēn evōdias*; for a sweetsmelling savour[37]) offering and sacrifice to God" (Eph 5:2); "I have received full payment, and more; I am filled, having received from Epaphroditus the gifts you sent, a fragrant offering (*osmēn evōdias*), a sacrifice acceptable and pleasing to God." (Phil 4:18) When one keeps in mind that the king, as son of God, was de facto the high priest, as is clear in the case of Solomon who, at the inauguration of the temple, both blessed the people (1 Kg 8:1) and prayed on and in behalf of them (vv.30-61) as well as for himself (vv.22-29),[38] then the result is that, as God's anointed (Christ), Jesus is both Son of God and high priest (Jn 17; Heb passim).

Looking closely at the 2 Corinthians passage we are discussing, we find the following. First, Paul writes of himself as having been "anointed (*khrisas*)" by God (1:21b); RSV has "and [God] has commissioned us" for the Greek *kai khrisas hēmas* (and has anointed us). *khrisas* (having anointed) is the aorist participle of the verb *khriō* (anoint) whence *Khristos* (anointed, Christ) and it

---

[36] Rom 1:8; 1 Cor 1:4; Eph 1:15-16; Phil 1:3; Col 1:3; 1 Thess 1:2; 2 Thess 1:3.
[37] KJV.
[38] Since the administration of the palace and public life took most of his time, a monarch would appoint at will one of the priests as high priest (1 Kg 2:35b), who would be his locum tenens in the temple service.

corresponds to the two aorist participles *aphorisas* (having set apart) and *kalesas* (having called) that Paul uses in Galatians to speak of God's having commissioned him to the apostolate (Gal 1:15).[39] Considering that in the entire New Testament the verb *khriō* occurs rarely and only in conjunction with Jesus Christ (Lk 4:18; Acts 4:27; 10:38; Heb 1:9), the conclusion is unavoidable: for the Corinthians, the Apostle Paul—and solely he—*is* Christ.[40] Given that the first and last instances (Lk 4:18 and Heb 1:9) are quotations from Isaiah 61 and Psalm 45, then it is only Luke who uses the verb *khriō* twice to speak of God's anointing Jesus in conjunction with the gospel being imparted to both Jews (Acts 4:27) and Gentiles (10:38). Consequently, its use is obviously programmatic: the anointment of God's chosen is in view of preaching the gospel through his apostles. That this is Luke's intention is evident in the quotation he uses early in his Gospel at the first occasion of Jesus' public ministry after his official assignment through "anointment" by God's spirit at his baptism (Lk 3:21-22), which quotation is imbued in the original with "apostolic" terminology:

> The Spirit of the Lord is upon me, because he has anointed (*ekhrisen*) me to preach good news (*evangelisasthai*; from the verb *evangelizomai* [evangelize, preach the gospel]) to the poor. He has sent (*apestalken*; from the verb *apostellō* [send as emissary] whence *apostolos* [apostle]) me to proclaim (*kēryxai*; from the verb *kēryssō*

---

[39] I just pointed out above the closeness in terminology between this passage of 2 Corinthians and Galatians.

[40] See Gal 1:16 where we hear that God's revealing his Christ took place "in (*en*) me [Paul]" which explains why the churches of Judea "glorified God in (*en*) me" (v.24). RSV changes the first "in me" into "to me" and the second into "because of me (on my account)." KJV has "in me" in both cases, while JB has "in me" in the first instance and "on my account" in the second.

[herald][41] that occurs in the New Testament as parallel to *evangelizomai*)[42] release to the captives and recovering of sight to the blind, to set (*aposteilai*; from the verb *apostellō*) at liberty those who are oppressed." (4:18; see Is 61:1-2)

But, if so, then what would be the difference, if any, between Jesus Christ and Paul? The answer to this lies in the background of Paul's metaphoric terminology concerning relationships, that is, the Roman household. The Roman household had only one *kyrios* (master; lord) or *oikodespotēs* (sovereign or absolute master of the house[hold]),[43] who has only one "heir." At the assigned time, this heir *alone* would become the new master (Gal 4:1-2). This is clearly represented in the parable of the tenants of the vineyard. The mistake of the tenants was to assume that they would automatically inherit the vineyard should they eliminate the heir:

> "But when the tenants saw the son, they said to themselves, 'This is the heir; come, let us kill him and have his inheritance.' And they took him and cast him out of the vineyard, and killed him. When therefore the owner (*kyrios*; lord, master) of the vineyard comes, what will he do to those tenants?" They said to him, "He will put those wretches to a miserable death, and let out the vineyard to other tenants who will give him the fruits in their seasons." (Mt 21:38-41)

---

[41] Paul has just used that verb in 2 Cor 1:19 to speak of his and his colleagues' preaching activity: "For the Son of God, Jesus Christ, whom we preached (*di' hēmōn kērykhtheis* [from *kēryssō*]; heralded by us) among you, Silvanus and Timothy and I, was not Yes and No; but in him it is always Yes."

[42] The two nouns *kērygma* and *evangelion* are also parallel in meaning in the New Testament.

[43] See Mt 10:25; 13:27, 52; 20:1, 11; 21:33; 24:43; Mk 14:14; Lk 12:39; 13:25; 14:21; 22:11.

What is interesting in this parable for our discussion is that the *kyrios* of v.40 was introduced at the beginning as *oikodespotēs*: "There was a householder (*oikodespotēs*) who planted a vineyard." (v.33) On the other hand, the *oikodespotēs* assigns one of his slaves to be the *oikonomos* (house[hold] ruler) to administer his household, and this is precisely how Paul systematically views himself.[44] Given that the same Paul considers not only his addressees but also himself as "fellow heirs with Christ," who alone is the "appointed heir of all things" (Heb 1:2), then the difference between him and Jesus becomes clear. Paul is God's plenipotentiary representative in Corinth *until* the coming of the heir, the Lord (*kyrios*) Jesus Christ, and thus of his full revelation (revealing; 1 Cor 1:7) as such.[45] Until then, the heir is, to plagiarize Galatians 4:2, *under* God's *oikonomos* Paul. It is Paul's teaching, the gospel, that makes Jesus Christ present among the Corinthians (1 Cor 4:15b). However, this teaching is not a compendium of abstract "theological" statements or propositions; rather it is a "law" (1 Cor 7:19; see also Rom 8:2; Gal 6:2), a rule of behavior that must be followed. That is why Paul started this passage with the words "For our boast is this, the testimony of our conscience that we have behaved (*anestraphēmen*) in the world" (2 Cor 1:12a).[46] The result is that really nothing is "all settled" for Paul nor for the Corinthians

---

[44] See especially 1 Cor 9; see my comments thereon in *C-1Cor*.
[45] See also 2 Thess 1:7; 1 Pet 1:7, 13; 4:13.
[46] The denotation of behavior connected with the verb *anastrephō* is confirmed in its other instance where it parallels the verb *peripatō* (walk) that occurs often in Paul with the consistent meaning of "behave": "And you he made alive, when you were dead through the trespasses and sins in which you once walked (*periepatēsate*), following the course of this world, following the prince of the power of the air, the spirit that is now at work in the sons of disobedience. Among these we all once lived (*anestraphēmen*) in the passions of our flesh, following the desires of body and mind, and so we were by nature children of wrath, like the rest of mankind." (Eph 2:1-3)

until the Lord's coming (1 Cor 4:1-5a) when "(Then) every man will receive his commendation from God" (v.5b).

That is why, at this juncture, Paul brings back into the picture what he stated right from the start, namely, that the assuredness is anchored in *hope*. Indeed, if his hope is unshaken (*bebaia*; firm, sure, assured; 2 Cor 1:7a) it is only because God is the one "who establishes (*bebaiōn*; ensures) us with you in (*eis*; toward, unto) Christ" (v.21a). This thought is central to Paul; he uses it at the beginning of his first letter as well and in a context similar to here where the Apostle is "leading" his addressees toward judgment day:[47]

> I give thanks to God always for you because of the grace of God which was given you in Christ Jesus, that in every way you were enriched in him with all speech and all knowledge—even as the testimony to Christ was confirmed (*ebebaiōthē*) among you—so that you are not lacking in any spiritual gift, as you wait for the revealing of our Lord Jesus Christ; who will sustain (*bebaiōsei*) you to the end, guiltless in the day of our Lord Jesus Christ. God is faithful,[48] by whom you were called into the fellowship of his Son, Jesus Christ our Lord. (1 Cor 1:4-9)

The corollary is that the gift of the Spirit is a guarantee (*arrabōna*; pledge, sure sign, 2 Cor 1:22b) for the fulfillment of God's promises rather than their full realization, a thought that is repeated in 5:5. It occurs once more in the New Testament in a passage dealing with the same topic and uses similar phraseology to render Paul's thought with utmost clarity:

---

[47] Hence I opted for taking the preposition *eis* before "Christ" literally as "unto, toward."
[48] Compare with 2 Cor 1:18.

> In him, according to the purpose of him who accomplishes all things according to the counsel of his will, we who first *hoped* in Christ have been destined and appointed to live for the praise of his glory. In him you also, who have heard the word of truth, the gospel of your salvation, and have believed in him, *were sealed* with the *promised* Holy Spirit, which is the *guarantee* (*arrabōn*) of our *inheritance* until we acquire possession of it, to the praise of his glory. (Eph 1:11-14)

The Greek *arrabōn* is a transliteration of the Hebrew *'erabon* that occurs in the Old Testament only three times, all in the same context, which will allow us to understand its function:

> When Judah saw her [Tamar], he thought her to be a harlot, for she had covered her face. He went over to her at the road side, and said, "Come, let me come in to you," for he did not know that she was his daughter-in-law. She said, "What will you give me, that you may come in to me?" He answered, "I will send you a kid from the flock." And she said, "Will you give me a pledge (*'erabon*), till you send it?" He said, "What pledge (*'erabon*) shall I give you?" She replied, "Your signet and your cord, and your staff that is in your hand." So he gave them to her, and went in to her, and she conceived by him. Then she arose and went away, and taking off her veil she put on the garments of her widowhood. When Judah sent the kid by his friend the Adullamite, to receive the pledge (*'erabon*) from the woman's hand, he could not find her. (Gen 38:15-21)

It is clear that *'erabon/arrabōn* is a "serious" pledge that holds its giver to fulfilling the promise made, and not just an "empty word." In Arabic the engagement in view of marriage is called *'urbun* (pledge; betrothal), which reflects the seriousness with which that commitment is taken: the "breaking" of an engagement in the East is not simply a "calling off" but is as serious as the "breaking" of a marriage. Yet, engagement is in no way tantamount to a realized marriage.[49] A contemporary equivalent is the down payment, which secures the use of a house or a car *as though* one owns it: besides the monthly payments, one is also responsible for the insurance and maintenance. And yet the ownership deed is in retainer; one does not "own" the house or car yet.[50] However, at the signing of the papers, one says already "the deal is sealed."

In order to bring home the teaching of scripture to his Gentile audience, Paul often combined scriptural and Roman society terminologies and metaphors.[51] In our case here, with the aim of making clear the "assuredness" of God's promise, Paul brings into the picture the metaphor of "seal" (2 Cor 1:22a; see also Eph 1:13).[52] Sealing was used to ensure the content of a letter or a given ware would reach its destination, in the same way as nowadays one seals a letter before mailing or a crate before shipping. The seal is no proof that the object already reached its destination; rather, as a pledge, it ensures that it would eventually reach its destination barring any mishap. The seal proved to be a perfect metaphor for Paul to speak of God's law as *promise* of life. The Corinthians' sharing in knowledge of this Law (2 Cor 1:13-14a) will not preclude their ending in death, also promised in that same Law to those who would not walk

---

[49] Even in Western contemporary societies where sexual intercourse and even pregnancy are "consummated" before and without marriage, the wedding still preserves its traditional "halo." The bride and groom make a big fuss about their "wedding" and prepare for it—in both energy and money—as though no other day can and will ever be one like it. Marriage Day is "the day!" It is as sacrosanct as "the Lord's Day." It is "it" in a way the engagement is not.

[50] One cannot at the same time own and not own something. Thus, technically speaking, the credit card companies' question as to whether the applicant "owns" a house should be rephrased!

[51] See especially Rom 6 and Gal 3:15-4:7.

[52] See also Eph 4:30: "And do not grieve the Holy Spirit of God, in whom you were sealed for the day of redemption."

according to its prescriptions (Lev 26 and Deut 28): "I warn you, as I warned you before, that those who do such things [the works of the flesh] shall not inherit the kingdom of God." (Gal 5:21b) However, without the seal, which is exclusively a divine prerogative (2 Cor 1:22a), there is not even the slightest hope that the letter or the ware would reach its destination or, conversely, that the Corinthians would attain co-heirship with Christ in the promised inheritance. The hope is "sure" (*bebaia*) to the extent that they abide by Paul's teaching as is clear from how Paul phrases the divine assurance: "But it is God who establishes (*ho bebaiōn*; who ensures) *us with you* toward Christ, and has commissioned (*khrisas*; anointed, chrismated) *us*." (v.21) Since the commissioning is confined to Paul, the Corinthians share in the assurance communicated to him.

Chapter 2

1:23-24 ²³Ἐγὼ δὲ μάρτυρα τὸν θεὸν ἐπικαλοῦμαι ἐπὶ τὴν ἐμὴν ψυχήν, ὅτι φειδόμενος ὑμῶν οὐκέτι ἦλθον εἰς Κόρινθον. ²⁴ οὐχ ὅτι κυριεύομεν ὑμῶν τῆς πίστεως ἀλλὰ συνεργοί ἐσμεν τῆς χαρᾶς ὑμῶν· τῇ γὰρ πίστει ἑστήκατε.

2:1-11 ¹Ἔκρινα γὰρ ἐμαυτῷ τοῦτο τὸ μὴ πάλιν ἐν λύπῃ πρὸς ὑμᾶς ἐλθεῖν. ² εἰ γὰρ ἐγὼ λυπῶ ὑμᾶς, καὶ τίς ὁ εὐφραίνων με εἰ μὴ ὁ λυπούμενος ἐξ ἐμοῦ; ³ καὶ ἔγραψα τοῦτο αὐτό, ἵνα μὴ ἐλθὼν λύπην σχῶ ἀφ' ὧν ἔδει με χαίρειν, πεποιθὼς ἐπὶ πάντας ὑμᾶς ὅτι ἡ ἐμὴ χαρὰ πάντων ὑμῶν ἐστιν. ⁴ ἐκ γὰρ πολλῆς θλίψεως καὶ συνοχῆς καρδίας ἔγραψα ὑμῖν διὰ πολλῶν δακρύων, οὐχ ἵνα λυπηθῆτε ἀλλὰ τὴν ἀγάπην ἵνα γνῶτε ἣν ἔχω περισσοτέρως εἰς ὑμᾶς. ⁵ Εἰ δέ τις λελύπηκεν, οὐκ ἐμὲ λελύπηκεν, ἀλλὰ ἀπὸ μέρους, ἵνα μὴ ἐπιβαρῶ, πάντας ὑμᾶς. ⁶ ἱκανὸν τῷ τοιούτῳ ἡ ἐπιτιμία αὕτη ἡ ὑπὸ τῶν πλειόνων, ⁷ ὥστε τοὐναντίον μᾶλλον ὑμᾶς χαρίσασθαι καὶ παρακαλέσαι, μή πως τῇ περισσοτέρᾳ λύπῃ καταποθῇ ὁ τοιοῦτος. ⁸ διὸ παρακαλῶ ὑμᾶς κυρῶσαι εἰς αὐτὸν ἀγάπην· ⁹ εἰς τοῦτο γὰρ καὶ ἔγραψα, ἵνα γνῶ τὴν δοκιμὴν ὑμῶν, εἰ εἰς πάντα ὑπήκοοί ἐστε. ¹⁰ ᾧ δέ τι χαρίζεσθε, κἀγώ· καὶ γὰρ ἐγὼ ὃ κεχάρισμαι, εἴ τι κεχάρισμαι, δι' ὑμᾶς ἐν προσώπῳ Χριστοῦ, ¹¹ ἵνα μὴ πλεονεκτηθῶμεν ὑπὸ τοῦ σατανᾶ· οὐ γὰρ αὐτοῦ τὰ νοήματα ἀγνοοῦμεν.

1:23-24 ²³But I call God to witness against me—it was to spare you that I refrained from coming to Corinth. ²⁴ Not that we lord it over your faith; we work with you for your joy, for you stand firm in your faith.

2:1-11 ¹For I made up my mind not to make you another painful visit. ²For if I cause you pain, who is there to make me glad but the one whom I have pained? ³And I wrote as I did, so that when I came I might not suffer pain from those who should have made me rejoice, for I felt sure of all of you, that my joy *would be the joy of you all.* ⁴*For I wrote you out of much affliction and anguish of heart and with many tears, not to cause you pain but to let you know the abundant love that I have for you.* ⁵*But if any one has caused pain, he has caused it not to me, but in some measure—not to put it too severely—to you all.* ⁶*For such a one this punishment by the majority is enough;* ⁷*so you should rather turn to forgive and comfort him, or he may be overwhelmed by excessive sorrow.* ⁸*So I beg you to reaffirm your love for him.* ⁹*For this is why I wrote, that I might test you and know whether you are obedient in everything.* ¹⁰*Any one whom you forgive, I also forgive. What I have forgiven, if I have forgiven anything, has been for your sake in the presence of Christ,* ¹¹*to keep Satan from gaining the advantage over us; for we are not ignorant of his designs.*

Now that he has established in the minds of his hearers that they are "on the way" toward the inheritance, Paul is at liberty to explain his change of plans, which is not whimsical, and actually allows them to proceed on that path without any hindrance. If they are standing firm in their trust in his teaching, he has no desire to lord over them or to dictate how they are to handle that trust. To the contrary, he is their fellow worker (*synergoi esmen;* we work with you) in that matter. However, he reminds them that the goal of that trust is not to bask in it, but rather to reach the full joy (*kharas*) of the Kingdom (v.24). In his judgment (*ekrina*; from the verb *krinō* [judge, estimate])[1] it would be better not to spoil their hope in that joy with a visit that would bring sorrow (*lypē*; grief, pain, 2:2). Since there is no mention of either joy or sorrow in 1 Corinthians, some exegetes assume that a previous sorrowful visit had taken place before the writing of 2 Corinthians and that this verse means that Paul

---

[1] RSV translates *ekrina* into "I made up my mind."

would pay them "a second sorrowful visit." Such a reading is no more than a "shot in the dark" given that the original can simply mean "I would not want my second visit to you to end up sorrowfully,"[2] which fits the context that is filled with terminology of sorrow versus joy.

The entire passage (2 Cor 1:23-2:11) revolves around the grief occasioned by the extreme stand he took toward the community regarding the adulterous man (1 Cor 5:1-8). What Paul is doing here is taking the opportunity created by his change of plans to give the community, as well as the culprit, time to implement his suggestion as to how to bring about healing before he would arrive at Corinth. In the way the statement is phrased, the suggested solution sounds ambiguous: "For if I cause you pain, who is there to make me glad but the one whom I have pained?" (2 Cor 2:2) This magisterial stroke gives the impression that the solution is to be found between the adulterer and Paul, thus lowering the guard of his hearers by making them an audience of watchers. Does this mean that the adulterer is to forgive Paul for having pained him or that he is to repent from his sin of harlotry in order for him to be reintegrated in the community (1 Cor 5:5)?[3] By the time the hearers realize that they are the ones who would have to do something about the situation, it is too late; they are already trapped. Indeed, although the latter part of 2 Corinthians 2:2b is phrased in the singular, the following two verses revert to the plural and more specifically the second person plural with which he started v.2a: "And I wrote[4] as I did, so that when I came I might not suffer pain from those who should have

---

[2] Compare with KJV (I would not come again to you with heaviness) and JB (my next visit to you would not be a painful one).
[3] See my comments in *C-1Cor* 101.
[4] This is not a reference to a previous writing, but rather to what he is writing now. See 1 Cor 5:11 and my comments thereon in *C-1Cor* 105-6.

made me rejoice, for I felt sure of all of you, that my joy would be the joy of you all. For I wrote[5] you out of much affliction and anguish of heart and with many tears, not to cause you pain but to let you know the abundant love that I have for you." (vv.3-4) Moreover, along with the phraseology of joy and pain, he throws in love, the key word he is about to capitalize on.

Love is the ingredient necessary to solve the dilemma and such love is required not so much of Paul or of the adulterer, but is required from the Corinthians themselves. The reason is that it is they who feel the sorrowful pain more than he (v.5): although Paul is the one who issued the verdict (1 Cor 5:3), it is they who had to implement the sentence of excommunicating one of their own (vv.4-5; 2 Cor 2:6). Yet, Paul is cleverly guiding them to not make of their pain an occasion for subconscious retaliation. Rather, as he himself took the opportunity of his own affliction to comfort others (1:3-7) and behaved toward others according to God's grace (*khariti*; v.12), he is asking them to do the same: "… so you should rather turn to forgive (*kharisasthai*; behave gracefully, deal with grace) and comfort (*parakalesai*) him, or he may be overwhelmed (*katapothē*; swallowed up [KJV]) by excessive sorrow." (2:7) Paul's use of the rare verb "swallow up" (*katapinō*) is obviously intentional. Out of its seven instances in the New Testament, four are found in the Pauline corpus, three of which occur in the Corinthian correspondence (1 Cor 15:54; 2 Cor 2:7; 5:4). Not only do the first and last passages deal with the same topic of death being swallowed up by life, but they also use the same terminology:

> For this perishable nature must put on the imperishable, and this mortal nature (*to thnēton*) must put on immortality. When the

---

[5] See previous fn.

perishable puts on the imperishable, and the mortal (*to thnēton*) puts on immortality, then shall come to pass the saying that is written: "Death is swallowed up in victory." (1 Cor 15:53-54)

For while we are still in this tent, we sigh with anxiety; not that we would be unclothed, but that we would be further clothed, so that what is mortal (*to thnēton*) may be swallowed up by life. (2 Cor 5:4)

Consequently, Paul is inviting the Corinthians to understand that their forgiveness would comfort the adulterer just as Paul was comforted in Asia, out of death into life, which was precisely the original aim of the punishment: "... you are to deliver this man to Satan for the destruction of the flesh, that his spirit may be saved in the day of the Lord Jesus." (1 Cor 5:5) That this thought is on Paul's mind is evident in that a few verses later we hear: "Any one whom you forgive (*kharizesthai*), I also forgive.[6] What I have forgiven (*kekharismai*), if I have forgiven (*kekharismai*) anything, has been for your sake in the presence of Christ, to keep Satan from gaining the advantage over us; for we are not ignorant of his designs." (2 Cor 2:10-11)[7] On the other hand, the close link between 2 Corinthians 2:7 and 5:4 is secured through the reference in 5:5 to "God, who has given us the Spirit as a guarantee" (see 1:22).

Immediately after bringing in the subject of comfort, Paul combines it with "love" with which he started his appeal: "So I beg (*parakalō*) you to reaffirm (*kyrōsai*; confirm, validate, ratify) your love for him." (2:8) Since the Greek *parakalō* means both "ask, summons, request" and "comfort, console," then Paul is asking the Corinthians to do for the adulterer (v.7) what he

---

[6] The original has simply "so do I" without the repetition of the verb *kharizomai*.
[7] The reference to Satan in the Corinthian correspondence is restricted to 1 Cor 5:5; 7:5; 2 Cor 2:11; 11:14; 12:7.

himself is doing for them (v.7) *in this letter*! Such forcefulness is evident in his use of the verb *kyrōsai* that is found only twice more in the New Testament in a passage where the topic is the "promises" and the "promise of the Spirit" (1:20-22; 5:5; 7:1):

> ... that in Christ Jesus the blessing of Abraham might come upon the Gentiles, that we might receive the promise of the Spirit through faith. To give a human example, brethren: no one annuls even a man's will, or adds to it, once it has been *ratified* (*kekyrōmenēn*). Now the promises were made to Abraham and to his offspring. It does not say, "And to offsprings," referring to many; but, referring to one, "And to your offspring," which is Christ. This is what I mean: the law, which came four hundred and thirty years afterward, does not annul a covenant *previously ratified* (*prokekyrōmenēn*) by God, so as to make the promise void. (Gal 3:14-17)

In this case, it is clear from the context that the ratification refers to something sealed *in writing*. Consequently, Paul is requesting no less of the Corinthians than he himself is doing. He is committing *in writing* his "request" (*parakalō*; 2 Cor 2:8) that they "comfort" (*parakalesai*; v.7) the adulterer through their love for him (vv.4, 8), and they are to commit themselves to this task *as though it were sealed in writing*. This intention is evident in that, in the following verse, he forces their hand by assuming they already passed the test. Thus they will be obedient to his request: "*For this is why I wrote*, that I might test you and know whether you are obedient in everything." (v.9) Such a statement is not a plea, but rather an order,[8] on the part of the plenipotentiary Apostle who earlier wrote:

---

[8] This is also the connotation of *parakalō* on the lips or pen of a senior; see my comments in *1 Thess* 133-4.

For though you have countless guides in Christ, you do not have many fathers. For I became your father in Christ Jesus through the gospel. I urge you, then, be imitators of me. Therefore I sent to you Timothy, my beloved and faithful child in the Lord, to remind you of my ways in Christ, as I teach them everywhere in every church. Some are arrogant, as though I were not coming to you. But I will come to you soon, if the Lord wills, and I will find out not the talk of these arrogant people but their power. For the kingdom of God does not consist in talk but in power. What do you wish? Shall I come to you with a rod, or with love in a spirit of gentleness? (1 Cor 4:15-21)

This is, in fact, what he says in continuation because he is their father in Christ Jesus: "Any one whom you forgive, I also forgive. What I have forgiven, if I have forgiven anything, has been for your sake *in the presence* (*en prosōpō* [face, person]) of Christ." (2 Cor 2:10) The Corinthians are to forgive and comfort the adulterer, thus reaffirming their love for him. If they do not do so it will be they and not the adulterer who will have succumbed to Satan and his devices (v.11).

Vv. 12-17 ¹² Ἐλθὼν δὲ εἰς τὴν Τρῳάδα εἰς τὸ εὐαγγέλιον τοῦ Χριστοῦ καὶ θύρας μοι ἀνεῳγμένης ἐν κυρίῳ, ¹³ οὐκ ἔσχηκα ἄνεσιν τῷ πνεύματί μου τῷ μὴ εὑρεῖν με Τίτον τὸν ἀδελφόν μου, ἀλλὰ ἀποταξάμενος αὐτοῖς ἐξῆλθον εἰς Μακεδονίαν. ¹⁴ Τῷ δὲ θεῷ χάρις τῷ πάντοτε θριαμβεύοντι ἡμᾶς ἐν τῷ Χριστῷ καὶ τὴν ὀσμὴν τῆς γνώσεως αὐτοῦ φανεροῦντι δι' ἡμῶν ἐν παντὶ τόπῳ· ¹⁵ ὅτι Χριστοῦ εὐωδία ἐσμὲν τῷ θεῷ ἐν τοῖς σῳζομένοις καὶ ἐν τοῖς ἀπολλυμένοις, ¹⁶ οἷς μὲν ὀσμὴ ἐκ θανάτου εἰς θάνατον, οἷς δὲ ὀσμὴ ἐκ ζωῆς εἰς ζωήν. καὶ πρὸς ταῦτα τίς ἱκανός; ¹⁷ οὐ γάρ ἐσμεν ὡς οἱ πολλοὶ καπηλεύοντες τὸν λόγον τοῦ θεοῦ, ἀλλ' ὡς ἐξ εἰλικρινείας, ἀλλ' ὡς ἐκ θεοῦ κατέναντι θεοῦ ἐν Χριστῷ λαλοῦμεν.

> *¹²When I came to Troas to preach the gospel of Christ, a door was opened for me in the Lord; ¹³but my mind could not rest because I did not find my brother Titus there. So I took leave of them and went on to Macedonia. ¹⁴But thanks be to God, who in Christ always leads us in triumph, and through us spreads the fragrance of the knowledge of him everywhere. ¹⁵For we are the aroma of Christ to God among those who are being saved and among those who are perishing, ¹⁶to one a fragrance from death to death, to the other a fragrance from life to life. Who is sufficient for these things? ¹⁷For we are not, like so many, peddlers of God's word; but as men of sincerity, as commissioned by God, in the sight of God we speak in Christ.*

Having referred to love for the lesser neighbor, which is the core of his gospel (1 Cor 13; see also Rom 13:8-10; Gal 5:13-15), and in order to block any complaint on their part, Paul hastens to remind them of the high cost of the gospel for the Gentiles of Macedonia and Achaia (2 Cor 8:2) since its beginning at Troas (1:12). Paul was hoping to find relief (*anesin*; rest) at Troas, and he was also hoping to find Titus there to take him along to Philippi (see Acts 16:11). Titus would have functioned for Paul there as he did at the council in Jerusalem (Gal 2:1-10). In Jerusalem, Paul showcased Titus, the uncircumcised Gentile, in his confrontation with the Jewish pillars regarding "the truth of the gospel" (v.5). At Philippi, the company of Titus was intended to be a showdown with Rome itself, that is, Paul was planning to have Rome submit in obedience to that same gospel (Rom 1:14-17). Titus was a classic Roman name, and its bearer would have challenged the Roman soldiers residing in or banished to Philippi to find relief and the aroma of freedom that the gospel offers to all those subjugated in any manner. As for the original Macedonians residing in Philippi, Titus, a quintessential Roman subjugated *"under* (the) grace" of the gospel (Rom 6:14-15), would have been a sign of hope for them that, in spite of all that points to the contrary, their Roman conquerors are ultimate "lords" only in this world: "Masters (*hoi kyrioi*; lords), treat your slaves justly and fairly, knowing that you also have a Master (*kyrion*; Lord) in heaven." (Col 4:1). Yet, Titus was nowhere to be found in Troas and Paul had to go it alone (2 Cor 2:13).

"But thanks be to God" writes Paul (v.14a). The original Greek *tō de Theō kharis* (But grace be to God) is skillfully composed. As Paul underscores time and again, the message of God as scripture which was handed to Israel as gratuitous gift (*kharis*) is now imparted, also as a free gift, to the Gentiles. As a "slave" commissioned for this task (1 Cor 9), whatever the affliction and the sufferings (2 Cor 1:4-5), it is with thanks*giving* (*evkharistia*; acknowledging the grace, returning the gift) that Paul is to accomplish his mission. As he himself has aptly put it:

> For if I preach the gospel, that gives me no ground for boasting. For necessity is laid upon me. Woe to me if I do not preach the gospel! For if I do this of my own will, I have a reward; but if not of my own will, I am entrusted with a commission. What then is my reward? Just this: that in my preaching I may make the gospel free of charge, not making full use of my right in the gospel. For though I am free from all men, I have made myself a slave to all, that I might win the more. To the Jews I became as a Jew, in order to win Jews; to those under the law I became as one under the law—though not being myself under the law—that I might win those under the law. To those outside the law I became as one outside the law—not being without law toward God but under the law of Christ—that I might win those outside the law. To the weak I became weak, that I might win the weak. I have become all

things to all men, that I might by all means save some. I do it all for the sake of the gospel, that I may share in it.⁹'" (1 Cor 9:16-23)

Thus, a plain "thank you" (*evkharistia*) to God for his graceful gift (*kharis*) does not cut it. The receiver of God's gift of love must thank him by sharing what one has received with those less fortunate. It is precisely Paul's choice of *kharis* (grace) over the plain *evkharistō* (I thank) in 2 Corinthians 2:14a that challenges his addressees whom he asked earlier to *kharisasthai* (deal gracefully and forgivingly) with the adulterer (v.7). Indeed, God's grace (*kharin*) comes to them with every apostolic visit (1:15), and if the Apostle himself is "bound" by that grace, then so are they! Since this is the case, why would the Corinthians not extend the same prodigality toward the Macedonians? If graceful dealing (*kharisasthai*) is required toward someone who is in need of "comfort" (2:7), then the Corinthians are to consider the Macedonians more in need of such than themselves, that is, to consider that the Macedonians are needier of God's grace because they are more "sinful" than themselves. Thus the Corinthians should be "grateful" to God that his "grace" reached Macedonia first! As for their potentially being robbed of the "double grace" originally planned by Paul (1:15), let the Corinthians realize that (1) divine grace is not quantitative; rather it carries the fullness of God's love at all times and (2) the postponement of Paul's visit will allow them extra time to forgive the adulterer and thus "spare them" (1:23). Should they not be ready at Paul's eventual coming, he "will not spare them": "I warned those who sinned before and all the others, and I warn them now while absent, as I did when present on my second visit, that if I come again I will not spare them." (13:2) In other

---

⁹ RSV has "in its blessings."

words, the Corinthians should count their blessings rather than complain!

Although alone, without Titus, Paul is led by God into Macedonia triumphantly (*thriambevonti*) in Christ (2:13b-14a), such triumph was assured since God had already "triumphed (*thriambevsas*) over the principalities and powers in Christ" (Col 2:15).[10] Given that the principalities and powers are subsumed in the office of the Roman emperor, accordingly his vanquishers—Paul as well as Christ—are themselves presented in metaphors fitting that office.[11] Since every monarch is also the high priest, Paul proceeds by referring to "fragrance" and "aroma" (2 Cor 2:14b-15a) which was discussed earlier in conjunction with 1:18-20. He then uses the imagery of imperial power over life and death which evokes the imagery of the gladiators in the arena, where the emperor decides who will be "saved" and who will "perish" (2:15b), even against the will of the people. Lastly, in an accomplished recapitulating statement, Paul combines the two metaphors of high priest and of master over life and death: "For we are the aroma of Christ to God among those who are being saved and among those who are perishing." (v.16a) With this thought concerning absolute power over life and death, Paul cannot but exclaim rhetorically: "Who is sufficient for (*hikanos*; worthy of [toward]) these things?" (v.16b) Even imperial power is assigned by God (Rom 13:1-2), let alone that of a mere "servant" (*doulos*; slave) such as Paul (Phil 1:1) and also Jesus (2:7). That Paul was referring to the apostolic assignment is corroborated in that a few chapters earlier he used the same *hikanos* in reference to his unworthiness of his calling to apostleship: "For I am the least of the apostles, unfit (*ouk*

---

[10] These are the only instances of the verb *thriambevō* in the New Testament.
[11] See my comments in *C-Col* 70.

hikanos; not worthy)¹² to be called an apostle, because I persecuted the church of God." (1 Cor 15:9) Finally, he ends with a critical assessment of his opponents, "peddlers of God's word" (2 Cor 2:17), a criticism he will develop later in the letter (2 Cor 11:1-15). For the time being, he proceeds to develop what "sincere" ministry entails.

---

[12] KJV has "not meet."

Chapter 3

Vv. 1-3 ¹Ἀρχόμεθα πάλιν ἑαυτοὺς συνιστάνειν; ἢ μὴ χρῄζομεν ὥς τινες συστατικῶν ἐπιστολῶν πρὸς ὑμᾶς ἢ ἐξ ὑμῶν; ² ἡ ἐπιστολὴ ἡμῶν ὑμεῖς ἐστε, ἐγγεγραμμένη ἐν ταῖς καρδίαις ἡμῶν, γινωσκομένη καὶ ἀναγινωσκομένη ὑπὸ πάντων ἀνθρώπων, ³ φανερούμενοι ὅτι ἐστὲ ἐπιστολὴ Χριστοῦ διακονηθεῖσα ὑφ' ἡμῶν, ἐγγεγραμμένη οὐ μέλανι ἀλλὰ πνεύματι θεοῦ ζῶντος, οὐκ ἐν πλαξὶν λιθίναις ἀλλ' ἐν πλαξὶν καρδίαις σαρκίναις.

¹Are we beginning to commend ourselves again? Or do we need, as some do, letters of recommendation to you, or from you? ²You yourselves are our letter of recommendation, written on your hearts, to be known and read by all men; ³and you show that you are a letter from Christ delivered by us, written not with ink but with the Spirit of the living God, not on tablets of stone but on tablets of human hearts.

The verb *synistanein* (commend) that Paul uses in the beginning sentence of chapter 3 is a staple of 2 Corinthians; it occurs nine times in this letter (compared to seven in the rest of the New Testament) and always in conjunction with either Paul or his opponents.[1] Such confirms that the entire letter, except for chapters 8 and 9 that deal with the "collection" and where the verb "commend" does not appear, is an expansion on the theme of 1 Corinthians 9: Paul's apologia of his apostleship and, more specifically, his being the sole Apostle for the Corinthians. However, from the beginning he makes it clear, just as he does in all his letters, that his apologia is not tantamount to self-defense as though he had to explain his actions; rather it is

---

[1] 2 Cor 3:1, 2 (*systatikōn epistolōn*, recommendation letters); 4:2; 5:12; 6:4; 7:11 (where RSV translates it as "prove"); 10:12, 18; 12:11. *systatikōn* is a participial form from the verb *synistanein*.

done *for the Corinthians' sake* in the sense that, were he a false apostle, "then our preaching is in vain and *your faith is in vain* ... your faith is futile and *you are still in your sins*" (1 Cor 15:14, 17). His stand is corroborated by the two opening rhetorical questions: Paul is in no need of commending himself nor is he in need of letters of recommendation "*to you, or from you*" (2 Cor 3:1). The reason is evident: the Corinthians' awareness of who God's Christ is and what he is all about is the *sealed* "proof" that Paul is an apostle. That is why, after the rhetorical question where reference is made to "*letters* of recommendation" (v.1), he switches to the singular: "You yourselves are our *letter* of recommendation." (v.2a)

Yet, how could a letter inscribed in their hearts be both known and read aloud,[2] no less, to all men? The explanation lies in the functionality of the metaphor and not in some mystical esoteric jargon. Paul's letters were meant to be read aloud to the gathered community (Phil 1:1). When he says "to (by) all men" he is obviously referring foremost to all residents of Achaia (1 Cor 1:2; 2 Cor 1:1). Since Corinth was the capital of Achaia, one of the most prestigious Roman provinces wherein lay Athens, then assumedly any major news heard there would be eventually known throughout the empire. A similar case nowadays would be major news concerning New York, Chicago, or Los Angeles, which are not even state capitals; such news would be printed in all major newspapers across the USA. So Paul is putting pressure on his addressees by letting them know that the content of his letter would be known not only to them, but also to all men (3:2). Put otherwise, they should be careful to abide by the teaching contained in his letter lest they be made by God "a desolation and an object of reproach among the nations round

---

[2] This is the meaning of the original *anaginōskomenē*.

about you and in the sight of all that pass by ... a reproach and a taunt, a warning and a horror, to the nations round about you" (Ezek 5:14-15).[3] Still, and beyond that, given that the apostolic teaching contained in the letter is "inscribed—as scripture would be— (*engegrammenē*)[4] on your hearts" (2 Cor 3:2a), they ultimately will be accountable to God himself "on the day of the Lord Jesus" (1:14). That such is Paul's intention is confirmed in the following verse (2 Cor 3:3) where he explains what he means by "written on your hearts" (v.2): "... written not with ink but with the Spirit of the living God, not on tablets of stone (*lithinais*; stony) but on tablets, (that is to say) hearts, (that are) fleshly (*sarkinais*)."[5] This is an outright reference to Ezekiel which is the only book of the Old Testament where we twice hear "heart of flesh" in opposition to "heart of stone" and in both instances in conjunction with the "spirit," which is precisely the case here. Furthermore, the "heart of flesh" under the aegis of the spirit is not the end of the line; it is an invitation to behave accordingly in view of ultimate divine judgment:

> And I will give them one heart, and put a new spirit within them; I will take the stony heart out of their flesh and give them a heart of flesh, that they may walk in my statutes and keep my ordinances and obey them; and they shall be my people, and I will be their God. But as for those whose heart goes after their detestable things and their abominations, I will requite their deeds upon their own heads, says the Lord God. (Ezek 11:19-21)

> A new heart I will give you, and a new spirit I will put within you; and I will take out of your flesh the heart of stone and give you a heart of flesh. And I will put my spirit within you, and cause you

---

[3] I referenced Ezekiel since he will be at the core of 2 Cor 3:2-3.
[4] From the verb *graphō* whence *graphē* (scripture)
[5] RSV has "on tablets of human hearts."

to walk in my statutes and be careful to observe my ordinances. (36:26-27)

It is precisely because of the impending judgment that Paul is not putting his hope in them, but rather in God. Given their record, the Corinthians may not be abiding by the Apostle's directives, and he is trying to spare them his coming, which is a foretaste of the Lord's coming (1 Cor 4:14-21). Such is evident in his explication that they are his letter of recommendation in their response to the message of the gospel (2 Cor 3:2a): "*Forasmuch as ye are* manifestly declared to be the epistle of Christ ministered by us." (3:3a; KJV)[6] A literal translation would be "(you) being shown (*phaneroumenoi*; being manifested) that you are the epistle of Christ ministered (*diakonētheisa*) by us." *phaneroumenoi* is the passive participle of the verb *phanerō* (manifest, show) whose active participle *phanerounti* has just been used of God as the agent of the advancement of the gospel "through us" (2:14). In 3:3a we have the same thought: it is God, through Paul, who is performing an action among the Corinthians who are thus mere recipients, yet they still have to respond. Moreover, Paul's action is that of table ministry (*diakonia* from the same root as *diakonētheisa*), which is precisely how he has introduced himself when he spoke of his activity in Corinth: "What then is Apollos? What is Paul? Servants (*diakonoi*; [table] ministers) through whom you believed, as the Lord assigned to each." (1 Cor 3:5) The reference to table ministry corroborates that Paul is not speaking here of any "action" on the part of the Corinthians. Rather they are to listen

---

[6] KJV italics is not in the original and added in the translation to make the English clearer. I opted against RSV that makes of the Corinthians the subject of the action of "showing" rather than the object of the divine action among them—"and *you show* that you are a letter from Christ delivered by us"—which is precisely the opposite of what Paul is communicating to them!

to his letter read aloud at the weekly "meal gathering", that is nothing other than the Lord's supper, during which his instruction is imparted. Such instruction prepares them for the divine judgment (1 Cor 11:17-34).[7] Thus, the Corinthians have not yet done anything of value except receive the gift (*kharis*; grace) of Paul's visit to them (2 Cor 1:15). Now, he is challenging them to respond to God's appeal by sharing this gift with the adulterer (*kharisasthai*; 2:7). Indeed, immediately after speaking of *his* letter "inscribed" in their hearts, he says his confidence is not in them but "Such (*toiavtēn*) is the confidence (*pepoithēsin*; assuredness) that we have through Christ *toward God*" (3:4),which is precisely how he earlier referred to his "graceful" visit to them: "Because I was sure of this (*tavtē tē pepoithēsei*; with this confidence/assuredness), I wanted to come to you first, so that you might have a double pleasure (*kharin*; grace)." (1:15) That his purview is his own ministry among them rather than their response to his preaching is confirmed in that, starting with 2:5 and through 6:10, he goes in detail over that ministry.

Vv. 4-11 ⁴Πεποίθησιν δὲ τοιαύτην ἔχομεν διὰ τοῦ Χριστοῦ πρὸς τὸν θεόν. ⁵ οὐχ ὅτι ἀφ' ἑαυτῶν ἱκανοί ἐσμεν λογίσασθαί τι ὡς ἐξ ἑαυτῶν, ἀλλ' ἡ ἱκανότης ἡμῶν ἐκ τοῦ θεοῦ, ⁶ ὃς καὶ ἱκάνωσεν ἡμᾶς διακόνους καινῆς διαθήκης, οὐ γράμματος ἀλλὰ πνεύματος· τὸ γὰρ γράμμα ἀποκτέννει, τὸ δὲ πνεῦμα ζῳοποιεῖ. ⁷ Εἰ δὲ ἡ διακονία τοῦ θανάτου ἐν γράμμασιν ἐντετυπωμένη λίθοις ἐγενήθη ἐν δόξῃ, ὥστε μὴ δύνασθαι ἀτενίσαι τοὺς υἱοὺς Ἰσραὴλ εἰς τὸ πρόσωπον Μωϋσέως διὰ τὴν δόξαν τοῦ προσώπου αὐτοῦ τὴν καταργουμένην, ⁸ πῶς οὐχὶ μᾶλλον ἡ διακονία τοῦ πνεύματος ἔσται ἐν δόξῃ; ⁹ εἰ γὰρ τῇ διακονίᾳ τῆς κατακρίσεως δόξα, πολλῷ μᾶλλον περισσεύει ἡ διακονία τῆς δικαιοσύνης δόξῃ. ¹⁰ καὶ γὰρ οὐ δεδόξασται τὸ δεδοξασμένον ἐν τούτῳ τῷ μέρει

---

[7] See my comments on this passage in *C-1Cor* 200-215.

εἵνεκεν τῆς ὑπερβαλλούσης δόξης. ¹¹ εἰ γὰρ τὸ καταργούμενον διὰ δόξης, πολλῷ μᾶλλον τὸ μένον ἐν δόξῃ.

⁴Such is the confidence that we have through Christ toward God. ⁵Not that we are competent of ourselves to claim anything as coming from us; our competence is from God, ⁶who has made us competent to be ministers of a new covenant, not in a written code but in the Spirit; for the written code kills, but the Spirit gives life. ⁷Now if the dispensation of death, carved in letters on stone, came with such splendor that the Israelites could not look at Moses' face because of its brightness, fading as this was, ⁸will not the dispensation of the Spirit be attended with greater splendor? ⁹For if there was splendor in the dispensation of condemnation, the dispensation of righteousness must far exceed it in splendor. ¹⁰Indeed, in this case, what once had splendor has come to have no splendor at all, because of the splendor that surpasses it. ¹¹For if what faded away came with splendor, what is permanent must have much more splendor.

When describing his "ministry," Paul begins by asserting that his worthiness is altogether an act of grace on God's part (Gal 1:15b), given that no one is worthy (*hikanos*; sufficient) of the call to apostleship (2 Cor 2:16). He does so with forcefulness since the root *hikan*— occurs thrice over two verses: "Not that we are competent (*hikanoi*) of ourselves to claim anything as coming from us; our competence (*hikanotēs*) is from God, who has made us competent (*hikanōsen hēmas*) to be ministers of a new covenant, not in a written code but in the Spirit; for the written code kills, but the Spirit gives life." (3:5-6) It would behoove us to linger on the statement concerning the new covenant and the opposition between the written code (*gramma*; letter [of the alphabet]) and the Spirit. This statement and similar statements in the New Testament were by and large misconstrued in classical theology that tended to hear scripture as though it were a Platonic dialogue dealing with abstract notions. It thus misinterpreted what Paul meant by "letter" and "spirit."[8] Let me begin by pointing out that the information we have concerning both the new covenant and the spirit is laid down as "letters" (*grammata*) in and as "scripture" (*graphē*), just as Paul's epistle conceived through God's spirit is nonetheless *written* (*engegrammenē*; v.3); all these Greek words are from the root *graphō* (write). In other words, both the spirit and the new covenant are as much "literal" as the letter and the old covenant. The difference lies in their functionality, and scriptural functionality cannot be perceived except within the story line itself since scripture is a "parable" (*mašal*), an instructional story. This is precisely what we find in v.3. The spirit is the expression of another chance, a renewed invitation to follow the ordinances of God. However, this invitation is the *final* one. That is why it is a promise rather than an actuality, and that is also why it shall entail a *final* judgment. The actual meaning of the original Hebrew *ḥadašah* behind the Greek *kainēs*, which qualifies "covenant," is precisely "final" rather than "new" in the sense that it may not be followed by another "newer" one later on; *ḥadašah* is the "newest" possible and thus "final."[9]

The clearest scriptural example of this is found at the end of Isaiah where in the prophet's description of the New Jerusalem, the heavenly city, we hear the Lord saying "For as the new (*ḥadašim*) heavens and the new (*ḥadašah*) earth which I will make *shall remain* (*'omedim*; shall stand) before me" (66:22). This in turn explains its use in Revelation (21:1-2). Yet the last statement in this "good" ending, which is at the same time the

---

[8] See further my comments on Rom 2:26-29 in *C-Rom* 71-74.
[9] Those who know Arabic will realize that the Arabic *ḥadath* refers to an event that just happened. Its plural *'aḥdath* is used to speak of the latest news in journalism.

last verse of Isaiah, is a reminder that those who entered God's city underwent his judgment: "And they shall go forth and look on the dead bodies of the men that have rebelled against me; for their worm shall not die, their fire shall not be quenched, and they shall be an abhorrence to all flesh." (66:24) Revelation follows suit. Just after we hear of the Spirit teaching the bride and its followers to pray that the Lord come (22:17), we are forewarned in the harshest possible manner by the author with as serious a "testimony" as the one with which he started (1:1-3):

> I warn (*martyrō*; bear witness [testimony] to) every one who hears the words of the prophecy of this book: if any one adds to them, God will add to him the plagues described (*gegrammenas*; inscribed [as scripture]) in this book, and if any one takes away from the words of the book of this prophecy, God will take away his share in the tree of life and in the holy city, which are described (*gegrammenōn*; inscribed [as scripture]) in this book. (22:18-19)

That Paul had such thought in mind in conjunction with the "new" covenant (2 Cor 3:6) is validated by what he will write later, again quoting Isaiah and referencing "ministry" that is the topic of chapter 3 (vv.3, 6, 7, 8, 9 [twice]; 4:1): "Therefore, if any one is in Christ, he is a new (*kainē*) creation; the old has passed away, behold, the new (*kaina*) has come.[10] All this is from God, who through Christ reconciled us to himself and gave us the ministry of reconciliation." (5:17-18) That the two passages 2 Corinthians 3:5-4:1, in which Paul discusses in detail his ministry, and 5:17-18 are closely linked is evident in that "ministry" (*diakonian*) in 5:18 is the first occurrence of that noun after 4:1.

---

[10] See Is 43:18-19a; "Remember not the former things, nor consider the things of old. Behold, I am doing a new thing (*ḥadašah*; *kaina* [LXX])."

So the following passage (3:7-11) is not disparaging the value of the "old covenant" (v.14), but is addressing the functionality of that covenant in the scriptural story that is leading *toward* the final covenant. "Toward" is underscored since, at the conclusion to his discussion of the two covenants (vv.7-11), Paul will revert to the element "hope" (v.12) which he introduced from the beginning (1:7, 10, 13). Paul could not have intended to denigrate the "old covenant" since he refers to it twice as "ministry" (3:7, 9a), the same word he uses to describe his own apostleship (vv.8, 9b).[11] In order to understand what Paul is saying in this passage, one should know what a covenant is all about. A covenant (Hebrew *berit*) is an agreement imposed by a monarch on his vassal who is treated as a "servant" (Hebrew *'ebed*, Greek *doulos*, both meaning literally slave) and is bound by certain rules he is to follow and conditions he is to fulfill. This is similar to the relation between the Roman master and the members of his household. That is why any covenant, including a new one (Jer 31:31-34), is sealed with a law. Life is promised to those who abide by it and death awaits those who do not (Lev 26; Deut 28). It is only because, *in the scriptural story*, the covenant dispensed through Moses ended with the destruction of Jerusalem and exile of its inhabitants that Paul refers to it as de facto "the ministry of death" (3:7a); in his precise description thereof he says that it was "carved" (*entetypōmenē*; engraven)— unique in the entire Bible in Greek—on stones[12] for two reasons: (1) to link its obsoleteness with the fact that the curses spoken of in the Mosaic law (Lev 26: Deut 28) *did take effect* with the

---

[11] I am opting purposely for "ministry" over RSV's "dispensation" to render *diakonia*. RSV is misleading since later, in the same letter, it translates the same apostolic *diakonia* into "ministry" (5:18). KJV is more nuanced in that it uses "ministration" in 3:7-9 and "ministry" in 5:18.

[12] The original has the plural *lithois*.

demise of the stony city buildings and (2) to differentiate between the Mosaic covenant and the new covenant that is "written" *in Paul's letter* on the Corinthians' hearts (2 Cor 3:2-3). Another sure indication that Paul is sticking to the scriptural story is reflected in the unusually lengthy wording of the second part of the verse (3:7b) which refers to the fact that the divine glory was perceived through its reflection on Moses' face, which reflection—not the divine glory!—is said to be fading: "Now if the dispensation of death, carved in letters on stones, came in (such) glory to the extent that the children of Israel could not look intently at Moses' face due to *the glory of his face*, in spite of the fact that it was bound to be done away with."[13] The intentional repetition of the reference to Moses' face is to prohibit the hearers from assuming that it is the divine glory that is fading. What faded was the glory reflected on Moses' face. Indeed, the skin of Moses' face did not shine all the time; it did so only when he came out of the tent of meeting to communicate to the people the conditions of the covenant.

The "perceived" difference between the (divine) glory of the old covenant and that of the new covenant is not, philosophically speaking, on an essential level, but rather on the practical, functional level of finality. Death does not preclude glory, but actually presupposes it (v.7a). Scriptural glory is nothing other than divine glory,[14] which is a reference to God seated on his throne of judgment[15] as is clear from "the ministry of death" being referred to also as "ministry of condemnation"

---

[13] This is my rendering of 2 Cor 3:7, which is closer to the original.
[14] Here again, by rendering the Greek *doxa* repeatedly as "splendor" (vv.7-13) and once as "brightness" (v.7) before reverting to "glory" (v.18), RSV misses the point completely and is definitely misleading by giving the impression that Paul was dealing with glory as though it is a piece of jewelry or a beauty contest!
[15] See, e.g., Is 2 and 6.

(v.9a). So Paul is not pinning one kind of glory against another kind of glory. To the contrary, he is forewarning the Corinthians that, this time round, the functional implementation of judgment by God's glory is final: "For if what fades away came with splendor (*doxēs*; glory), what is *permanent* must have much more splendor (*doxē*; glory)." (v.11) In other words, the finality does not mean that everything is bound to be fine. To the contrary, should matters go wrong, then it is not the stone tablets that will be shattered (Ex 32:19) though they are "the work of God" (v.16), but it will be the people's fleshly stones, their hearts, that will be broken, which is tantamount to final condemnation!

Clearly Paul's intention is not to lessen the value of the divine glory but rather to heighten it in his hearers' minds in view of the following "how (rather) much more" statement (2 Cor 3:8). The full parallelism in the original is evinced by the use of the same phrase "in glory" (*en doxē*) without any comparative in both verses (vv.7 and 8): the ministry of death *egenēthē en doxē* (happened [came] in glory; v.7) and that of the Spirit *estai en doxē* (will be in glory; v.8). There is absolutely no mention of a "greater" glory.[16] Such is further confirmed in v.9 (in Greek): "For if there was glory in the dispensation of condemnation, the dispensation of righteousness must far exceed it in glory." The meaning is that the same glory will be more evident[17] as is corroborated in the following verses: "For, regarding this matter (of glory), that which is supposed to appear glorious (*to dedoxasmenon*) was not fully shown as such (*ou dedoxastai*)— since it was only reflected through Moses' face—in view of the

---

[16] Notice RSV's blatant "philosophico-theological" bias (will not the dispensation of the Spirit be attended with *greater* splendor?) compared to KJV's more literal rendering (How shall not the ministration of the spirit be *rather* glorious?) of v.8.

[17] See Rom 5:15-21 where we have the same kind of comparisons.

(coming) surpassing (*hyperballousēs*) glory. For if what fades away—from Moses' face—(came) through glory, how much more the permanent (will be) in glory." (v.10-11) In other words, earlier through Moses the divine glory was manifested as divine righteousness only among the children of Israel, whereas now through Paul the same divine glory is bound to be manifested among all nations and thus in a more impressive or showy manner (*hyperballousēs*). Since divine righteousness amounted to divine condemnation due to Israel's disobedience, Paul is hoping (v.12) that this time around, should the Corinthians heed the lesson and be obedient, divine righteousness would express itself as salvation rather than destruction (2:15).

Looking closely at the entire passage in the original, we discover the importance of Paul's specific and, at face value, unwarranted choice of *diakonia* (table service) to speak of Moses' mission as well as of his own. This will help us understand *how* he is expressing himself here in 2 Corinthians 3 and, consequently, *what* he is saying. One cannot stress enough the importance of differentiating between "slave" (*doulos*) and "minister" (*diakonos*) in the Roman household. The *diakonos* was still a slave, however, one specifically assigned to serve at meals. In the case of a *symposion* which was essentially a social festivity around a common table where socio-political and philosophical ideas were debated, one can imagine the importance of that "ministry" (*diakonia*). Consequently, whenever Paul speaks of himself as "slave" he is stressing the aspect of total obedience to his master, God or Christ. Whenever he refers to himself as "minister" he is stressing his "service" or "ministry" to the master within the setting of table fellowship. One can see how the high incidence of "ministry" and "minister" in chapter 3 fits the larger context of 2 Corinthians which deals with Paul's coming to

Corinth (chs.1-2) in order to "minister" to the Corinthians (chs.3-6) in view of what he is about to ask them (chs.8-9) concerning the "offering (*diakonias*) for the saints (of Jerusalem and Judea)"[18] that was to take place at the weekly gatherings (1 Cor 16:2) revolving around a common meal (11:17-22). So Paul's aim was to bring his "ministry" to its final fruition by having the Corinthians share in that "ministry" and thus be partakers with him of God's promises (2 Cor 1:20) through the guarantee of his spirit (1:22). That goal was so essential for his understanding of the "ministry of the new covenant" that, in spite of his colleagues' betrayal (Gal 2:11-14) after the sealing of the deal with his promise to remember the brothers in Judea (v.10), Paul abided by that promise to maintain the oneness of table fellowship to the extent that he actually imposed it, willy-nilly, on his Gentile following.

The question that remains is, "How was Paul able to bring into *this* picture the Mosaic covenant?" Sealing agreements and deals in conjunction with a common meal is an age long tradition encountered in all civilizations. The reason is obvious: food being the staple of human life, it is ultimately the common meal that is the tangible sign of the oneness of a family, clan, or tribe. When an outsider is invited to sit at the same table and share the same food, then that person becomes de facto part of the unit presided over by the patriarch who heads the table and provides the food.[19] If the patriarch acknowledges the visitor as "one of the family," then who could argue, especially since that same patriarch has the authority to excise a blood member of his family into an outcast and thus a "stranger"? This is precisely the background behind the otherwise outlandish statement regarding

---

[18] 1 Cor 16:3; 2 Cor 1:16.
[19] An avid watcher of Western movies will have often noticed this scenario.

table fellowship at the sealing of the covenant between the Lord and Israel:

> And he said to Moses, "Come up to the Lord, you and Aaron, Nadab, and Abihu, and seventy of the elders of Israel, and worship afar off. Moses alone shall come near to the Lord; but the others shall not come near, and the people shall not come up with him." Moses came and told the people all the words of the Lord and all the ordinances; and all the people answered with one voice, and said, "All the words which the Lord has spoken we will do." And Moses wrote all the words of the Lord. And he rose early in the morning, and built an altar at the foot of the mountain, and twelve pillars, according to the twelve tribes of Israel. And he sent young men of the people of Israel, who offered burnt offerings and sacrificed peace offerings of oxen to the Lord. And Moses took half of the blood and put it in basins, and half of the blood he threw against the altar. Then he took the book of the covenant, and read it in the hearing of the people; and they said, "All that the Lord has spoken we will do, and we will be obedient." And Moses took the blood and threw it upon the people, and said, "Behold the blood of the covenant which the Lord has made with you in accordance with all these words." Then Moses and Aaron, Nadab, and Abihu, and seventy of the elders of Israel went up, and they saw the God of Israel; and there was under his feet as it were a pavement of sapphire stone, like the very heaven for clearness. And he did not lay his hand on the chief men of the people of Israel; they beheld God, and ate and drank. (Ex 24:1-11)

The "sealing" value of table fellowship is corroborated a few chapters later in the description of betrayal by the people—and more specifically by Aaron who had just sat at the Lord's table:

> When the people saw that Moses delayed to come down from the mountain, the people gathered themselves together to Aaron, and said to him, "Up, make us gods, who shall go before us; as for this Moses, the man who brought us up out of the land of Egypt, we do not know what has become of him." And Aaron said to them, "Take off the rings of gold which are in the ears of your wives, your sons, and your daughters, and bring them to me." So all the people took off the rings of gold which were in their ears, and brought them to Aaron. And he received the gold at their hand, and fashioned it with a graving tool, and made a molten calf; and they said, "These are your gods, O Israel, who brought you up out of the land of Egypt!" When Aaron saw this, he built an altar before it; and Aaron made proclamation and said, "Tomorrow shall be a feast to the Lord." And they rose up early on the morrow, and offered burnt offerings and brought peace offerings; and the people sat down to eat and drink, and rose up to play.[20] (Ex 32:1-6)

Paul's choice of *diakonia* to speak of his "ministry" was due to the fact that table fellowship was at the heart of his gospel preaching, and this allowed him to draw into the same picture the parallelism between the old and new covenants. That this matter was on his mind all along is evident in that, in drawing another parallelism between the scriptural story and the situation in the church of Corinth regarding idolatry in conjunction with

---

[20] The Hebrew verb is from the root *ṣḥq* whose meaning is "laugh" as in the name *yiṣḥaq* (Isaac; he laughs).

common meals (1 Cor 10:1-22), he expressly quotes Exodus 32:6: "Now these things are warnings for us, not to desire evil as they did. Do not be idolaters as some of them were; as it is written, 'The people sat down to eat and drink and rose up to dance.'" (1 Cor 10:6-7)

Now one can better understand the function of "glory" which is the main concern of 2 Corinthians 3:7-11. In scripture, glory refers to God's full presence among his followers. Although such entails his function as judge among his people, it does not however preclude his being the "parent" around whose table the same people congregate to be fed by his teaching (the Law) as well as by the bread he provides and breaks with them; hence the importance of table fellowship. Notice how in the above quoted text from Exodus the presence of God is underscored through the double mention of "seeing" and "beholding" him:

> Then Moses and Aaron, Nadab, and Abihu, and seventy of the elders of Israel went up, and they *saw* the God of Israel; and there was under his feet as it were a pavement of sapphire stone, like the very heaven for clearness. And he did not lay his hand on the chief men of the people of Israel; they *beheld* God, and ate and drank. (Ex 24:9-11)

Seeing has not the meaning it was given later in mystical theology which developed under the influence of Platonism and, more so, Plotinism. The basic connotation of seeing is that of closeness and intimacy and, at the extreme, of privacy. That verb still bears such connotation in common language. One says, "The bishop gave me an audience and I was able to see him." Such sight would not be more valuable than speaking with him over the phone if the audience did not entail any conversation! Consequently, the value of "seeing" the bishop lies in that one was able to be "in his presence" and *converse* with him "face to face" or, more à propos, listen to him at close range. That this is definitely the intention of the Exodus passage is evident in the use of *wayyeḥezu* "beheld" (24:11) from *ḥazah* which is a staple verb of the prophetic literature where God's assignee is alone privy to a correct "vision"—audience with—of God.[21] In the entire Pentateuch the use of the verb *ḥazah* and even of any cognate from the root *ḥzh* is restricted to five instances (Ex 24:11; Num 24:4 [twice], 16 [twice]). The latter verses consist of a virtually verbatim repetition of a statement related to the "seer" Balaam:

> … and he [Balaam] took up his discourse, and said, The oracle of Balaam the son of Beor, the oracle of the man whose eye is opened, the oracle of him who hears the words of God, who sees (*yeḥezeh*) the vision (*maḥazeh*) of the Almighty, falling down, but having his eyes uncovered. (Num 24:3-4)

> And he [Balaam] took up his discourse, and said, "The oracle of Balaam the son of Beor, the oracle of the man whose eye is opened, the oracle of him who hears the words of God, and knows the knowledge of the Most High, who sees (*yeḥezeh*) the vision (*maḥazeh*) of the Almighty, falling down, but having his eyes uncovered." (vv.15-16)

Although not an Israelite, Balaam was privy to the right "vision," as were Isaiah and Ezekiel, and that is why he communicated the Lord's will (v.13) even against the will of Balak who commissioned him (v.10). Thus the function of the lengthy pericope concerning Balaam just before the passage into the land of the divine promise is a reminder to the Israelites that the scriptural God is the universal deity of all nations or, as Paul will

---

[21] See, e.g., (in Hebrew) Is 1:1; 2:1; Jer 14:14; Ezek 12:22-24, 27; 13:16; Ob 1; Nah 1:1.

later phrase it: "Or is God the God of Jews only? Is he not the God of Gentiles also? Yes, of Gentiles also." (Rom 3:29) Consequently, in 2 Corinthians 3:7-11, Paul is saying that the Mosaic common table of Exodus 24:11 encompassing only Israelites did not reflect the fullness of God's glory, whereas the Pauline common table shared by both Gentiles and Jews does reflect that fullness. Put in scriptural terms, the one and same glory of the scriptural God, which was shown to Israel through the *diakonia* of Moses, will be shown as that of the universal God of both the nations and Israel through the *diakonia* of Paul. On the other hand, that glory will still be no less than God's true glory as judge of all, a glory that brings with it curse as well as blessing, death as well as life: "For we are the aroma of Christ to God among those who are being saved and among those who are perishing, to one a fragrance from death to death, to the other a fragrance from life to life." (2 Cor 2:15-16)

Vv. 12-18 ¹² Ἔχοντες οὖν τοιαύτην ἐλπίδα πολλῇ παρρησίᾳ χρώμεθα ¹³ καὶ οὐ καθάπερ Μωϋσῆς ἐτίθει κάλυμμα ἐπὶ τὸ πρόσωπον αὐτοῦ πρὸς τὸ μὴ ἀτενίσαι τοὺς υἱοὺς Ἰσραὴλ εἰς τὸ τέλος τοῦ καταργουμένου. ¹⁴ ἀλλὰ ἐπωρώθη τὰ νοήματα αὐτῶν. ἄχρι γὰρ τῆς σήμερον ἡμέρας τὸ αὐτὸ κάλυμμα ἐπὶ τῇ ἀναγνώσει τῆς παλαιᾶς διαθήκης μένει, μὴ ἀνακαλυπτόμενον ὅτι ἐν Χριστῷ καταργεῖται· ¹⁵ ἀλλ' ἕως σήμερον ἡνίκα ἂν ἀναγινώσκηται Μωϋσῆς, κάλυμμα ἐπὶ τὴν καρδίαν αὐτῶν κεῖται· ¹⁶ ἡνίκα δὲ ἐὰν ἐπιστρέψῃ πρὸς κύριον, περιαιρεῖται τὸ κάλυμμα. ¹⁷ ὁ δὲ κύριος τὸ πνεῦμά ἐστιν· οὗ δὲ τὸ πνεῦμα κυρίου, ἐλευθερία. ¹⁸ ἡμεῖς δὲ πάντες ἀνακεκαλυμμένῳ προσώπῳ τὴν δόξαν κυρίου κατοπτριζόμενοι τὴν αὐτὴν εἰκόνα μεταμορφούμεθα ἀπὸ δόξης εἰς δόξαν καθάπερ ἀπὸ κυρίου πνεύματος.

¹² *Since we have such a hope, we are very bold,* ¹³*not like Moses, who put a veil over his face so that the Israelites might not see the end of the fading splendor.* ¹⁴*But their minds were*

hardened; for to this day, when they read the old covenant, that same veil remains unlifted, because only through Christ is it taken away. ¹⁵Yes, to this day whenever Moses is read a veil lies over their minds; ¹⁶but when a man turns to the Lord the veil is removed. ¹⁷Now the Lord is the Spirit, and where the Spirit of the Lord is, there is freedom. ¹⁸And we all, with unveiled face, beholding the glory of the Lord, are being changed into his likeness from one degree of glory to another; for this comes from the Lord who is the Spirit.

It is traditionally and still commonly believed that in 3:12-18 Paul was speaking of all believers and not just of himself as Apostle.[22] However, such an assumption is dubious since (1) the subject throughout 2:14-4:15 is Paul, and (2) 3:12-18 is a continuation of the argument begun in vv.7-11 in that both passages deal with the parallelism between Moses and Paul (or Christ). Having dealt in principle with the difference between two covenants (vv.7-11), Paul moves on to tackle the difference between him and his opponents, the other Jewish leaders he alluded to in 2:17-3:1, showing that in spite of everything they are handling the new covenant promised by Jeremiah and Ezekiel as though it was still the old covenant (3:12-17). He then invites them to join him in his endeavor (v.18).

Since he is about to deal with his peers who are unrelenting in their opposition to him, Paul combines "boldness" with "hope" (v.12). The boldness is rooted in his unwavering assuredness (1:15) of the truth of the gospel he is preaching (Gal 2:5, 14) in spite of the multitude of afflictions and sufferings, given that "the Father of mercies and God of all comfort" has consistently

---

[22] The same is usually done with "Woe to me if I do not preach the gospel!" (1 Cor 9:16) and "Since we have the same spirit of faith as he had who wrote, 'I believed, and so I spoke,' we too believe, and so we speak" (2 Cor 4:13).

sustained him through and out of such (2 Cor 1:3-11). However, not being God, Paul could only hope that the other leaders would be convinced. The following verse (3:13) obviously points to the dissimilarity (and not like [*kai ou kathaper*]; v.13) between Moses, the minister of the old covenant, and Paul, the minister of the new covenant; however, it also opposes (But [*alla*]; v.14) the stand of Moses with that of Paul's opponents whose "minds were hardened" (v.14).[23] Since the dissimilarity between Moses and Paul is only a repetition of what was said earlier (vv.7-11), it is actually the opposition between Moses and Paul's contemporaries (to this day; v.14) that is the new point brought into the picture. Thus it is this opposition that is the matter under discussion here (vv.12-18), especially in view of the fact that the phrase "to this day" is reprised after another "But [*alla*]" (v.15).[24]

The primacy of this matter is ingeniously prepared for in the way Paul rephrases what he wrote earlier concerning Moses and the glory reflected on his face:

> Now if the dispensation of death, carved in letters on stone, came with such splendor (*doxē*; glory) that the Israelites could not look at Moses' face because of its brightness (*doxan*; glory), fading as this was. (v.7)

> ... not like Moses, who used to put a veil over his face so that the children of Israel might not look directly (at his face) until the end (*telos*; goal, aim, objective, purpose, intention) of what is bound to fade.[25] (v.13)

---

[23] See Rom 11:7 and 25 regarding the "hardening" on the part of "some of Israel" and my comments thereon in *C-Rom*.

[24] In order to avoid the redundancy of the second "But," which is preserved in the Vulgate and KJV, it is stylistically smoothed out into a "Yes" in both RSV and JB.

[25] My translation. RSV completely misses the point.

Two striking differences are immediately detectable. On the one hand, the glory in conjunction with Moses' face, which is central in the first instance, is totally absent in the second. On the other hand, instead of the glory, it is now the veil on Moses' face that is the subject of interest as is evident in its occurrence four consecutive times (vv.13, 14, 15, 16) This is further underscored by the scriptural reference (Ex 34:34) Paul uses to bolster his point concerning the veil (2 Cor 3:16). The centrality of the "veil" in this passage lies in that it is, at the same time, the element of dissimilarity between Paul and Moses, on the one hand, and the element of parallelism between Moses and Paul's opponents, on the other hand. So Paul is not repeating here (vv.12-17) the same argument he just made in vv.7-11; rather he is moving from the level of scripture to the plane of his contemporary reality. The scripture teaching emboldens him, whereas the harsh reality of his own times requires hope on his part that eventually the word of the scriptural God will prevail over all hardening (Rom 11:25). The end goal is Christ, through whom Gentile as well as Jew will sit at the same table of the one God (2 Cor 3:14c). This rejoins what Paul writes in Romans 9-11 in the same context where he refers to the Jewish leaders' "hardening": "For Christ is the end (*telos*) of the law, that every one who has faith may be justified (*eis dikaiosynēn panti tō pistevonti*; unto the righteousness [justification] of everyone who believes)." (10:4) Here, "every one" means "Gentile as well as Jew" as is clear from an earlier statement that uses the same vocabulary: "For I am not ashamed of the gospel: it is the power of God for salvation to every one who has faith (*panti tō pistevonti*), to the Jew first and also to the Greek. For in it the righteousness (*dikaiosynē*) of God is revealed through faith for faith." (1:16-17a) For Paul, there is not an open-ended Christ, but a specific Christ conveyed exclusively in the gospel preached *à la* as well as by Paul. He will make this matter incontrovertibly clear later:

> I feel a divine jealousy for you, for I betrothed you to Christ to present you as a pure bride to her one husband. But I am afraid that as the serpent deceived Eve by his cunning, your thoughts will be led astray from a sincere and pure devotion to Christ. For if some one comes and preaches another Jesus than the one we preached, or if you receive a different spirit from the one you received, or if you accept a different gospel from the one you accepted, you submit to it readily enough. (2 Cor 11:2-4)

By keeping "that same veil" (3:14b) now that the true Christ has been revealed through Paul's gospel, his opponents are maintaining the value of the Mosaic table fellowship of Exodus 24:11, which is the common table of the elders of Israel, and consequently are intently blocking God's glory to shine as it really is—that of the one universal God of both Jews and Gentiles. In so doing, they are misconstruing the meaning of the Mosaic veil as well, which was used for a specific purpose; once the purpose was reached it was no longer needed:

> And when Moses had finished speaking with them, he put a veil on his face; but whenever Moses went in before the Lord to speak with him, he took the veil off, until he came out; and when he came out, and told the people of Israel what he was commanded, the people of Israel saw the face of Moses, that the skin of Moses' face shone; and Moses would put the veil upon his face again, until he went in to speak with him. (Ex 34:33-35)

Because "their minds were hardened" (2 Cor 3:14a), in the sense of they refused to understand, "the veil remains (*keitai*) upon their heart" (v.15).[26] In other words, those who opted, against

---

[26] This is the literal translation.

the directive of scripture, for the veil to remain on Moses' face succeed only to "blind themselves" to the fullness of God's glory that is revealed at the Pauline table fellowship between Jew and Gentile.

It would be worthwhile to linger on how Paul constructs his argument. The first passage in which Paul discusses the Mosaic covenant (vv.7-11) is replete with the root *dox—* (10 times in 5 verses)[27] that completely disappears in the second passage (vv.12-17) then reappears thrice in the verse concluding the argument encompassing both passages (v.18).[28] This disappearance of the root *dox—* in vv.12-17 goes hand in hand with the double announcement that the glory of the old covenant was bound to fade away (vv.7 and 11). Thus, the addressees are made to experience that fading away through the hearing of the letter. At the beginning of the second passage one hears of "the *end* of what is bound to fade" (v.13), with Christ being the one who brings that end (v.14). All seems to be flowing according to plan until the hearers realize that a new root, *kalypt—* (cover, hide), which was not present in vv.7-11, starts taking the place (5 times in vv.12-17) of the root *katarg—* (fade away). The most important feature of the root *kalypt—* is the noun *kalymma* (veil) that takes center stage; besides its use in vv.13, 14, 15, it appears also in v.16 in a quotation from Exodus (34:34). Whereas *katargō* is an intransitive verb describing a situation, *kalyptō* is a transitive verb requiring an object complement. In other words, the latter verb reflects the intentionality of the action on the part of a subject: someone is covering (hiding) the veil instead of the

---

[27] In the original Greek.
[28] In the original Greek. RSV has "from one degree of glory to another" for the original "from glory to glory."

veil fading away.²⁹ This, in turn, corroborates the difference in attitude between Moses and Paul's contemporaries. Moses used the veil functionally, whereas Paul's contemporaries gave it a perennial and thus intrinsic value, and Paul underscores this oppositional behavior by masterfully weaving Exodus 34:34 into his argument. He prepares for this quotation in 2 Corinthians 3:16 by using the same conjunction *hinika an* (whenever) found in Exodus to describe his opponents' action (Yes, to this day whenever [*hinika an*] Moses is read a veil lies over their minds; v.15) and recasting it into *hiniken ean* (when) in the quotation itself (but when a man turns to the Lord the veil is removed; v.16). Then he slightly rephrases Exodus to turn it into an invitation to his opponents to follow the example of their master, Moses:

> ... but whenever Moses went in before the Lord to speak with him, he took the veil off (*periēreito to kalymma*). (Ex 34:34)

> ... but when a man turns to the Lord (*epistrepsē pros kyrion*) the veil is removed (*periaireitai to kalymma*). (2 Cor 3:16.)

Paul uses the classic phrase "turn to the Lord," which describes someone's acceptance of the gospel message,³⁰ to speak of Moses' return to the tent of meeting and standing in presence of the Lord. In so doing, Paul was obliquely inviting the opponents to endorse his gospel. This is corroborated in that, in the original, the verb "turns to" does not have a subject. Consequently one can either supply a general "someone"—whence RSV's "a man"—or a previously occurring noun as the subject, which in

---

²⁹ Notice how Paul writes that the veil "remains" (*menei*) *because* it is "unlifted" (*anakalyptomenon*; a compound verb of the verb *kalyptō*).

³⁰ See Acts 9:35; 11:21; 14:15; 15:19; 26:20. This assumption is endorsed by the *Traduction Oecuménique de la Bible*: "C'est seulement par la *conversion* au Seigneur que le voile tombe." (v.16)

our case would be the "veil" (v.15). This is how KJV understands it: "Nevertheless when it [the veil] shall turn to the Lord, the veil shall be taken away." (v.16) Since the veil "lies over their minds (hearts)" the actual subject of the "return" is anyone who has not yet, or not yet fully, endorsed Paul's gospel, but more specifically Paul's opponents.

What is intended in v.16 is the Pauline gospel. This is confirmed in the following verse: "Now the Lord is the Spirit, and where the Spirit of the Lord is, there is freedom." (v.17) This statement, combining Spirit and freedom, is vintage Galatians, which is the blue print for the entire Pauline corpus. Indeed, we have here the only instance of the root *elevther*— (free[dom]) in the entire 2 Corinthians letter. Its sudden appearance and disappearance must be explained by its connection with Spirit that is the most prominent term in chapter 3 and is at the heart of Galatians. It is important to understand that the spirit is not a "person" as is understood in classical trinitarian theology. The spirit is the mighty destructive "wind"—God's breath—that is prominent in the prophetic literature. Its function is to bring to naught the temple-palace complex which is the product of the hands of man. Once this has been eliminated and the people are scattered to the "four winds" by that same spirit, God in his mercy transforms his mighty spirit into a soft breath that blows life into dry bones and raises them into a new people.[31] Earlier Paul spoke of the Corinthians as a building and, more specifically, as the "temple of the Spirit" (1 Cor 3:10-16) and no less in conjunction with his criticism of his opponents, the defenders of Jerusalem and its temple (vv.17-23), as is the case here in 2 Corinthians 3. Consequently, v.17, which unwarrantedly became a classic *crux*

---

[31] See Ezek 37:1-14.

interpretum, is much simpler than traditionally understood. "The Lord is the spirit" (v.17) means that the (scriptural) Lord, who has no icon or statue and therefore has no need of a temple, is (active, apparent) as the wind (Greek *pnevma*, Hebrew *ruaḥ*) is (active, apparent); in other words, in scripture the Lord behaves as the wind does. However, that spirit (wind) in scripture is the spirit *of the Lord* (v.17b) who thus remains in control of it and, whenever he wills, can subdue it into a life-breathing breeze (Gen 2:7; Ezek 37:1-14). The Lord can act thusly toward Israel and, being the God of all (Rom 3:29), he can do the same among the nations, granting them true freedom not only from Jerusalem, but also from Rome and even from their own sins, a freedom that would place them on a par with Israel (Eph 2:10-22).[32] This reading is not as farfetched as it may seem. The immediate previous reference to "freedom" in the Corinthian correspondence is the passage where the Spirit is the "star" just as it is in 2 Corinthians 3:

> Now concerning spiritual gifts, brethren, I do not want you to be uninformed. You know that when you were heathen, you were led astray to dumb idols, however you may have been moved. Therefore I want you to understand that no one speaking by the Spirit of God ever says "Jesus be cursed!" and no one can say "Jesus is Lord" except by the Holy Spirit. Now there are varieties of gifts, but the same Spirit; and there are varieties of service, but the same Lord; and there are varieties of working, but it is the same God who inspires them all in every one. To each is given the manifestation of the Spirit for the common good. To one is given through the Spirit the utterance of wisdom, and to another the utterance of knowledge according to the same Spirit, to another faith by the same Spirit, to another gifts of healing by the one Spirit, to another the working of miracles, to another prophecy, to

---

[32] Notice how the Spirit is eminently functional in this process (vv.18 and 22).

another the ability to distinguish between spirits, to another various kinds of tongues, to another the interpretation of tongues. All these are inspired by one and the same Spirit, who apportions to each one individually as he wills. For just as the body is one and has many members, and all the members of the body, though many, are one body, so it is with Christ. *For by one Spirit we were all baptized into one body—Jews or Greeks, slaves or free—and all were made to drink of one Spirit.* (1 Cor 12:1-13)

Notice in this passage that deals in general with church community how Paul shifts suddenly and unexpectedly to a theme central to Galatians (3:27-28), bringing into the picture the equality between Jew and Gentile in conjunction with both freedom and the Spirit as well as with baptism.

The dependence of 1 Corinthians on Galatians is evident. In both cases we have the unique instance of the plural personal pronoun emphasized with "all": "for *you* (*hymeis*) are *all* (*pantes*) one in Christ Jesus" (Gal 3:28b); "*we* (*hēmeis*) were *all* (*pantes*) baptized into one body" (1 Cor 12:13a). However, in Galatians the phrase has been prepared for in v. 26: "for in Christ Jesus you[33] are *all* (*pantes*) sons of God, through faith." (3:27). In 1 Corinthians, on the other hand, one would have expected a mere "all (are)" after the lengthy passage (12:1-12) where the reference to the individual members is made through the impersonal "one"; at the most one would have expected a non-emphatic "we" assumed in the verb as was the case, twice in a row, earlier in 10:17: "Because there is one bread, (we) who are many *are* (*esmen*) one body, for (we) all *partake* (*metekhomen*) of the one bread." So the inclusiveness in 1 Corinthians 12:13 is

---

[33] The pronoun is not found in the original. In the Greek verbal conjugation the pronoun is implied in the ending of the verb; when the pronoun is added, it is for emphasis. Thus, in v.26 what is said is "you are *all* sons of God" whereas in v.28 the intended is "for it is indeed *you all* that are one in Christ Jesus."

intentionally underscored. Turning to 2 Corinthians we encounter the same phenomenon. After a lengthy passage (2:14-3:17) where he is referring to himself in the inclusive apostolic "we" either as a simple pronoun or systematically assumed in the Greek verbal form (2:15, 16 [twice]; 3:1 [twice], 4, 5, 12) Paul uses the emphatic "we (*hēmeis*) all (*pantes*)" before the verb "(we) are being changed" (*metamorphoumetha*) in the concluding verse 18 of chapter 3, only to revert in chapter 4 to either the non-emphasized Greek verbal form where the "we" is assumed, not spelled out (vv.1, 2, 5, 8, 13, 16), or the simple "we" (*hēmeis*) without "all" (*pantes*) (vv.11).

But whom is Paul trying to include in his "we all" (3:18)? Given that (1) throughout chapters 3 and 4 the subject matter is his apostleship, (2) he is leveling criticism at his opponents in 3:14-15, and (3) he is opening the possibility for them to "return" to the true gospel in the verse 16, then the most convincing answer is that Paul is using "we all" to also include his opponents with the hope that their "face be unveiled" and "all the apostles" (see 1 Cor 9:5; 15:7) would "return" to the initial agreement sealed at Jerusalem (Gal 2:7-10). Only then will the Lord's glory, reflected in total table fellowship without restrictions, be "beheld as in a mirror."[34] Since the root *optr—*, whence *esoptron* (mirror), is confined to three instances in the New Testament (1 Cor 13:12; 2 Cor 3:18; Jam 1:23), it is reasonable to assume that the first two should be closely related. Consequently, it is only in the light of 1 Corinthians 13:12 that one is to fathom 2 Corinthians 3:18:

> For our knowledge is imperfect and our prophecy is imperfect; but when the perfect comes, the imperfect will pass away ... For now

---

[34] RSV mistranslates *katoptrizomenoi* as simply "beholding."

we see in a mirror dimly, but then face to face. Now I know in part; then I shall understand fully, even as I have been fully understood. (1 Cor 13:9-10, 12)

And we all, with unveiled face, beholding as in a mirror[35] the glory of the Lord, are being changed into the same[36] likeness from glory to glory.[37] (2 Cor 3:18) (my translation)

In the first passage "the perfect" (1 Cor 13:10b) refers to the Lord at his coming.[38] What Paul is saying in 2 Corinthians 3:18 is that the common table fellowship is not a once and for all deal, but has to be maintained until the Lord comes. He knew only too well that table fellowship could be mishandled at any time by his Corinthians (1 Cor 8:7-13; 10:14-33; 11:17-22, 27-33) as well as by his colleagues (Gal 2:11-14). He used "beholding as in a mirror" in conjunction with the Lord's glory to prepare for the phrase "from glory to glory," intimating that the ultimate fullness of table fellowship is always ahead and will take place in the Kingdom at the Lord's coming. Furthermore, there is no foolproof guarantee that one will reach the Kingdom (1 Cor 11:31-33). That is why one is to be *constantly* changed (transformed)[39] into that same image reflected in the mirror, which he will discuss momentarily (2 Cor 4:4). And lest anyone should "boast" of one's accomplishment "as if it were not a gift" (1 Cor 4:7), he ends by saying that such continual change "comes (*kathaper*; as though indeed it is) from the Lord who is

---

[35] RSV has simply "beholding."
[36] RSV has 'his" instead of "the same" (*tēn avtēn*).
[37] RSV has "from one degree of glory to another."
[38] See *C-1Cor* 240-1.
[39] This is reflected in the present tense of the original *metamorphoumetha* (we are being changed, metamorphosed).

the Spirit" or "comes (*kathaper*; as though indeed it is) from the Spirit of the Lord" (2 Cor 3:18).[40]

---

[40] The original Greek *apo kyriou pnevmatos* allows either possibility.

Chapter 4

Vv. 1-6 ¹Διὰ τοῦτο, ἔχοντες τὴν διακονίαν ταύτην καθὼς ἠλεήθημεν, οὐκ ἐγκακοῦμεν ²ἀλλὰ ἀπειπάμεθα τὰ κρυπτὰ τῆς αἰσχύνης, μὴ περιπατοῦντες ἐν πανουργίᾳ μηδὲ δολοῦντες τὸν λόγον τοῦ θεοῦ ἀλλὰ τῇ φανερώσει τῆς ἀληθείας συνιστάνοντες ἑαυτοὺς πρὸς πᾶσαν συνείδησιν ἀνθρώπων ἐνώπιον τοῦ θεοῦ. ³εἰ δὲ καὶ ἔστιν κεκαλυμμένον τὸ εὐαγγέλιον ἡμῶν, ἐν τοῖς ἀπολλυμένοις ἐστὶν κεκαλυμμένον, ⁴ἐν οἷς ὁ θεὸς τοῦ αἰῶνος τούτου ἐτύφλωσεν τὰ νοήματα τῶν ἀπίστων εἰς τὸ μὴ αὐγάσαι τὸν φωτισμὸν τοῦ εὐαγγελίου τῆς δόξης τοῦ Χριστοῦ, ὅς ἐστιν εἰκὼν τοῦ θεοῦ. ⁵Οὐ γὰρ ἑαυτοὺς κηρύσσομεν ἀλλὰ Ἰησοῦν Χριστὸν κύριον, ἑαυτοὺς δὲ δούλους ὑμῶν διὰ Ἰησοῦν. ⁶ὅτι ὁ θεὸς ὁ εἰπών· ἐκ σκότους φῶς λάμψει, ὃς ἔλαμψεν ἐν ταῖς καρδίαις ἡμῶν πρὸς φωτισμὸν τῆς γνώσεως τῆς δόξης τοῦ θεοῦ ἐν προσώπῳ [Ἰησοῦ] Χριστοῦ.

> ¹Therefore, having this ministry by the mercy of God, we do not lose heart. ²We have renounced disgraceful, underhanded ways; we refuse to practice cunning or to tamper with God's word, but by the open statement of the truth we would commend ourselves to every man's conscience in the sight of God. ³And even if our gospel is veiled, it is veiled only to those who are perishing. ⁴In their case the god of this world has blinded the minds of the unbelievers, to keep them from seeing the light of the gospel of the glory of Christ, who is the likeness of God. ⁵For what we preach is not ourselves, but Jesus Christ as Lord, with ourselves as your servants for Jesus' sake. ⁶For it is the God who said, "Let light shine out of darkness," who has shone in our hearts to give the light of the knowledge of the glory of God in the face of Christ.

Chapter 4 is a portrayal of Paul's behavior in carrying out his ministry. It is presented as a fitting conclusion to the preceding discussion of Paul's gospel in conjunction with the Mosaic law (ch. 3). This is confirmed by the similar phrase that brackets the entire chapter as an *inclusio*: "Therefore ... we do not lose heart" (*Dia touto ... ouk enkakoumen*; 4:1); "So we do not lose heart" (*Dio ouk enkakoumen*; v.16). At the outset, Paul repeats what he wrote earlier concerning his unworthiness (3:5-6): "... having this ministry as through mercy[1] (*kathōs eleēthēmen*; as we have received mercy)." (4:1) The thought that his assignment as apostle is through sheer divine mercy is an essential conviction on his part. This can be gathered from the use of the verb *eleoumai* (receive mercy) which occurs only one other time in the Corinthian correspondence (1 Cor 7:25).[2] What is striking in that case is that at the height of his argumentation, where he needs all the weight of his apostolic authority to introduce a command not extant in scripture, he refers to his authority in the most humble terms: "To the married I give charge, not I but the Lord, that the wife should not separate from her husband ... Now concerning the unmarried, I have no command of the Lord, but I give my opinion as one who by the Lord's mercy (*eleēmenos*) is trustworthy."[3] (7:10, 25) Such phraseology becomes even more stunning when compared to the end of the chapter where he concludes his directives to the unmarried with the assertive statement: "And I think that I have the Spirit of God." (v.40b)[4]

That 2 Corinthians 4 is dealing with behavior is confirmed by the verb "walk" (*peripatountes*) which is rendered as "practice" in

---

[1] RSV has "by the mercy of God."
[2] Actually, with the exception of 1 Cor 15:19 (If for this life only we have hoped in Christ, we are of all men most to be pitied [*eleeinoteroi*]), 1 Cor 7:25 and 2 Cor 4:1 are the sole instances of the root *eleo*— in these two letters.
[3] Trustworthiness was earlier directly linked with apostleship (4:2).
[4] See my comments on all three verses in *C-1Cor*.

RSV and by Paul's appeal to "commend ourselves to every man's conscience in the sight of God" (v.2). It is inconceivable that a plenipotentiary apostle who judges all men (1 Cor 2:15) in the matter of the wisdom of the gospel teaching (vv.6-14) would appeal to them to appraise him on that level. However, they could assess him on the plane of comportment, that of "disgraceful, underhanded ways," "cunning," and "guile"[5] (2 Cor 4:2). In order not to misconstrue what Paul is saying, it is imperative to understand all the terminology of vv.1-6, including that of "hidden things (*krypta*; underhanded ways in RSV)," "manifestation" (*phanerōsei*; open statement in RSV), "truth," "light," "glory," "likeness," and even "knowledge,"[6] on the level of behavior rather than in terms of an intellectual understanding of a theoretical gospel cast in philosophical terminology. In a nutshell, verse 2 is saying that Paul's behavior is obvious both to God and to men and is devoid of any hidden cunning or guile. The reason is that "the word of God," that is to say, "the gospel" Paul is preaching, is intrinsically linked to the "truth" (Gal 2:5, 14) of God's teaching as laid down in scripture (2:15-3:29; 4:23-31). Since divine truth (Greek *alētheia*) is the Hebrew *'emet* which means "truth of the matter," its "indeed-ness," then

---

[5] The original *dolountes* rendered as "tamper" in RSV is from the same root as *dolos* (guile) which is used elsewhere in a passage similar to ours in both content and intent: "For our appeal does not spring from error or uncleanness, nor is it made with guile (*dolō*); but just as we have been approved by God to be entrusted with the gospel, so we speak, not to please men, but to please God who tests our hearts. For we never used either words of flattery, as you know, or a cloak for greed, as God is witness; nor did we seek glory from men, whether from you or from others, though we might have made demands as apostles of Christ." (1 Thess 2:3-6) Notice how his appeal here is to the addressees *before God* as is the case in 2 Cor 4:2.

[6] Concerning "knowledge" see especially Col 1:9-10 (And so, from the day we heard of it, we have not ceased to pray for you, asking that you may be filled with *the knowledge of his will* in all spiritual wisdom and understanding, *to lead a life worthy of the Lord, fully pleasing to him, bearing fruit in every good work* and increasing in the knowledge of God) and my comments thereon in *C-Col*.

handling it with any cunning or guile would readily be "made manifest" (*phanerōsei*). Furthermore, if "(the truth of) the gospel is veiled, it is so only to those who are perishing" (2 Cor 4:3; see also 2:15) because they decided to harden their minds (3:14b; see Jer 5:21 and Ezek 12:2).

In order to preserve God's control over everything and in order not let the hearers assume that matters happen outside his will, scripture uses two stratagems. The first is that God allows the people to go their way and contravene his will by opting for an earthly king (1 Sam 8), only to let them pay for their misguided choice by orchestrating the end of their kingdoms: the demise of Samaria (2 Kg 17) and the fall of Jerusalem (2 Kg 24-25). The second and more extreme fashion is to flatly say that God "shut" the ears of the people and "blinded" their minds (Is 6:9-10), which is what Paul opted for here (2 Cor 4:4).

To soften the blow on his hearers, Paul ascribes the (misleading) action to "the god *of this world* (*tou aiōnos toutou*)." The phrase "this world (age)" occurred repeatedly at the beginning of 1 Corinthians:

> Where is the wise man? Where is the scribe? Where is the debater of this age? Has not God made foolish the wisdom of the world? (1:20)

> Yet among the mature we do impart wisdom, although it is not a wisdom of this age or of the rulers of this age, who are doomed to pass away. But we impart a secret and hidden wisdom of God, which God decreed before the ages for our glorification. None of the rulers of this age understood this; for if they had, they would not have crucified the Lord of glory. (2:6-8)

Let no one deceive himself. If any one among you thinks that he is wise in this age, let him become a fool that he may become wise. (3:18)

In all these instances, "this world (age)" clearly denotes a reality that is opposed to God. In 2:8 in particular the reference is to "the rulers" of this age, which points to the Roman emperor and authorities that crucified the Lord whom Paul was preaching. That same power, assigned by God to rule within the boundaries of "this world" (Rom 13:1-7), is depicted by Paul as having been lured by Satan to assume the position of God (2 Thess 2:3-4, 9). Satan's ability to deceive human powers, and thus all humans, presents itself as a quasi-divine authority with features similar to those conferred by God upon his Christ:

> Now concerning the *coming* (*parousias*) of our Lord Jesus Christ and our assembling to meet him, we beg you, brethren, not to be quickly shaken in mind or excited, either by spirit or by word, or by letter purporting to be from us, to the effect that the day of the Lord has come. Let no one deceive you in any way; for (that day will not come,)[7] unless the rebellion *comes* (*elthē*) first, and the man of lawlessness is *revealed* (*apokalyphthē*), the son of perdition, who opposes and exalts himself against every so-called god or object of worship, so that he *takes his seat in the temple of God, proclaiming himself to be God* ... And then the lawless one *will be revealed* (*apokalyphthēsetai*), and the Lord Jesus will slay him with the breath of his mouth and destroy him by his appearing (*epiphaneia*) and his coming (*parousias*). The coming (*parousia*) of the lawless one by the *activity* (*energian*; impowering) of Satan will be with all *power* (*dynamei*) and with pretended *signs and wonders* (*sēmeiois kai terasin*),[8] and with all wicked deception for those who

---

[7] This is an addition to the original to make the verse clearer.
[8] See also Mt 24:24 and Mk 13:22 and compare with Jn 4:48; Acts 2:22, 43; 4:30; 5:12; 6:8; 14:3; 15:12; Rom 15:19; 2 Cor 12:12, where this phrase is used to speak of either Jesus or the gospel preaching.

are to perish, because they refused to love the truth and so be saved. (2 Thess 2:1-4, 8-10)

So it is Satan that Paul is referring to in the phrase "the god of this world" (2 Cor 4:4). This roundabout approach serves to remind the hearers that, ultimately, Satan is not God and whatever he can do, he is allowed to do by God himself in order to test the humans.[9] However, the responsibility lies with those who make the choice as to whom they follow (2 Thess 2:10; see also Gen 2). That is why those, whose "minds are blinded" by the god of this world (2 Cor 4:4), are the same as those who *chose* to "harden their minds" (3:14). Later in the letter, Paul will refer to opponents of his gospel as being "ministers" (*diakonoi*) of Satan instead of being "ministers" (*diakonoi*) of the righteousness (11:13-15), which righteousness is the staple of the "ministry" of the new covenant carried on by Paul (3:1-11). Notice, moreover, the direct correspondence between 4:4 and 11:13-15 in that both refer to "light" in conjunction with Satan and his deception:

> In their case the god of this world has blinded the minds of the unbelievers, to keep them from seeing the *light* (*phōtismon*; enlightenment; illumination) of the gospel of the glory of Christ, who is the likeness of God. (4:4)

> For such men are false apostles, deceitful workmen, disguising themselves as apostles of Christ. And no wonder, for even Satan disguises himself as an angel of *light* (*phōtos*). So it is not strange if his servants also disguise themselves as servants of righteousness. Their end will correspond to their deeds. (11:13-15)

---

[9] See especially Job 1:6-11 where Satan is referred to as one of the council of "the sons of God" (v.7).

One is not to understand 2 Corinthians 4:4 as a statement standing on its own and thus as proof text regarding the "person" of Christ. Instead, it is to be viewed as an integral part of chapters 3 and 4 where Paul is contrasting his ministry to that of his opponents. In such case, both "glory" and "image" are to be taken in the same vein as in 3:18 where they appeared together. In other words, 4:4 is an elaboration on 3:18; it is as though 3:18 functions as a "teaser" whose solution is to be found in the "enlightenment" (*phōtismon*) provided in 4:4. This is corroborated in a later passage (11:13-15) which elaborates on 4:4. There we hear the only three instances in this letter of the verb "disguise" (*metaskhēmatizomai*; change one's appearance) that totally parallels in meaning "be changed" (*metamorphoumai*; undergo change in shape, appearance) found only in 3:17 in the entire Corinthian correspondence.[10]

There has never been—except in the mind of "theologians"—an ethereal self-standing "gospel" that is hanging out there between heaven and earth, to which each and every "apostle" is privy.[11] Rather "our gospel" (4:3) that 4:4 is speaking of is none other than the Pauline gospel. It is Paul's preaching (*kyrēssomen*; v.5) and nothing else that provides both the glory of Christ, who is the image of God, and the enlightenment to perceive that glory (v.4). In order to understand this verse one should remember the centrality of the figure of the Servant in Isaiah in

---

[10] The full parallelism between *skhēma* and *morphē* is evident from Phil 2:6-11 where the first occurs in v.7b and the second twice in vv.6 and 7a; see my comments in *C-Phil* 116-7.

[11] See my comments on 1 Cor 15:1-11 in *C-1Cor* 260-73.

the Pauline letters.[12] In the first of the four Servant hymns we hear:

> Behold my servant, whom I uphold, my chosen, in whom my soul delights; I have put my Spirit upon him, he will bring forth justice to the nations. He will not cry or lift up his voice, or make it heard in the street; a bruised reed he will not break, and a dimly burning wick he will not quench; he will faithfully bring forth justice. He will not fail or be discouraged till he has established justice in the earth; and the coastlands wait for his law. Thus says God, the Lord, who created the heavens and stretched them out, who spread forth the earth and what comes from it, who gives breath to the people upon it and spirit to those who walk in it: "I am the Lord, I have called you in righteousness, I have taken you by the hand and kept you; I have given you as a covenant to the people, a light to the nations, to open the eyes that are blind, to bring out the prisoners from the dungeon, from the prison those who sit in darkness. I am the Lord, that is my name; my glory I give to no other, nor my praise to graven images." (Is 42:1-8)

One can readily hear that this passage is behind 2 Corinthians 3:1-4:6 and accounts for its vocabulary: Spirit, God's (Mosaic) law, covenant, light, "opening the eyes of the blind," and glory. Add to this that, in a similar passage later in Isaiah, which appears on Jesus' lips at the outset of his ministry in Luke (4:18-19), reference is made to the two verbs Paul uses to describe his preaching activity as well as to "consolation" and "anointing": "The Spirit of the Lord God is upon me, because the Lord has anointed me to *bring good tidings* (*evangelisasthai*;[13] evangelize; preach the gospel) to the afflicted; he has sent (*ekhrisen*;[14]

---

[12] I showed this to be the case in my commentaries on Romans, Philippians, and Colossians, as well as in my discussion of 2 Corinthians 1:5.
[13] From the same root as *evangelion* (gospel).
[14] The same verb Paul used in 2 Cor 1:21b: "… and [God] has commissioned (*khrisas*; anointed) us."

anointed) me to bind up the brokenhearted, to proclaim (*kēryxai*;[15] herald) liberty to the captives, and the opening of the prison to those who are bound; to proclaim (*kalesai*; call [out]) the year of the Lord's favor, and the day of vengeance of our God; to comfort (*parakalesai*) all who mourn." (Is 61:1-2)

The Isaianic Servant's commission consists in sharing with the nations the divine law that was granted to Israel (Is 42:1-7; 49:1-6). This commission does not consist of sharing with them something over and above what God himself graced Israel with. It is precisely this divine law that will enlighten the path of the Gentiles just as it does that of Israel, as Isaiah himself has announced at the start of his mission to Jerusalem and Judah:

> The word which Isaiah the son of Amoz saw concerning Judah and Jerusalem. It shall come to pass in the latter days that the mountain of the house of the Lord shall be established as the highest of the mountains, and shall be raised above the hills; and all the nations shall flow to it, and many peoples shall come, and say: "Come, let us go up to the mountain of the Lord, to the house of the God of Jacob; that he may teach us his ways and that we may walk in his paths." For out of Zion shall go forth the law, and the word of the Lord from Jerusalem. He shall judge between the nations, and shall decide for many peoples; and they shall beat their swords into plowshares, and their spears into pruning hooks; nation shall not lift up sword against nation, neither shall they learn war any more. O house of Jacob, come, let us walk in the light of the Lord. (Is 2:1-4)

One is in the light to the extent one submits to be enlightened by this message. The message reflects as well as announces the full glory of God as the one deity of all nations, a glory sealed at the common table fellowship. However, given that, for the time

---

[15] From the same root as *kēryssomen* in 2 Cor 4:5.

being, such fellowship is taking place only in the Pauline gatherings, the fullness of that glory is not readily seen by all. Thus, according to Paul, this fullness is postponed in the church gatherings under the aegis of his opponents until they recognize full table fellowship. Paul is toiling for that aim and is asking the full support of his churches in spite of any adversity:

> At present, however, I am going to Jerusalem with aid for the saints. For Macedonia and Achaia have been pleased to make some contribution for the poor among the saints at Jerusalem; they were pleased to do it, and indeed they are in debt to them, for if the Gentiles have come to share in their spiritual blessings, they ought also to be of service to them in material blessings. When therefore I have completed this, and have delivered to them what has been raised, I shall go on by way of you to Spain; and I know that when I come to you I shall come in *the fulness of the blessing of Christ*. I appeal to you, brethren, by our Lord Jesus Christ and by the love of the Spirit, to strive together with me in your prayers to God on my behalf, that I may be delivered from the unbelievers in Judea, and that my service for Jerusalem may be acceptable to the saints, so that by God's will I may come to you with joy and be refreshed in your company. The God of peace be with you all. Amen. (Rom 15:25-33)

The fullness of God's glory is detectable in the Pauline gatherings through the image of God, that is to say, through his plenipotentiary representative, Christ (2 Cor 4:4), *as preached by Paul* (v.5). Although Paul himself was "anointed" into his commission (1:21), nevertheless he does not preach himself but *the* anointed (*Khristos*; Christ) of God as "lord" and thus "master of the house" (*oikodespotēs*); even Paul, as "house manager" (*oikonomos*), is his "slave." As such and in this sense, Paul is also the "slave" of the Corinthians "for Jesus' sake" (4:5), as he elaborated earlier in 1 Cor 9:16-23.

In order to make incontrovertible in his addressees' minds his point that God's glory is already shining in all its brightness in "the church of God which is at Corinth" (1 Cor 1:2; 2 Cor 1:1), Paul recasts his assertion (2 Cor 4:4-5) as the realization of the divine promise in Isaiah:

> For it is the God who said, "Let light (*phōs*) shine (*lampsei*)[16] out of darkness (*skotous*)," who has shone (*elampsen*) in our hearts to give the light (*phōtismon*; enlightenment) of the knowledge of the glory of God in the face of Christ. (2 Cor 4:6)

> The people who walked in darkness (*skotei*) have seen a great light (*phōs*); those who dwelt in a land of deep darkness, on them has light (*phōs*) shined (*lampsei*).[17] (Is 9:2; LXX 9:1)

Since Paul follows the LXX text that has "light will shine (*lampsei*)" and then says that God "has shone (*elampsen*)," the hearer perceives that the promise of God has been realized, at least in Corinth in particular and the Pauline churches in general. Unfortunately, "our hearts" (2 Cor 4:6) is usually taken as being inclusive of the addressees, and the entire verse is understood as though God "has shone" *directly* in the heart of each believer through the "person" of Christ. However, such goes against the grain of the entire passage (2 Cor 3:1-4:15) on two counts: (1) from the outset Paul is speaking of *his* "ministry," and (2) his entire argument, as was the case in 1 Corinthians 9, is to remind his addressees that they got to know God and his Christ *exclusively* through him. Indeed, God's shining is *pros phōtismon*, "unto enlightenment (of others)", "to give light (unto others)" (4:6). Earlier (4:4) in conjunction with criticism of his opponents, Paul spoke of the enlightenment that

---

[16] The Greek *lampsei* actually means "will shine."
[17] See previous footnote.

the gospel message (of the glory of Christ) provided for the Gentiles which the opponents did not trust in (*apistōn*); in v.6 he refers to the enlightenment provided those same Gentiles so that they could get to know God's glory.[18] Moreover, the Corinthians are to understand—to acquiesce to Paul's teaching—that such glory is apparent in the face of the Christ *as the head of the common table fellowship.*[19] The use of "face" is intentional; it posits Christ in a position similar to that of Moses when it comes to God's glory. The corollary is that Christ is present among the Corinthians through his "law" (Gal 6:2) which is "the law of the Spirit of life" (Rom 8:2). Conversely, Paul is their only father who not only can bestow the Spirit, but can also wield the "rod" (1 Cor 4:21).[20]

Vv. 7-15 ⁷ Ἔχομεν δὲ τὸν θησαυρὸν τοῦτον ἐν ὀστρακίνοις σκεύεσιν, ἵνα ἡ ὑπερβολὴ τῆς δυνάμεως ᾖ τοῦ θεοῦ καὶ μὴ ἐξ ἡμῶν· ⁸ ἐν παντὶ θλιβόμενοι ἀλλ' οὐ στενοχωρούμενοι, ἀπορούμενοι ἀλλ' οὐκ ἐξαπορούμενοι, ⁹ διωκόμενοι ἀλλ' οὐκ ἐγκαταλειπόμενοι, καταβαλλόμενοι ἀλλ' οὐκ ἀπολλύμενοι, ¹⁰ πάντοτε τὴν νέκρωσιν τοῦ Ἰησοῦ ἐν τῷ σώματι περιφέροντες, ἵνα καὶ ἡ ζωὴ τοῦ Ἰησοῦ ἐν τῷ σώματι ἡμῶν φανερωθῇ. ¹¹ ἀεὶ γὰρ ἡμεῖς οἱ ζῶντες εἰς θάνατον παραδιδόμεθα διὰ Ἰησοῦν, ἵνα καὶ ἡ ζωὴ τοῦ Ἰησοῦ φανερωθῇ ἐν τῇ θνητῇ σαρκὶ ἡμῶν. ¹² ὥστε ὁ θάνατος ἐν ἡμῖν ἐνεργεῖται, ἡ δὲ ζωὴ ἐν ὑμῖν. ¹³ Ἔχοντες δὲ τὸ αὐτὸ πνεῦμα τῆς πίστεως κατὰ τὸ γεγραμμένον· ἐπίστευσα, διὸ ἐλάλησα,

---

[18] In the first case, "of the gospel" (*tou evangeliou*) is a genitive subjective whereas, in the latter case, "of the knowledge" (*tēs gnōseōs*) is a genitive objective.

[19] See 1 Cor 11:17-25 and my comments thereon in *C-1Cor* 202-11.

[20] Notice the closeness between Gal 5:22-23 and 6:1-2 (But the fruit of the Spirit is *love*, joy, peace, patience, kindness, goodness, faithfulness, *gentleness*, self-control; against such there is *no law* ... Brethren, if a man is overtaken in any trespass, you who are spiritual should restore him in *a spirit of gentleness*. Look to yourself, lest you too be tempted. Bear one another's burdens, and so fulfil *the law of Christ*), on the one hand, and 1 Cor 4:21 (What do you wish? Shall I come to you with *a rod*, or with love in *a spirit of gentleness*?), on the other hand.

καὶ ἡμεῖς πιστεύομεν, διὸ καὶ λαλοῦμεν, ¹⁴εἰδότες ὅτι ὁ ἐγείρας τὸν κύριον Ἰησοῦν καὶ ἡμᾶς σὺν Ἰησοῦ ἐγερεῖ καὶ παραστήσει σὺν ὑμῖν. ¹⁵τὰ γὰρ πάντα δι' ὑμᾶς, ἵνα ἡ χάρις πλεονάσασα διὰ τῶν πλειόνων τὴν εὐχαριστίαν περισσεύσῃ εἰς τὴν δόξαν τοῦ θεοῦ.

> ⁷But we have this treasure in earthen vessels, to show that the transcendent power belongs to God and not to us. ⁸We are afflicted in every way, but not crushed; perplexed, but not driven to despair; ⁹persecuted, but not forsaken; struck down, but not destroyed; ¹⁰always carrying in the body the death of Jesus, so that the life of Jesus may also be manifested in our bodies. ¹¹For while we live we are always being given up to death for Jesus' sake, so that the life of Jesus may be manifested in our mortal flesh. ¹²So death is at work in us, but life in you. ¹³Since we have the same spirit of faith as he had who wrote, "I believed, and so I spoke," we too believe, and so we speak, ¹⁴knowing that he who raised the Lord Jesus will raise us also with Jesus and bring us with you into his presence. ¹⁵For it is all for your sake, so that as grace extends to more and more people it may increase thanksgiving, to the glory of God.

In 2 Corinthians 4:7-12 Paul describes the difficulties he went through to bring the gospel to the Corinthians. He does this along similar lines as those in 1 Corinthians 4:6-13, using the imagery of the Roman arena.[21] The terminology of 2 Corinthians 4:7 harks back to the passage where Paul was referring to his near death experience that had taken place in the Roman arena in Ephesus:[22]

> For we do not want you to be ignorant, brethren, of the affliction (*thlipseōs*) we experienced in Asia; for we were so utterly (*kath'*

---

[21] See my comments in *C-1Cor* 88-94.
[22] See earlier my comments on 2 Cor 1:8-10.

hyperbolēn; beyond transcendence, beyond excessive measure), unbearably (*hyper dynamin*; beyond [our] human] power) crushed that we despaired (*exaporēthēnai*) of life itself. (2 Cor 1:8)

But we have this treasure in earthen vessels, to show that the transcendent power (*hē hyperbolē tēs dynameōs*; the transcendence of the power) belongs to God and not to us. We are afflicted (*thlibomenoi*; from the same root as *thlipseōs*) in every way, but not crushed; perplexed, but not driven to despair (*exaporoumenoi*; from the same verb as *exaporēthēnai*)... (4:7-8)

Paul begins by correcting any impression of arrogance in depicting himself as the only valid apostle, at least in Corinth. Regardless of all appearances, the power exhibited in the apostolic office is God's (2 Cor 4:7a); the apostle is only the vessel holding the true treasure (v.7b); and in spite of its apparent solidity, this vessel is made of clay and thus can easily break at any time and be replaced by another (Rom 9:21-23). This rejoins what Paul wrote earlier concerning the expendability of an apostle (1 Cor 3:5-7; 21-22). The fragility of the messenger is detailed further in an impressive foursome of couples: "We are afflicted (*thlibomenoi*) in every way, but not crushed; perplexed, but not driven to despair; persecuted, but not forsaken; struck down, but not destroyed (*apollymenoi*)." (2 Cor 4:8-9) As was the case earlier (1 Cor 4:10-13), this long series is not meant to be dissected one item at a time—which would be a sheer impossibility for the hearers of a text being read aloud to them without interruption. Its aim is to impress upon the hearers the unbearable difficulty of the apostolic office, humanly speaking. The series is intelligently constructed in order to produce an intended effect.[23] In our case, the remaining aural impression is controlled by the first and last element of the series. *thlibomenoi*

---

[23] See my discussion of 1 Cor 4:10-13 in *C-1Cor* 91-92.

(afflicted; v. 8) is from the same root *thlib—* as the noun *thlipsis* (affliction) which defines the perilous situation that warrants God's comforting intervention:

> Blessed be the God and Father of our Lord Jesus Christ, the Father of mercies and God of all comfort, who comforts us in all our *affliction*, so that we may be able to comfort those who are in any *affliction*, with the comfort with which we ourselves are comforted by God ... If we are *afflicted* (*thlibomenoi*), it is for your comfort and salvation; and if we are comforted, it is for your comfort, which you experience when you patiently endure the same sufferings that we suffer ... For we do not want you to be ignorant, brethren, of the *affliction* we experienced in Asia; for we were so utterly, unbearably crushed that we despaired of life itself. (2 Cor 1:3-4, 6, 8)

As is usual, the last word in the series, *apollymenoi*, is the key that brings the different elements together. That *ouk apollymenoi* (not destroyed) in 4:9 is intended to be the culmination of the series is evident in that its counterpart, *kataballomenoi* (struck down), is from the same root *ball—* that was used to speak of God's power (*hyperbolē;* transcendence) in v. 7.[24] The contrast between "those who are being saved (*sōzomenois*)" and "those who are perishing (*apollymenois*)" is Roman arena terminology. In the arena the gladiators are slated either to perdition (*apōleia*)[25] or to salvation (*sōtēria*),[26] both ultimately through the "power" of the emperor who is able and has the right to decide their fate, even against the people's preference.[27] Thus, the

---

[24] The Greek preposition *hyper* connotes "being over and above" whereas the preposition *kata* connotes "bringing down."
[25] From the same root as *apollymenois*.
[26] From the same root as *sōzomenois*.
[27] See 1 Cor 1:18 where the same wording of the contrast occurs also in conjunction with the preaching of the gospel.

intention of 4:7-9 is to say that if the apostle is not struck down it is due to God's transcendent power that cannot be checked even by "the god of this world" (v.4), whose medium is the Roman authorities. The term *apollymenoi* was used twice earlier to describe the fate of those who refuse to put their trust in the gospel and thus are slated to perdition: "For we are the aroma of Christ to God among those who are being saved and among those who are perishing (*apollymenois*), to one a fragrance from death to death, to the other a fragrance from life to life" (2:15-16b); "And even if our gospel is veiled, it is veiled only to those who are perishing (*apollymenois*)." (4:3) These three occurrences account for all the instances of the verb *apollymi* in this letter. By using the phrase *ouk apollymenoi* to speak of himself, Paul was distancing himself from his opponents as well as from any Corinthian who would side with them. At the same time he was impressing on his hearers that, in spite of his appearance as one who is "perishing," they should continue to endorse his teaching that is bringing them true salvation.

The following two verses (2 Cor 4:10-11) are often understood as speaking of resurrection to life after death in the vein of 1 Corinthians 15. However, such cannot be the case since the concluding verse clearly states: "So (*hōste*; so then, therefore, in such way that) death is at work *in us*, but life *in you*." (2 Cor 4:12) Thus, Paul's continual battles with death are for the sake of the others, to produce life through Christ in others. Since this verse concludes the previous two verses, then these must have prepared for it. This reading goes hand in hand with verses 7-9 that parallel in content and scope 1 Corinthians 4:6-12 where Paul was contrasting his attitude with that of the Corinthians *in order to* show the effect of his apostleship among them and to prepare for the following verses where he would use the example of sacrificial fatherhood to underscore that his authority over them is exercised *for their own good* (vv.14-21). In 2 Corinthians 4:10-11, the combination of "always" (*pantote*) and "putting to death," which is the literal meaning of the Greek *nekrōsin*,[28] (v.10) cannot possibly be referring to the once for all actual death. The recurrence of the action subsumed in the adverb "always" is obviously essential given its repetition, under the different Greek form *aei*, in the parallel statement (v.11). In order to make sense of these two verses, one is to hear them against the background of the Roman arena.

Let us begin with the most striking feature of these two verses, that is, the use of "Jesus," without "Christ," no less than four times in a row. The entire passage (vv.7-15) accounts for six occurrences of "Jesus" without "Christ," which is rare in the Pauline corpus.[29] Given that the name Jesus in Hebrew means "the Lord saves," Paul is using it here to reflect God's decision to "save" someone (*sōzomenos*) who has been condemned to death (*apollymenos*) by imperial decision.[30] This is verified by the term "putting to death" (*nekrōsin*) used in conjunction with the death of Jesus, which is unique in the New Testament. One would have expected "death of Jesus" as counterpart to "life of Jesus." Consequently, "putting to death" (*nekrōsin*) was purposely used with Paul in mind, rather than Jesus, as is discernible from the parallel statement:

---

[28] KJV's "the dying of Jesus" is more accurate than RSV's "the death of Jesus."
[29] 1 Thess 1:10; 4:14. "Jesus" (Rom 3:26) is preceded by "Christ Jesus" (v.24) and in 8:11 "Jesus" is followed by "Christ Jesus." The multiple occurrence of the plain "Jesus" in Hebrews confirms that the letter's intention is to appeal to the Jews as counterpart of the letter to the Romans (see *NTI₄* 80-2).
[30] The intentionality of the reference to the Hebrew meaning of Jesus is corroborated by the high incidence of the instances of "Jesus" in the letter known as "Letter to the Hebrews" (Heb 2:9; 3:1, 3; 4:14; 5:7; 6:20; 7:22; 10:19; 12:12, 24; 13:12, 20).

... always carrying in the body the (putting to) death of Jesus, so that the life of Jesus may also be manifested in our bodies. For while we live we are always being given up to death for Jesus' sake, so that the life of Jesus may be manifested in our mortal flesh. (vv. 10-11)

While verse 11b is virtually a verbatim repetition of verse 10b, verse 11a is an explication of verse 10a: "carrying the putting to death of Jesus" is to be understood as "being given up to death *for Jesus' sake*." Moreover, the resulting "manifestation of the life of Jesus," repeated twice to underscore its centrality in the argument, is linked to the preaching of the gospel that gives life through its teaching. This is confirmed by the previous three instances of the root *phaner*— (manifest; 2:14; 3:3; 4:2)[31] used to underscore that the "life of Jesus" is not a mystical reality; rather it is the life granted by the Pauline Jesus *preached in his gospel* (1 Cor 4:15; 2 Cor 11:4a), which is precisely the concern of the immediately preceding verses (2 Cor 4:7-9). The experience the Corinthians have of Jesus is exclusively through the life and tribulations of Paul.[32] This is corroborated in the concluding statement: "So *death* is at work *in us*, but *life in you*." (v.12) As was the case in 1 Corinthians 4:6-13, Paul and his addressees are *not* on equal footing. A closer look at the original will reveal that "is at work" (*energeitai*; is energized, is implemented) is the verb used by Paul to speak of God's action among the Galatians (Gal 3:5) and also to speak of Paul's and Peter's commissioning *as apostles* (2:8).

---

[31] Translated differently in each case in RSV. KJV is closer to the original in that it keeps the root "manifest—" in all three instances.
[32] See my comments on 1:3-7.

Why does Paul switch from "our bodies"[33] (2 Cor 4:10) to "our mortal flesh" (v.11)? As a reminder for my readers, the Greek *sōma* refers to the "body" of someone or something and thus to the reality in its functionality. An example in English would be to say that "an actual table" has "body"; if one bumps into it, one feels the shock and even may get bruised. The opposite of *sōma* would be *skia* (shadow). The reflection of an actual table into a shadow is still a "table" however without "body"; one can see a table, yet cannot touch it, let alone bump into it. So by using "body" to speak of himself, Paul was underscoring the reality of his tribulations and sufferings within and without the arena (1:3-9). Still the matter of his body is "flesh" (Greek *sarx*; Hebrew *baśar*) which, in scripture, refers to the meaty substance of mammals, human as well as animal, and as such is bound to disintegrate. Thus it is by definition *thnētē* (death bound, mortal). By switching to "mortal flesh" Paul wanted to impress on the hearers that he was saved from "sure death" in the arena—nowadays, we would say he should not even be around. Yet Paul is alive and well and, in fact, penning another lengthy letter to be read aloud in his Corinthian congregation. Indeed, the life of Jesus *is* manifested in Paul's "death bound" flesh! Moreover, Paul's experiences enhance his trust in God and embolden him to continue "speaking (*laloumen*; speaking the gospel word)"[34] with "the same spirit of faith (*pisteōs*; trust)" (4:13). In so doing, he will not be boasting since he will be following the dictate of scripture itself: "I believed (trusted), and so I spoke" (LXX 115:1a), corresponding to the Hebrew Ps 116:10.[35] When one hears the entire passage in

---

[33] "our body" (as in KJV) in the original.
[34] See e.g. Rom 15:18; 2 Cor 2:17; 4:13-14; 7:14; 12:19; Eph 6:19-20; Phil 1:14; Col 4:3-4; 1 Thess 2:2, 4, 16.
[35] Translated in RSV as "I kept my faith, even when I said…"

Psalm 116 one realizes that the quotation is not haphazardly chosen, but is very much à propos in that it corresponds to 2 Corinthians 4:7-12 (see also 1:3-7).

> I love the Lord, because he has heard my voice and my supplications. Because he inclined his ear to me, therefore I will call on him as long as I live. The snares of death encompassed me; the pangs of Sheol laid hold on me; I suffered distress and anguish. Then I called on the name of the Lord: "O Lord, I beseech thee, save my life!" Gracious is the Lord, and righteous; our God is merciful. The Lord preserves the simple; when I was brought low, he saved me. Return, O my soul, to your rest; for the Lord has dealt bountifully with you. For thou hast delivered my soul from death, my eyes from tears, my feet from stumbling; I walk before the Lord in the land of the living. *I kept my faith, even when I said,* "I am greatly afflicted"; I said in my consternation, "Men are all a vain hope." What shall I render to the Lord for all his bounty to me? I will lift up the cup of salvation and call on the name of the Lord, I will pay my vows to the Lord in the presence of all his people. (Ps 116:1-14)

Still, the ultimate reason that Paul continues his ministry is his trust that, beyond the actual end of his "bodily" life, he will be raised just as Jesus was; however, in Paul's case, it will be for him to stand before (*parastēsai*) God who will judge as to whether he has accomplished his mission (2 Cor 4:14). Nonetheless, his concern is not so much for himself since, as "house manager" (*oikonomos*), he has no choice (1 Cor 9:16-17). Rather, his concern is for those who have been entrusted to his care: they also will be raised to stand trial: "… knowing that he who raised the Lord Jesus will raise us also with Jesus and bring us *with you* into his presence (*parastēsai*)." (2 Cor 4:14) This is corroborated in the following verse: "For it is all for your sake." (v.15a) In turn, the result of Paul's persevering apostolic endeavor will make God's grace abound among a larger number of people who will join in thanksgiving to God unto his glory, that is to say, will be making his presence known at an ever more encompassing table fellowship (v.15).[36] This verse corresponds in content to 1:11 which was the opening verse of Paul's lengthy apologia in defense of his delay in visiting the Corinthians (1:12-4:15) and thus ends the *inclusio*.

---

[36] I read this verse with KJV along the lines of 1:12 that opened Paul's lengthy apologia for his delay in coming to Corinth. RSV has a different reading of the original, which I consider incorrect.

Chapter 5

4:16-18 ¹⁶Διὸ οὐκ ἐγκακοῦμεν, ἀλλ' εἰ καὶ ὁ ἔξω ἡμῶν ἄνθρωπος διαφθείρεται, ἀλλ' ὁ ἔσω ἡμῶν ἀνακαινοῦται ἡμέρᾳ καὶ ἡμέρᾳ. ¹⁷ τὸ γὰρ παραυτίκα ἐλαφρὸν τῆς θλίψεως ἡμῶν καθ' ὑπερβολὴν εἰς ὑπερβολὴν αἰώνιον βάρος δόξης κατεργάζεται ἡμῖν, ¹⁸ μὴ σκοπούντων ἡμῶν τὰ βλεπόμενα ἀλλὰ τὰ μὴ βλεπόμενα· τὰ γὰρ βλεπόμενα πρόσκαιρα, τὰ δὲ μὴ βλεπόμενα αἰώνια.

¹⁶So we do not lose heart. Though our outer nature is wasting away, our inner nature is being renewed every day. ¹⁷For this slight momentary affliction is preparing for us an eternal weight of glory beyond all comparison, ¹⁸because we look not to the things that are seen but to the things that are unseen; for the things that are seen are transient, but the things that are unseen are eternal.

After having exhausted all that pertains to his apostleship and having explained why he cannot afford to "lose heart" in his ministry to and for them (4:1), Paul reprises this same statement in 4:16. However, this time he includes his addressees in the movement ahead, inviting them to join him in looking forward for the coming of the Lord when they all will be raised as was Jesus (v.14a), and all, they as well as he, will be brought into his presence (v.14b). In 4:16-5:5 Paul develops the thought he hinted at in 4:14: he and the Corinthians are on a path which will end in divine judgment (5:10). If Paul seems to be "dragging" them into his picture of "not losing heart" and encouraging them to proceed on that path, the reason is clear: if even the apostle himself, "the spiritual man" who "judges all things but is himself to be judged by no one" (1 Cor. 2:15), is not exempt from final judgment (4:1-5), then this certainly holds true for the "fleshly" Corinthians (3:1-3). Nevertheless, the

121

pressure he is putting on them is not "undue" since he has already presented himself as an example of someone not losing heart (2 Cor 4:1). Actually, as their "father in Christ Jesus through the gospel" (1 Cor 4:15b), he is not "dragging" them along but rather holding them by the hand.

What is Paul saying in 2 Corinthians 4:16? Although the statement is constructed in the present tense, it should not be understood as describing a factual situation, that is, as though the Corinthians, regardless of their input, are mere passive recipients of what is automatically taking place. That would be, at best, highly non-Pauline. Parallel texts using a terminology similar to that found in 2 Corinthians 4:16-5:5 confirm this understanding:

> You did not so learn Christ!—assuming that you have heard about him and were taught in him, as the truth is in Jesus. Put off your old nature which belongs to your former manner of life and is corrupt through deceitful lusts, and be renewed in the spirit of your minds, and put on the new nature, created after the likeness of God in true righteousness and holiness. Therefore, putting away falsehood, let every one speak the truth with his neighbor, for we are members one of another. (Eph 4:20-25)

> When Christ who is our life appears, then you also will appear with him in glory. Put to death therefore what is earthly in you: fornication, impurity, passion, evil desire, and covetousness, which is idolatry. On account of these the wrath of God is coming. In these you once walked, when you lived in them. But now put them all away: anger, wrath, malice, slander, and foul talk from your mouth. Do not lie to one another, seeing that you have put off the old nature with its practices and have put on the new nature, which is being renewed in knowledge after the image of its creator. Here there cannot be Greek and Jew, circumcised and uncircumcised, barbarian, Scythian, slave, free man, but Christ is

all, and in all. Put on then, as God's chosen ones, holy and beloved, compassion, kindness, lowliness, meekness, and patience, forbearing one another and, if one has a complaint against another, forgiving each other; as the Lord has forgiven you, so you also must forgive. And above all these put on love, which binds everything together in perfect harmony. And let the peace of Christ rule in your hearts, to which indeed you were called in the one body. And be thankful. (Col 3:4-15)

So we do not lose heart. Though our outer nature is wasting away, our inner nature is being renewed every day. For this slight momentary affliction is preparing for us an eternal weight of glory beyond all comparison, because we look not to the things that are seen but to the things that are unseen; for the things that are seen are transient, but the things that are unseen are eternal. (2 Cor 4:16-18)

For we know that if the earthly tent we live in is destroyed, we have a building from God, a house not made with hands, eternal in the heavens. Here indeed we groan, and long to put on our heavenly dwelling, so that by putting it on we may not be found naked. For while we are still in this tent, we sigh with anxiety; not that we would be unclothed, but that we would be further clothed, so that what is mortal may be swallowed up by life. He who has prepared us for this very thing is God, who has given us the Spirit as a guarantee. (2 Cor 5:1-5)

In both Colossians and Ephesians the tenor clearly summons the addressees to behave according to God's will as they learned from Paul and to desist from their previous comportment lest they incur divine wrath. This is also what we hear in 2 Corinthians: because the spirit of trust in God (4:13) that he himself "has given us," the longing for something that lies ahead is a "guarantee" (*arrabōn*: down payment, promise), yet only a "guarantee" (5:5).[1]

Taking all this into consideration, we can understand more clearly 4:16. The verb "wasting away" (*diaphtheiretai*) is from the same root as the noun *phthora* used twice in 1 Corinthians 15 (vv.42, 50) in conjunction with the rotting (corruption) a seed undergoes on its way to becoming a full-fledged plant or tree. Such an imagery of "corruption" is used in Ephesians and fits perfectly the erstwhile behavior of the Ephesian Gentiles; there RSV translated *phtheiromenon* into "corrupt" (Eph 4:22). The parallelism in thought between 2 Corinthians and Ephesians is evident in that, in both cases, the verb *ananeousthai* that describes the opposite of corruption means "renewed" (Eph 2:23). In Ephesians 4:22-24, it is very clear that corruption is not so much an automatic phenomenon, but is linked to "deceitful lusts" expressing a "former manner of life" to which belongs the "old nature" that is to be "put off" (*apothesthai*; put away). In other words, it is only to the extent that the "old nature" (old man) is "thrown aside" that the Ephesians will be "renewed." They will "put on" (*endysasthai*) their "new nature" (new man) through actions reflecting "true righteousness and holiness."[2] The same thought is found in the parallel passage of Colossians (3:8-10) where we encounter the same verb connoting "renewal" (*anakainoumenon*; v.9) as the one in 2 Corinthians 4:16 (*anakainoutai*). The conclusion is that the two verbs—*diaphtheireitai* (is wasting away) and *anakainoutai* (is renewed)—used here in 2 Corinthians are describing neither a matter of fact situation nor an automatic, taken for granted, state of affairs.

---

[1] See earlier my comments on 1:22.
[2] Notice that the verb *endysasthai* is of the same root as *ependysasthai* (put on over) translated as "put on" (2 Cor 5:2) and "further clothed" (v.4).

Both are qualified by "every day" (*hēmera kai hēmera*; day and day, day after day, day in day out). It is then the day to day renewal of the "inner nature" (inner man; 2 Cor 4:16a), corresponding to the "new nature" (new man; Eph 4:22), which ensures that the "outer nature" (outer man; 2 Cor 4:16b), corresponding to the "old nature" (old man; Eph 4:24), will be wasting away day by day. How? By "walking" (2 Cor 5:7a)—that is to say, "behaving"—day by day in a manner "pleasing to him" (v.9b), since "we must all appear before the judgment seat of Christ, so that each one may receive good or evil, according to what he has done in the body" (v.10). Thus, just as Paul was describing a potential situation in 1 Corinthians 15:51-55[3] rather than matter-of-fact one, here also (2 Cor 4:16-5:5) he is doing the same thing.[4]

Still, the path of renewal that is to be walked is not always smooth. One can discern this from Paul's immediate reference to "affliction" (4:17), a thought that pervaded the beginning of the epistle in conjunction with his testing experience in Asia (1:3-8). That he had this in mind is corroborated by the use of the phrase *kath' hyperbolēn eis hyperbolēn* (beyond all comparison; 4:17) which he used earlier (*kath' hyperbolēn*; transcendent, 1:8).[5] The

---

[3] See my comments on 1 Cor 15:51-58 in *C-1Cor*.
[4] The parallelism in intention between these two passages is corroborated through the use of the rare verb *katapinomai* (be swallowed up) in both instances and in conjunction with the similar thought: "Death (*thanatos*) is swallowed up (*katepothē*) in victory" (1 Cor 15:54); "so that what is mortal (*to thnēton*) may be swallowed up (*katepothē*) by life." (2 Cor 5:4) The closeness of the two passages is sealed through the broader parallelism in terminology. In the same verse (1 Cor 15:54) "death (*thanatos*)" parallels the earlier "what is mortal (*to thnēton*)," which is found in 2 Cor 5:4. Moreover, the verb "put on (over, further)" (*ependysasthai*) of 2 Cor 5:2, 4 is found no less than four times as "put on" (*endysasthai*) in 1 Cor 15:53-54. The verb *katapinō/omai* occurs only once more in the Pauline corpus (Heb 11:29) and three more times in the rest of the New Testament (Mt 23:24; 1 Pet 5:3; Rev 12:16).
[5] These are the only two instances of *kath' hyperbolēn* in 2 Corinthians.

linkage is further sealed by the unexpected tautology of "weight" (*baros*) before "glory" (*doxēs*; 4:17).[6] The addition of the unnecessary *baros* is used to remind the hearer of the earlier *ebarēthēmen* (we were crushed [by the weight]; 1:8) that is from the same root as *baros*. The intentionality of the addition of *baros* (4:17) is further corroborated in the equally superfluous *baroumenoi* (with anxiety; being overwhelmed [by the weight]) of 5:4a: "For while we are still in this tent, we sigh with anxiety." One can safely conclude that, in speaking of daily renewal as well as fading away, Paul is referring to the actuality he just described in 4:7-12 where "afflicted" is the first element in the description of the apostolic way of life (v.8a). This being the case, then the first element of the pair "wasting away" and "renewed" (v.16) is a compressed rendition of vv.8-9 and by the same token of vv.10a, 11a, and 12a. The second element (renewed) recalls vv.10b, 11b, and 12b. This is corroborated in v.18 where one hears of the "unseen" that lies beyond the "seen." In the immediate context the "seen" is the actual distresses that the bare eye can behold (vv.8-9, 10a, 11a, 12a); whereas the "unseen" one awaits on hope with patience: "For in this hope we were saved. Now hope that is seen is not hope. For who hopes for what he sees? But if we hope for what we do not see, we wait for it with patience." (Rom 8:24-25). Put otherwise, the "unseen" is the "life" of Jesus "among the Corinthians" (2 Cor 4:12b) as well as "the life of Jesus manifested in our mortal flesh" (v.11b). So, by including the Corinthians with him (4:16-5:5), Paul is reminding them that having their share of affliction and suffering *for the others' sake* will not be automatically and immediately gratified; they will have to undergo them while "looking intently ahead" (*skopountōn*; 4:18) and forgetting what

---

[6] The Greek *doxa* is the rendering of the Hebrew *kabod* that means "heaviness, weight."

lies behind: "Let each of you *look* not only *to* (*skopountes*) his own interests, but also to the interests of others" (Phil 2:4); "I press on toward the goal (*skopon*) for the prize of the upward call of God in Christ Jesus." (3:14)

In the meantime, they are to take the consolation in Paul's example as invitation to proceed as he did, while trusting fully in the apostolic word despite all afflictions. While he is giving himself as the example to follow, Paul often points at his opponents' attitude as the path not to be trodden. As was the case in 2 Corinthians 3:1-3 where Paul was indirectly aiming at the other Jewish leaders, so also in 4:18 he is hinting at the change of heart in Antioch of his nemesis, Peter. At least that is how Mark, followed by Matthew, understood it. Outside Hebrews 11:25 that relates to Moses and his times, the only instances of the adjective *proskairos* in the New Testament are relegated to 2 Corinthians 4:18 and the two parallel Gospel verses, Mark 4:17 and Matthew 13:21:

> ... persecuted (*diōkomenoi*), but not forsaken; struck down, but not destroyed ... For this slight momentary *affliction* (*thlipseōs*) is preparing for us an eternal weight of glory beyond all comparison, because we look not to the things that are seen but to the things that are unseen; for the things that are seen are *transient* (*proskaira*), but the things that are unseen are eternal. (2 Cor 4:9, 17-18)

> And these in like manner are the ones sown upon rocky ground, who, when they hear the word, immediately receive it with joy; and they have no root in themselves, but endure *for a while* (*proskairoi*); then, when *tribulation* (*thlipseōs*) or persecution (*diōgmou*) arises on account of the word, immediately they fall away. (Mk 4:16-17)

As for what was sown on rocky ground, this is he who hears the word and immediately receives it with joy; yet he has no root in himself, but endures *for a while* (*proskairos*), and when *tribulation* (*thlipseōs*) or persecution (*diōgmou*) arises on account of the word, immediately he falls away (*skandalizetai*: is scandalized). (Mt 13:20-21)

The parallelism in terminology is unmistakable considering that the root *diōk—* connoting persecution occurs only once more in 2 Corinthians in a series of Paul's apostolic misfortunes (12:10). Add to this that in the Gospel parable about sowing, the seed has to "rot, deconstruct" (*phtheirō*) before producing fruit, which is precisely the verb found earlier as *diaphtheiretai* (is wasting away; 2 Cor 4:16). Further, in the parable of the sower in both Mark and Matthew, the "rocky ground" (*petrōdē*) is a mitigated reference to Peter (*Petros*; rock).[7] In Matthew the connection is at its clearest since later in the Gospel one hears within the same context:

And I tell you, you are Peter, and on this rock (*petra*) I will build my church, and the powers of death shall not prevail against it ... And Peter took him and began to rebuke him, saying, "God forbid, Lord! This shall never happen to you." But he turned and said to Peter, "Get behind me, Satan! You are a hindrance (*skandalon*) to me; for you are not on the side of God, but of men." (16:18, 22-23)

5:1-5 *¹Οἴδαμεν γὰρ ὅτι ἐὰν ἡ ἐπίγειος ἡμῶν οἰκία τοῦ σκήνους καταλυθῇ, οἰκοδομὴν ἐκ θεοῦ ἔχομεν, οἰκίαν ἀχειροποίητον αἰώνιον ἐν τοῖς οὐρανοῖς. ² καὶ γὰρ ἐν τούτῳ στενάζομεν τὸ οἰκητήριον ἡμῶν τὸ ἐξ οὐρανοῦ ἐπενδύσασθαι ἐπιποθοῦντες, ³ εἴ γε καὶ ἐκδυσάμενοι οὐ γυμνοὶ εὑρεθησόμεθα. ⁴ καὶ γὰρ οἱ ὄντες ἐν τῷ σκήνει στενάζομεν βαρούμενοι, ἐφ' ᾧ οὐ θέλομεν ἐκδύσασθαι ἀλλ' ἐπενδύσασθαι,*

---

[7] See *NTI₁* 158.

ἵνα καταποθῇ τὸ θνητὸν ὑπὸ τῆς ζωῆς. ⁵ ὁ δὲ κατεργασάμενος ἡμᾶς εἰς αὐτὸ τοῦτο θεός, ὁ δοὺς ἡμῖν τὸν ἀρραβῶνα τοῦ πνεύματος.

¹For we know that if the earthly tent we live in is destroyed, we have a building from God, a house not made with hands, eternal in the heavens. ²Here indeed we groan, and long to put on our heavenly dwelling, ³so that by putting it on we may not be found naked. ⁴For while we are still in this tent, we sigh with anxiety; not that we would be unclothed, but that we would be further clothed, so that what is mortal may be swallowed up by life. ⁵He who has prepared us for this very thing is God, who has given us the Spirit as a guarantee.

Before concluding with the assuredness of the guarantee (2 Cor 5:5), a matter he pointed out earlier (1:22), that requires of one to keep walking on the way (5:6), Paul reprises the image "inner-unseen" versus "outer-seen" (4:16-18). To do this he uses a richer encompassing imagery (5:1-4) that combines three different metaphors he used previously: the building-temple (1 Cor 3:10-17), the arena (4:6-13), and the resurrection (15:35-55). However, he gives the lion's share to the building-temple metaphor. The reason is that the other two metaphors on their own give the impression that Paul is speaking of each individual believer, which unfortunately is how traditional exegesis up to our own times has usually handled this passage (2 Cor 4:16-5:5). So by giving precedence to the metaphor of the building-temple, he is leading his hearers away from two pitfalls that work hand in hand: the first is the belief in the certainty of glorification of the individual beyond death as though there were no final judgment (1 Cor 3:12-15), and the second is the belief that individual accountability will be reckoned with at the time of one's demise and not collectively at the end (15:51-52).

The first verse (2 Cor 5:1) essentially controls the entire passage extending over verses 1-10, after which Paul reverts to speaking again of his own apostolic mission (vv.11-14). The controlling word is the noun "house" (*oikia*) that occurs twice in 5:1.[8] Its root *oik*— is found in both "building" (*oikodomēn*; v.1) and "dwelling" (*oikētērion*; v.2), while its meaning of residence is further encountered later in the passage several times:

> So we are always of good courage; we know that while we are at home (*endēmountes*; reside at home) in the body we are away (*ekdēmoumen*; reside abroad) from the Lord, for we walk by faith, not by sight. We are of good courage, and we would rather be away (*ekdēmēsai*) from the body and at home (*endēmēsai*) with the Lord. So whether we are at home (*endēmountes*) or away (*ekdēmountes*), we make it our aim to please him. (vv.6-9)

The hearers cannot escape the impression that, in spite of all the adversities surrounding him in foreign land away from his home (Cilicia and Syria) for the sake of Macedonians and Hellenes, which adversities he is suffering at the hands of the equally Gentile Romans, Paul is "heading home" to "the Father of mercies and God of all comfort" (1:3b). By including the Corinthians with him, he is inviting them to understand, as he delineated in the beginning of the letter (1:3-7), that there is no other path to reach the same "home."

Paul adroitly begins with an imagery that is developed in Hebrews. His itinerary is none other than the scriptural one: it starts with the freedom granted by God's spirit (2 Cor 3:17) from the earthly powers, Egypt and Rome, respectively. Through acceptance of the gospel, the Corinthians have become children

---

[8] RSV omits the first instance. The original Greek is better reflected in KJV: "For we know that if our earthly house of *this* tabernacle were dissolved, we have a building of God, an house not made with hands, eternal in the heavens."

of the scriptural fathers, and accordingly they are bound to the wilderness trek (1 Cor 10:1-13) when the Father's house was a *foldable* tent (2 Cor 5:1, 3), and thus "bound to destruction" (*katalythē*; v.1). However, the scriptural story ends with a promise of a residence in heaven, not made with human hands (v.1),[9] and those heading for this home groan and long until they reach that dwelling (v.2). In speaking of that dwelling Paul uses the unexpected verb "put on" (*ependysasthai*; put on over, above), to complement the following verse: "so that, though having being stripped (*ekdysamenoi*; unclothed),[10] we may not be found naked." (v.3) At face value, this statement sounds superfluous after *ependysasthai* which has the connotation "put on over what one has already on"; moreover, its superfluity is underscored in that verse 4a reverts to the terminology of verses 1-2: "For while we are still in this tent, we sigh with anxiety." However, the intent of the statement in v.3 lies in its finality: "so that… we may not be found naked (*gymnoi*)." In realizing that "nakedness" occurred earlier only twice, once in conjunction with the arena (To the present hour we hunger and thirst, we are ill-clad [*gymnitevomen*] and buffeted and homeless; 1 Cor 4:11) and the other time in reference to the resurrection (And what you sow is not the body which is to be, but a bare [*gymnon*] kernel, perhaps of wheat or of some other grain; 15:37), one can begin to fathom where Paul is heading: subsuming all three metaphors in his conclusion, "For while we are still in this tent, we sigh with anxiety; not that we would be unclothed, but that we would be further clothed (*ependysasthai*), so that what is mortal may be swallowed up by life" (2 Cor 5:4).

---

[9] See Is 66:1-2a; Acts 7:48-50; see also Ezek 48:35b and Rev 21:1-4.
[10] RSV has "by putting it on," which is an accommodating translation. Strangely enough, KJV follows a similar path: "If so be that being clothed we shall not be found naked." (v.3)

Still, a word should be said concerning the ingenuity of how nakedness is introduced into the picture. Instead of using the simple "put on" (*endysasthai*) to contrast "be stripped; be unclothed" (*ekdysasthai*), Paul uses twice "put on over, above" (*ependysasthai*) which occurs only here in the entire Pauline corpus. Paul's intention in using this verb is to allude to the victorious gladiator who, though naked while fighting, would don not his regular garb after the fight, but instead would be clothed with the mantle of victory at the emperor's or the governor's hand. The thought of victory prepares for "so that what is mortal (*to thnēton*) may be *swallowed up* by life" (v.4) which, in turn, is reminiscent of the end of the resurrection metaphor: "When the perishable puts on the imperishable, and the mortal (*to thnēton*) puts on immortality, then shall come to pass the saying that is written: 'Death is *swallowed up* in victory.'" (1 Cor 15:54)

Vv. 6-10 ⁶ Θαρροῦντες οὖν πάντοτε καὶ εἰδότες ὅτι ἐνδημοῦντες ἐν τῷ σώματι ἐκδημοῦμεν ἀπὸ τοῦ κυρίου· ⁷ διὰ πίστεως γὰρ περιπατοῦμεν, οὐ διὰ εἴδους· ⁸ θαρροῦμεν δὲ καὶ εὐδοκοῦμεν μᾶλλον ἐκδημῆσαι ἐκ τοῦ σώματος καὶ ἐνδημῆσαι πρὸς τὸν κύριον. ⁹ διὸ καὶ φιλοτιμούμεθα, εἴτε ἐνδημοῦντες εἴτε ἐκδημοῦντες, εὐάρεστοι αὐτῷ εἶναι. ¹⁰ τοὺς γὰρ πάντας ἡμᾶς φανερωθῆναι δεῖ ἔμπροσθεν τοῦ βήματος τοῦ Χριστοῦ, ἵνα κομίσηται ἕκαστος τὰ διὰ τοῦ σώματος πρὸς ἃ ἔπραξεν, εἴτε ἀγαθὸν εἴτε φαῦλον.

> ⁶ *So we are always of good courage; we know that while we are at home in the body we are away from the Lord,* ⁷*for we walk by faith, not by sight.* ⁸*We are of good courage, and we would rather be away from the body and at home with the Lord.* ⁹*So whether we are at home or away, we make it our aim to please him.* ¹⁰*For we must all appear before the judgment seat of Christ, so that each one may receive good or evil, according to what he has done in the body.*

Paul then reminds the Corinthians that, on the one hand, all that happens for the good is ultimately wrought by God himself (2 Cor 5:5a; see Phil 2:12-13) who also gives the guarantee that what was started will be brought to full fruition (2 Cor 5:5b). On the other hand, such guarantee requires that they and he continue to walk "toward home," in "good courage," while pleasing the Lord by doing his bidding (vv.6-9). The reason is that "we must all appear before the judgment seat of Christ, so that each one may receive good or evil, according to what he has done *in the body*," that is to say, during our earthly lives (v.10; see also Rom 2:6-8). This conclusion corroborates the understanding of 1 Corinthians 15 as being concerned with final judgment rather than as a defense of the possibility and "reality" of the resurrection followed by a description thereof.[11] In referring to the judgment Paul uses the same verb *phanerōthēnai* (appear, be revealed; 2 Cor 5:10) he used to speak repeatedly of the "revelation" brought about through his preaching of the gospel: "But thanks be to God, who in Christ always leads us in triumph, and through us spreads (*phanerounti*) the fragrance of the knowledge of him everywhere" (2:14); "and you show that you are (*phaneroumenoi*; are shown to be)[12] a letter from Christ delivered by us, written not with ink but with the Spirit of the living God, not on tablets of stone but on tablets of human hearts" (3:3); "We have renounced disgraceful, underhanded ways; we refuse to practice cunning or to tamper with God's word, but by the open statement (*phanerōsei*) of the truth we would commend ourselves to every man's conscience in the sight of God." (4:2). Consequently, the final judgment will take place *in the light of* the gospel teaching, which is precisely what Paul writes elsewhere: "They [the Gentiles] show that what the law

---

[11] See my comments in *C-1Cor* 294-5.
[12] See earlier my comments on that verse.

requires is written on their hearts, while their conscience also bears witness and their conflicting thoughts accuse or perhaps excuse them on that day when, according to my gospel, God judges the secrets of men by Christ Jesus." (Rom 2:16)

Vv. 11-21 ¹¹ Εἰδότες οὖν τὸν φόβον τοῦ κυρίου ἀνθρώπους πείθομεν, θεῷ δὲ πεφανερώμεθα· ἐλπίζω δὲ καὶ ἐν ταῖς συνειδήσεσιν ὑμῶν πεφανερῶσθαι. ¹² οὐ πάλιν ἑαυτοὺς συνιστάνομεν ὑμῖν ἀλλὰ ἀφορμὴν διδόντες ὑμῖν καυχήματος ὑπὲρ ἡμῶν, ἵνα ἔχητε πρὸς τοὺς ἐν προσώπῳ καυχωμένους καὶ μὴ ἐν καρδίᾳ. ¹³ εἴτε γὰρ ἐξέστημεν, θεῷ· εἴτε σωφρονοῦμεν, ὑμῖν. ¹⁴ ἡ γὰρ ἀγάπη τοῦ Χριστοῦ συνέχει ἡμᾶς, κρίναντας τοῦτο, ὅτι εἷς ὑπὲρ πάντων ἀπέθανεν, ἄρα οἱ πάντες ἀπέθανον· ¹⁵ καὶ ὑπὲρ πάντων ἀπέθανεν, ἵνα οἱ ζῶντες μηκέτι ἑαυτοῖς ζῶσιν ἀλλὰ τῷ ὑπὲρ αὐτῶν ἀποθανόντι καὶ ἐγερθέντι. ¹⁶ Ὥστε ἡμεῖς ἀπὸ τοῦ νῦν οὐδένα οἴδαμεν κατὰ σάρκα· εἰ καὶ ἐγνώκαμεν κατὰ σάρκα Χριστόν, ἀλλὰ νῦν οὐκέτι γινώσκομεν. ¹⁷ ὥστε εἴ τις ἐν Χριστῷ, καινὴ κτίσις· τὰ ἀρχαῖα παρῆλθεν, ἰδοὺ γέγονεν καινά· ¹⁸ τὰ δὲ πάντα ἐκ τοῦ θεοῦ τοῦ καταλλάξαντος ἡμᾶς ἑαυτῷ διὰ Χριστοῦ καὶ δόντος ἡμῖν τὴν διακονίαν τῆς καταλλαγῆς, ¹⁹ ὡς ὅτι θεὸς ἦν ἐν Χριστῷ κόσμον καταλλάσσων ἑαυτῷ, μὴ λογιζόμενος αὐτοῖς τὰ παραπτώματα αὐτῶν καὶ θέμενος ἐν ἡμῖν τὸν λόγον τῆς καταλλαγῆς. ²⁰ Ὑπὲρ Χριστοῦ οὖν πρεσβεύομεν ὡς τοῦ θεοῦ παρακαλοῦντος δι' ἡμῶν· δεόμεθα ὑπὲρ Χριστοῦ, καταλλάγητε τῷ θεῷ. ²¹ τὸν μὴ γνόντα ἁμαρτίαν ὑπὲρ ἡμῶν ἁμαρτίαν ἐποίησεν, ἵνα ἡμεῖς γενώμεθα δικαιοσύνη θεοῦ ἐν αὐτῷ.

¹¹Therefore, knowing the fear of the Lord, we persuade men; but what we are is known to God, and I hope it is known also to your conscience. ¹²We are not commending ourselves to you again but giving you cause to be proud of us, so that you may be able to answer those who pride themselves on a man's position and not on his heart. ¹³For if we are beside ourselves, it is for God; if we are in our right mind, it is for you. ¹⁴For the love of Christ controls us, because we are convinced that one has died

> *for all; therefore all have died. ¹⁵And he died for all, that those who live might live no longer for themselves but for him who for their sake died and was raised. ¹⁶From now on, therefore, we regard no one from a human point of view; even though we once regarded Christ from a human point of view, we regard him thus no longer. ¹⁷Therefore, if any one is in Christ, he is a new creation; the old has passed away, behold, the new has come. ¹⁸All this is from God, who through Christ reconciled us to himself and gave us the ministry of reconciliation; ¹⁹that is, in Christ God was reconciling the world to himself, not counting their trespasses against them, and entrusting to us the message of reconciliation. ²⁰So we are ambassadors for Christ, God making his appeal through us. We beseech you on behalf of Christ, be reconciled to God. ²¹ For our sake he made him to be sin who knew no sin, so that in him we might become the righteousness of God.*

Therefore (*oun*) to conclude his previous remarks Paul reverts to his own ministry to the Corinthians (2 Cor 5:11-21). After having mentioned the judgment (v.10) he refers to "the fear of the Lord" which is the classic scriptural phrase connected with doing his will.[13] In view of the judgment of all, Paul continues his efforts of persuasion hoping that, just as he is "known" (*phanerōmetha*; revealed) to God, so too and in the same way he would be "known" (*phanerōmetha*; revealed) to the Corinthians' conscience (v.11), that is to say, that they would see him just as God does, as his truthful apostle. This does not mean that he is in need of their commendation; to the contrary, he wants to equip them to stand up for him in front of his opponents who are trying to impress them with the position they hold rather than with their "heart" that is known only to God (v.12). As for

---

[13] See *OTI₃* 130.

Paul, his heart is "known" to God and should be "known" to them (v.11) who "show that you are (*phaneroumenoi*; shown to be) a letter from Christ delivered by us, written not with ink but with the Spirit of the living God, not on tablets of stone but on tablets of human hearts" (3:3).

The usual translation of 5:13, including that in the Vulgate and KJV, is "For if *we are beside ourselves* (*exestēmen*), it is for God; if *we are in our right mind* (*sōphronoumen*), it is for you" (RSV). This understanding of *exestēmen* as "being beside oneself" is problematic. It is readily taken as such because it opposes *sōphronoumen* that is translated elsewhere as "(be) sober" (Vulgate, KJV). However, later in the letter, no less than four times Paul uses *aphrōn* (fool; 11:16 [twice]; 12:6, 11), the opposite of *sōphrōn* (sensible, prudent, wise), in reference to himself to qualify his behavior or attitude toward the Corinthians, not God. In the same context he equates his "foolishness" toward the Corinthians with "boasting":

> On behalf of this man I will boast, but on my own behalf I will not boast, except of my weaknesses. Though if I wish to boast, I shall not be a fool, for I shall be speaking the truth. But I refrain from it, so that no one may think more of me than he sees in me or hears from me ... I have been a fool! You forced me to it, for I ought to have been commended by you. (vv.5-6, 11a)

That "boast" was on the mind of Paul in 5:13 is corroborated by its use twice in the preceding verse: "We are not commending ourselves to you again but giving you cause for boasting (*kavkhēmatos*) regarding us, so that you may be able to answer those who boast (*kavkhōmenous*) in a man's position and not on his heart." (v.12)[14] By reminding the Corinthians that he does not need to commend himself to them, he is forcing them to realize that it is they who should boast of him before others. Consequently one must understand *exestēmen* (5:13), a unique instance of the verb *existēmi* in the Pauline corpus, in the way that best fits the context of the entire epistle. Since the literal meaning of that verb is "stand out" and *exestēmen* is in the aorist (fulfilled) tense while *sōphronoumen* (we are sensible) is in the present tense, the intention of the verse is the following: "We already stood out before God when we delivered to you the gospel as his ministers; we do not need to pursue this matter anymore. However, we are using all possible prudence and wisdom to communicate to you the following." And the following (vv.14-19) is a reminder of the gospel in a nutshell along the same lines as those used in Romans 5:1-11.

Paul is following the example of Christ whose love—or rather God's love through Christ (Rom 8:35-39)—for him and for the Corinthians required that Christ, as God's ambassador, die for the sake of "all," that is to say, go the opposite way of boasting (2 Cor 5:14a). By the same token "all" are bound to heed his example and die (v.14b).[15] The corollary is that the Corinthians' life is no more theirs but Christ's (v.15) since "you were bought with a price" (1 Cor 6:20a; 7:23a). On the other hand, since the resurrection entails the dismissal of the fleshly (soul-ly, earthly)

---

[14] In translating the original Greek here into "to be proud of us" and "pride themselves," RSV misleads the hearers into not perceiving the connection between 2 Cor 5:12-13 and chapters 11 and 12.

[15] As I repeatedly explained in my commentaries, the aorist—in this case *apethanon* (died)—does not necessarily indicate a past action, but rather the assuredness that it need to be so. Compare with Rom 6:1-11 where after a series of aorist verbs in reference to the baptized having died with Christ, Paul concludes with an imperative: "So you also *consider* (*logizesthe*) dead to sin and alive to God in Christ Jesus." (v.11) RSV translates the imperative into a forceful "must consider."

for the spiritual (1 Cor 15:39-55), now that Christ is raised (2 Cor 5:15b) he is no more "from a human point of view" (*kata sarka*; according to the flesh, v.16), which rejoins what Paul writes in Rom 9:5 where he is addressing the Jerusalemite Jewish leadership.[16] The statement concerning the new creation (*kainē ktisis*; 2 Cor 5:17) reflects Romans 6, especially "we too might walk in newness (*kainotēti*) of life" (v.4), but more importantly recalls "For neither circumcision counts for anything, nor uncircumcision, but a new creation (*kainē ktisis*)" (Gal 6:15). Given that these are the only two instances of the phrase "a new creation" in the New Testament, one would expect a correlation between the two, and there is. The indications are the following:

1. 2 Corinthians 5:16 reflects the tension between Paul and his opponents, which is also evident in the verse 17 "the old has passed away, behold, the new has come" that is reminiscent of the "old" and "new" covenants (2 Cor 3).

2. Each of these two covenants are said to be served through a "ministry," which term is found in the verse (5:18) that follows immediately the reference to "the old and the new" as well as "a new creation" (v.16). Paul's (table fellowship) ministry was inclusive of Jews and Gentiles.[17]

3. The phrase *ta panta*, translated usually as "all" (2 Cor 5:18), means "all the aforementioned series." When there are only two items, the translation should be "both."[18] Thus, in our case here, *ta*

---

[16] See my comments on that verse in *C-Rom* 164-5.
[17] See especially my comments on 3:18.
[18] See *Gal* 157-9.

panta is inclusive of "both the old and the new," that is to say, both the followers of the old covenant and those pertaining to the new. Actually *ta de panta ek tou Theou* (And all are from God; 2 Cor 5:18) is verbatim what we find in 1 Corinthians where the intended is clearly the pair "man and woman" (11:12).[19]

4. However, Paul speaks of his ministry as one "of reconciliation" (*katallagēs*); this theme was so essential in his eyes at this juncture that the root *katallag—* occurs no less than five times in three verses (5:18-20) and only here in the entire letter! Although the phraseology of this passage is reminiscent of Romans 5, it is also very close to that found in Ephesians where the reconciliation is said to be not only between God and man, but also between Jew and Gentile: "But now in Christ Jesus you who once were far off have been brought near in the blood of Christ. For he is our peace, who has made us both one, and has broken down the dividing wall of hostility, by abolishing in his flesh the law of commandments and ordinances, that he might create in himself one new man in place of the two, so making peace, and might reconcile us both to God in one body through the cross, thereby bringing the hostility to an end." (2:13-16) Notice how reconciliation is also understood as "creating (*ktisē*) one new (*kainon*) man in place of the

---

[19] See my comments in *C-1Cor* 195.

two," which is precisely the phraseology found in 2 Corinthians 5:17-19.

Hence, by bringing into the picture *his* "ministry" (vv.18 and 20) Paul, as God's plenipotentiary ambassador (v.20), was inviting the Corinthians to reconcile with God *through* their reconciliation with "the whole world" (v.19).[20] Finally, by referring to God as *parakalountos*—which has the double meaning of "consoling, comforting" and "exhorting, making his appeal"—instead of simply *kalountos* (calling) through him, Paul was drawing the Corinthians' attention to the beginning of the letter (1:3-7) and thus inviting them to do his bidding to reconcile with everyone in spite of all the difficulties this may entail. Rendering *parakalountos* as simply "beseech" (KJV), "making his appeal" (RSV) or "exhorting" (JB), hides the double-entendre of the original.

How is one to understand 5:21, especially that God "made" (*epoiēsen*) the sinless Christ "(to be) a sin" (*hamartian*) "for our sake"? The answer lies in Leviticus where the same noun "sin" applies to both the act of sinning and the atoning sacrificial offering required for its expiation:

> When a ruler *sins*, doing unwittingly any one of all the things which the Lord his God has commanded not to be done, and is guilty (*'ašem*), if the *sin* (Hebrew *ḥaṭṭa't*; Greek *hamartia*) which he has committed (*sinned*) is made known to him, he shall bring as his offering a goat, a male without blemish, and shall lay his hand upon the head of the goat, and kill it in the place where they kill

---

[20] Compare with 1 Cor 10:31-11:1: "So, whether you eat or drink, or whatever you do, do all to the glory of God. Give no offense to Jews or to Greeks or to the church of God, just as I try to please all men in everything I do, not seeking my own advantage, but that of many, that they may be saved. Be imitators of me, as I am of Christ."

Chapter 5

the burnt offering before the Lord; it is a *sin offering* (*ḥaṭṭa't*; *hamartia*). (4:22-24)

So, if Christ "knew no sin" (2 Cor 5:21; see also Heb 4:15; 1 Pet 2:22) then he was in no need of a sin offering for his own sake, but he became the sin offering for the sake of others. That thought is precisely the centerpiece of the fourth Servant passage in Isaiah (52:13-53:12) which is an axial text in the New Testament view of Christ:

> Surely he has borne our griefs and carried our sorrows; yet we esteemed him stricken, smitten by God, and afflicted. But he was wounded for our transgressions, he was bruised for our iniquities; upon him was the chastisement that made us whole, and with his stripes we are healed. All we like sheep have gone astray; we have turned every one to his own way; and *the Lord has laid on him the iniquity of us all.* He was oppressed, and he was afflicted, yet he opened not his mouth; like *a lamb* (Hebrew *śeh*; Greek *probaton*) that is led to the slaughter, and like a sheep that before its shearers is dumb, so he opened not his mouth. By oppression and judgment he was taken away; and as for his generation, who considered that he was cut off out of the land of the living, stricken for the transgression of my people? And they made his grave with the wicked and with a rich man in his death, *although he had done no violence, and there was no deceit in his mouth.* Yet it was the will of the Lord to bruise him; he has put him to grief; when he makes himself an *offering for sin* (*'ašam*, guilt offering; *peri hamartias*), he shall see his offspring, he shall prolong his days; the will of the Lord shall prosper in his hand; he shall see the fruit of the travail of his soul and be satisfied; by his knowledge shall the *righteous one* (*dikaion*), my servant, *make many to be accounted righteous* (*dikaiōsai*); and he shall bear their iniquities. Therefore I will divide him a portion with the great, and he shall divide the spoil with the strong; because he poured out his soul to death, and was numbered with the transgressors; yet he bore the *sin* (*ḥeṭe'*;

hamartias) of many, and made intercession for the transgressors. (53:4-12)[21]

Considering the vocabulary of 2 Corinthians 5:21, it becomes clear that it is a compact rendition of Isaiah 53. Through the sacrifice of Christ, willed by God himself, Paul and the Corinthians have become tangible proof of God's power to implement his righteousness in spite of their being sinners. This rejoins what the Apostle writes in Romans: "… our wickedness (*adikia*; unrighteousness) serves to show the justice (*dikaiosynēn*; righteousness) of God." (3:5a) The link with Romans is forceful since in the previous verses (2 Cor 5:18-20) Paul speaks of "reconciliation," which is the topic of the concluding verses of Romans 5:1-11 that describes God's mercy and forgiveness to the sinners through the sacrifice of Christ.

---

[21] The difference between guilt and sin does not affect my argument.

Chapter 6

Vv. 1-2 ¹Συνεργοῦντες δὲ καὶ παρακαλοῦμεν μὴ εἰς κενὸν τὴν χάριν τοῦ θεοῦ δέξασθαι ὑμᾶς· ²λέγει γάρ· καιρῷ δεκτῷ ἐπήκουσά σου καὶ ἐν ἡμέρᾳ σωτηρίας ἐβοήθησά σοι. ἰδοὺ νῦν καιρὸς εὐπρόσδεκτος, ἰδοὺ νῦν ἡμέρα σωτηρίας. ³ Μηδεμίαν ἐν μηδενὶ διδόντες προσκοπήν, ἵνα μὴ μωμηθῇ ἡ διακονία,

¹Working together with him, then, we entreat you not to accept the grace of God in vain. ²For he says, "At the acceptable time I have listened to you, and helped you on the day of salvation." Behold, now is the acceptable time; behold, now is the day of salvation. ³We put no obstacle in any one's way, so that no fault may be found with our ministry,

In chapter 6 Paul describes his ministry in Corinth along the lines of Isaiah's "servant" whose mission was to share God's teaching unto their salvation not only with the faithful remnant of Israel but also with the nations (Is 42:1-7; 49:1-12). He starts the chapter with a quotation from Isaiah 49:8 (2 Cor 6:2) which is part of the second Servant "hymn" (Is 49:1-12) and concludes with a series of quotations (2 Cor 6:16-18), the second of which (v.17) is taken from Isaiah 52:11 that is only one verse away from the beginning of the fourth Servant "hymn" (52:13-53:12). Paul depicts himself as the true servant (*'ebed*; slave) who "works together" with his master, just as Isaiah does. Paul also "entreats" (*parakaloumen*) the Corinthians not to accept God's grace in vain (2 Cor 6:1),[1] for "now is the time" and they should not miss that opportunity which may not return (v.2). Should they not "make the most of the time, because the days are evil" (Eph 5:16), they would be at fault, and not Paul; he is carrying out his

---

[1] See 1 Cor 15:12-19 and my comments thereon in *C-1Cor* 274-7.

ministry[2] to perfection (2 Cor 6:3, 6-7) in spite of all possible obstacles (vv.4-6, 8-10).

Vv. 4-10 ⁴ ἀλλ' ἐν παντὶ συνιστάντες ἑαυτοὺς ὡς θεοῦ διάκονοι, ἐν ὑπομονῇ πολλῇ, ἐν θλίψεσιν, ἐν ἀνάγκαις, ἐν στενοχωρίαις, ⁵ ἐν πληγαῖς, ἐν φυλακαῖς, ἐν ἀκαταστασίαις, ἐν κόποις, ἐν ἀγρυπνίαις, ἐν νηστείαις, ⁶ ἐν ἁγνότητι, ἐν γνώσει, ἐν μακροθυμίᾳ, ἐν χρηστότητι, ἐν πνεύματι ἁγίῳ, ἐν ἀγάπῃ ἀνυποκρίτῳ, ⁷ ἐν λόγῳ ἀληθείας, ἐν δυνάμει θεοῦ· διὰ τῶν ὅπλων τῆς δικαιοσύνης τῶν δεξιῶν καὶ ἀριστερῶν, ⁸ διὰ δόξης καὶ ἀτιμίας, διὰ δυσφημίας καὶ εὐφημίας· ὡς πλάνοι καὶ ἀληθεῖς, ⁹ ὡς ἀγνοούμενοι καὶ ἐπιγινωσκόμενοι, ὡς ἀποθνῄσκοντες καὶ ἰδοὺ ζῶμεν, ὡς παιδευόμενοι καὶ μὴ θανατούμενοι, ¹⁰ ὡς λυπούμενοι ἀεὶ δὲ χαίροντες, ὡς πτωχοὶ πολλοὺς δὲ πλουτίζοντες, ὡς μηδὲν ἔχοντες καὶ πάντα κατέχοντες.

> ⁴*but as servants of God we commend ourselves in every way: through great endurance, in afflictions, hardships, calamities,* ⁵*beatings, imprisonments, tumults, labors, watching, hunger;* ⁶*by purity, knowledge, forbearance, kindness, the Holy Spirit, genuine love,* ⁷*truthful speech, and the power of God; with the weapons of righteousness for the right hand and for the left;* ⁸*in honor and dishonor, in ill repute and good repute. We are treated as impostors, and yet are true;* ⁹*as unknown, and yet well known; as dying, and behold we live; as punished, and yet not killed;* ¹⁰*as sorrowful, yet always rejoicing; as poor, yet making many rich; as having nothing, and yet possessing everything.*

The series of phrases detailing the description of Paul's ministry is obviously not intended to be "exegeted" word for word. Such would have been the case if the letter were addressed

---

[2] Having translated *diakonia* as "ministry" (2 Cor 6:3) RSV unwarrantedly opts for "servants" instead of "ministers" to render *diakonoi* (v.4). This is a classic sample of RSV's "colorful" tendency in translation.

to individuals for their own perusal and study. However, the letter was written to be read aloud to the congregated community (3:2) where the individual hearers would be listening to long sentences read in tandem without interruption. Clusters of interrelated words were meant to leave an "impression" of magnitude upon the hearer. In Revelation, for example, we find: "Worthy art thou, our Lord and God, to receive glory and honor and power" (4:11b); "Worthy is the Lamb who was slain, to receive power and wealth and wisdom and might and honor and glory and blessing!" (5:12); "… to kill with sword and with famine and with pestilence and by wild beasts of the earth" (6:8); "Amen! Blessing and glory and wisdom and thanksgiving and honor and power and might be to our God for ever and ever! Amen" (7:12). Nevertheless, the number of items within such lists is intentional in that certain numbers such as three, four, and seven, are symbolic.[3] Here in the lengthy series of twenty eight phrases (2 Cor 6:4-10), whose immediate and foremost intention is to say that Paul ministered "in every way" (*en panti*; 3a), was not haphazardly constructed. In the original, it is divided into eighteen phrases each introduced with *en* (in), followed by three phrases each starting with *dia* (through), and then ends with seven phrases each beginning with *hōs* (as). Moreover, the first eighteen are divided into ten "adversities" followed by eight "positive features." The numeral three and seven are easy to explain in that they are both reflective of the divine;[4] in ending with them Paul was stressing that he was indeed a "minister of God" (6:4a). As for the numerals ten and eight, I am proposing that they are meant as the doubles of five and four, respectively. In a text intended to be received aurally, repetition—in this case through doubling—usually reflects

---

[3] See my "Excursus on Number Symbolism" in *NTI₃* 22-25.
[4] See previous fn.

stressing a point, similar to our contemporary italicization, underscoring, or bold characters. As for five and four they are classic scriptural devices. Five is reminiscent of the Law, the five books of Moses, and as such reflects the Jews, whereas four is a symbol of universalism (the four geographical directions) and as such of the nations.[5] This reading fits the differentiation between the first ten "adversities" reflecting the attitude of the Jewish leadership at odds with Paul, and the eight "positive elements" reflecting his demeanor during his apostolate to the Gentiles.

Vv. 11-13 *11 Τὸ στόμα ἡμῶν ἀνέῳγεν πρὸς ὑμᾶς, Κορίνθιοι, ἡ καρδία ἡμῶν πεπλάτυνται· 12 οὐ στενοχωρεῖσθε ἐν ἡμῖν, στενοχωρεῖσθε δὲ ἐν τοῖς σπλάγχνοις ὑμῶν· 13 τὴν δὲ αὐτὴν ἀντιμισθίαν, ὡς τέκνοις λέγω, πλατύνθητε καὶ ὑμεῖς.*

11 Our mouth is open to you, Corinthians; our heart is wide. 12 You are not restricted by us, but you are restricted in your own affections. 13 In return—I speak as to children—widen your hearts also.

Verses 11-13 are a state of the art description of a parent's feeling and the request that the children reciprocate. Through his teaching mouth, it is Paul's heart that is wide open to the Corinthians (v.11), the heart being the Hebrew *leb* that is the mental center of the human being with which he thinks and wills. Such may be putting a restriction on them, however, only insofar as how they "feel" toward him (v.12).[6] Still, he is asking them to make the effort to reciprocate fully by opening wide their hearts to him, for in so doing they will show that they are truly his grown up children (v.13; see 1 Cor 4:14), that is to say,

---

[5] See, e.g., the feeding of the 5000 (Mk 6:30-44) followed by that of the 4000 (8:1-10). See my comments in *NTI₁* 175-6 and 182-3.
[6] What RSV translates as "affections" is actually *splankhna* whose literal meaning is "entrails," the seat of feelings. KJV has "bowels."

no longer "babes" (3:1). These three verses use the literary *topos* (device) of *philia* (friendship) that Paul elaborates on magisterially in Galatians 4:12-20 and 1 Thessalonians 2:7-12.[7]

Friendly adulation has a purpose. In 2 Cor 6:11-13 it serves as an introduction to the following (6:14-7:1) where Paul is laying a heavy demand on them: they must turn their back completely on their previous way of life. Given that Paul reprises and expands on the *topos* of friendship in 7:2-16, starting with a request "Open your hearts to us" (7:2a) which is similar to how he ended 6:11-13 (widen your hearts also; v.13b), many commentators consider 6:14-7:2 a later insertion that does not fit the context and even hints at extreme exclusivism which is non-Pauline, if not anti-Pauline, and that has no parallel in the entire letter.[8] However, one need not take such stance.

Before going into the two lengthy chapters (8 and 9) dealing with the collection among his churches as "the offering (*diakonias*; ministry) to the saints (of Jerusalem)" (9:1), Paul was wrapping up the discussion covering chapters 1-6. The bulk of the discussion dealt with the tension between him and his opponents. Suddenly asking the Corinthians to support those in Jerusalem without any preparation would have looked dubious. So Paul opted to remind them in the strictest possible manner of their previous way of life from which they were delivered by the "word of truth"[9]—the gospel—brought to them with "the power of God" (6:7a). This same word of God (*ho logos tou Theou*) did not originate with them (1 Cor 14:36a) but came to them

---

[7] See *Gal* 231-2.
[8] Such attitude recalls the one commentators have toward 1 Corinthians 14:33b-36, a passage I have shown to fit perfectly the context of chapter 14.
[9] RSV waters the original down to "truthful speech."

through Paul, who spoke out of the oracles of God (*ta logia tou Theou*) entrusted to the Jews (Rom 3:2).

Vv. 14-18 ¹⁴ Μὴ γίνεσθε ἑτεροζυγοῦντες ἀπίστοις· τίς γὰρ μετοχὴ δικαιοσύνῃ καὶ ἀνομίᾳ, ἢ τίς κοινωνία φωτὶ πρὸς σκότος; ¹⁵ τίς δὲ συμφώνησις Χριστοῦ πρὸς Βελιάρ, ἢ τίς μερὶς πιστῷ μετὰ ἀπίστου; ¹⁶ τίς δὲ συγκατάθεσις ναῷ θεοῦ μετὰ εἰδώλων; ἡμεῖς γὰρ ναὸς θεοῦ ἐσμεν ζῶντος, καθὼς εἶπεν ὁ θεὸς ὅτι ἐνοικήσω ἐν αὐτοῖς καὶ ἐμπεριπατήσω καὶ ἔσομαι αὐτῶν θεὸς καὶ αὐτοὶ ἔσονταί μου λαός. ¹⁷ διὸ ἐξέλθατε ἐκ μέσου αὐτῶν καὶ ἀφορίσθητε, λέγει κύριος, καὶ ἀκαθάρτου μὴ ἅπτεσθε· κἀγὼ εἰσδέξομαι ὑμᾶς ¹⁸ καὶ ἔσομαι ὑμῖν εἰς πατέρα καὶ ὑμεῖς ἔσεσθέ μοι εἰς υἱοὺς καὶ θυγατέρας, λέγει κύριος παντοκράτωρ.

7:1 ¹ταύτας οὖν ἔχοντες τὰς ἐπαγγελίας, ἀγαπητοί, καθαρίσωμεν ἑαυτοὺς ἀπὸ παντὸς μολυσμοῦ σαρκὸς καὶ πνεύματος, ἐπιτελοῦντες ἁγιωσύνην ἐν φόβῳ θεοῦ.

¹⁴Do not be mismated with unbelievers. For what partnership have righteousness and iniquity? Or what fellowship has light with darkness? ¹⁵What accord has Christ with Belial? Or what has a believer in common with an unbeliever? ¹⁶What agreement has the temple of God with idols? For we are the temple of the living God; as God said, "I will live in them and move among them, and I will be their God, and they shall be my people. ¹⁷ Therefore come out from them, and be separate from them, says the Lord, and touch nothing unclean; then I will welcome you, ¹⁸and I will be a father to you, and you shall be my sons and daughters, says the Lord Almighty."

7 ¹Since we have these promises, beloved, let us cleanse ourselves from every defilement of body and spirit, and make holiness perfect in the fear of God.

The function of 2 Corinthians 6:14-7:1 is to put in front of his hearers the essential reality that they are "indebted" to the Jewish leaders in Jerusalem and they should understand that. This is corroborated in the starting verse that is filled with Law terminology. The original for "mismated" (6:14) is *heterozygountes* (unequally yoked; KJV), yoke being a clear reference to the Law (Acts 15:10; Gal 5:1),[10] as are righteousness and iniquity. "Light" and "darkness" have earlier been used in conjunction with "unbelievers" as well as the gospel (2 Cor 4:4-6), just as is the case here. By using "fellowship" (*koinōnia*) Paul is bringing to mind what he earlier wrote concerning the table of God and that of idols (1 Cor 10:14-22), and also preparing for two verses later (2 Cor 6:16) where he introduces the metaphor of temple. This allows him to handle his subject head on. If God's temple, which the Corinthians together with Paul are (v.16), is to be defended against the Jewish opponents (1 Cor 3:10-17) how much more so is it to be protected from the Gentile mores. This is a matter that Paul had broached several times earlier (1:20-24; 5:1-8; 6:1-11, 12-20; 7:14; 10:14-22; 11:2-16; 14:33b-36; 15:32-34). He then uses a series of quotations whose overall tenor is very clear: since God resides among his people (2 Cor 6:16b) they will have to be rid of anything that is unworthy of him (v.17) in order for him and them to be a true family (v.18). However, as is usual with Paul, the quotations are not haphazardly thrown together. They are ingeniously collected on both the level of content and that of location. First and foremost, the series of the chosen quotations spans the spectrum of the Law and the Prophets. Short quotations in Paul are always an invitation for the hearers to recall the entire passages surrounding them, which passages will

---

[10] The same applies to the "law of Christ" (Gal 6:2) in Mt 11:28-30: "Come to me, all who labor and are heavy laden, and I will give you rest. Take my yoke upon you, and learn from me; for I am gentle and lowly in heart, and you will find rest for your souls. For my yoke is easy, and my burden is light."

secure the full and correct understanding of what the Apostle is aiming at.[11] So it would be worth our while to delve into the structure as well as content of verses 16b-18.

The entire section is constructed as a chiasm A [v.16b] B [v.17] A'[v.18]. The first and third elements are parallel in that they speak of God's community using the related metaphors of people and family. The central element is the requirement to join that community: one is to leave one's previous allegiance. When one includes into the picture the introductory "God said" (v.16a), which corresponds to the concluding "says the Lord Almighty" (v.18b), then one notices a wider chiasm—A, B, C, B', A'. The effect is that the Gentile Corinthians are hearing the scripture of Israel addressed to them.[12] This is confirmed in the quotation from Leviticus that is transformed from an address in the second person plural "you" (26:12) into one in the third person plural "they, them" (2 Cor 6:16b); once the literary inclusion of the Gentiles is made and they have become part of the addressed divine congregation, the following two quotations (vv.17-18) are retained in their original. Paul is in essence repeating 1 Corinthians 10:1-11 where the concluding remark is: "Now these things happened to them as a warning, but they were written down for our instruction, upon whom the end of the ages has come." (v.11)[13]

A closer look at the first quotation (2 Cor 6:16b) will reveal that it starts with the addition of "I will abide (dwell; *enoikēsō*)

---

[11] I showed that this was the case in my discussion of the end of 1 Cor 1; see *C-1Cor* 47-8.
[12] The true "God" of the Gentiles is none other than the scriptural "Lord Almighty" (*yahweh ṣeba'ot*; the Lord of hosts).
[13] See also "Now these things are warnings for us, not to desire evil as they did" (v.6).

among them"[14] that is not extant in the original. Considering that the verb *enoikēsō* is from the root *oikos* (house; household), it becomes clear that it was added with a double aim (1) to connect the quotations with "the temple of God," which is the reason behind them in the first place (v.16a), and (2) to tie in with the metaphor of household in the last quotation (v.18). Thus, the imagery of "dwelling among" underpins the movement from a building of stones to one of family or flock, which is so often underscored in the prophetic teaching. Still, the choice of *enoikēsō* is not as outlandish as it may sound. Its choice is very astute. On the one hand, it is found in Leviticus 26:32 "And I will devastate the land, so that your enemies who *settle* (*enoikountes*) in it shall be astonished at it. And I will scatter you among the nations, and I will unsheathe the sword after you; and your land shall be a desolation, and your cities shall be a waste." (vv.32-33) Since this is the only instance of that verb in the entire Pentateuch (LXX), Paul's use of it cannot possibly be regarded as happenstance. But what is the intention in the actual setting of the letter? Just as its counterpart Deuteronomy 28, Leviticus 26 is divided between blessings (vv.3-13), should Israel abide by God's ordinances, and curses (vv.14-43) in the opposite scenario. In the latter instance, the punishment will be so severe that the desolation of the land will be such that even its conquerors will not be able to dwell in it! So, if the Corinthians want the scriptural God to dwell among them, they will have to desist of their corrupt ways, just as Israel had to do. This is precisely what is required of them (2 Cor 6:17): notice how this verse starts with "Therefore" (*dio*). This stipulation is taken from a quotation in the second part of Isaiah (Is 52:11) that is just two verses before the fourth Servant passage (52:13-53:12) which

---

[14] RSV has the unwarranted "I will live in them," especially in view of the fact that, in continuation, it translates *emperipatēsō* as "[I will] move among them."

promises restoration to the punished should they follow the teaching of God's emissary who is bringing them the divine law (42:1-7; 49:1-6).

In order to pressure his hearers to do his bidding Paul uses a double stratagem. On the one hand, he calls them "beloved" (2 Cor 7:1) as a father would his children. This term occurs only once more in this letter (12:19). On the other hand, he reminds them that their becoming "sons and daughters" in God's family and he abiding among them are "promises" yet to be fulfilled. For them to be worthy of such, they will have to "cleanse ourselves from every defilement of body and spirit, and make holiness perfect in the fear of God" (7:1). The phrase "fear of God" is intimately connected with abiding by his law in scripture.[15]

---

[15] *OTI₃* 130.

Chapter 7

Vv. 2-16 ²Χωρήσατε ἡμᾶς· οὐδένα ἠδικήσαμεν, οὐδένα ἐφθείραμεν, οὐδένα ἐπλεονεκτήσαμεν. ³πρὸς κατάκρισιν οὐ λέγω· προείρηκα γὰρ ὅτι ἐν ταῖς καρδίαις ἡμῶν ἐστε εἰς τὸ συναποθανεῖν καὶ συζῆν. ⁴ πολλή μοι παρρησία πρὸς ὑμᾶς, πολλή μοι καύχησις ὑπὲρ ὑμῶν· πεπλήρωμαι τῇ παρακλήσει, ὑπερπερισσεύομαι τῇ χαρᾷ ἐπὶ πάσῃ τῇ θλίψει ἡμῶν. ⁵ Καὶ γὰρ ἐλθόντων ἡμῶν εἰς Μακεδονίαν οὐδεμίαν ἔσχηκεν ἄνεσιν ἡ σὰρξ ἡμῶν ἀλλ᾽ ἐν παντὶ θλιβόμενοι· ἔξωθεν μάχαι, ἔσωθεν φόβοι. ⁶ ἀλλ᾽ ὁ παρακαλῶν τοὺς ταπεινοὺς παρεκάλεσεν ἡμᾶς ὁ θεὸς ἐν τῇ παρουσίᾳ Τίτου, ⁷ οὐ μόνον δὲ ἐν τῇ παρουσίᾳ αὐτοῦ ἀλλὰ καὶ ἐν τῇ παρακλήσει ᾗ παρεκλήθη ἐφ᾽ ὑμῖν, ἀναγγέλλων ἡμῖν τὴν ὑμῶν ἐπιπόθησιν, τὸν ὑμῶν ὀδυρμόν, τὸν ὑμῶν ζῆλον ὑπὲρ ἐμοῦ ὥστε με μᾶλλον χαρῆναι. ⁸ Ὅτι εἰ καὶ ἐλύπησα ὑμᾶς ἐν τῇ ἐπιστολῇ, οὐ μεταμέλομαι· εἰ καὶ μετεμελόμην, βλέπω [γὰρ] ὅτι ἡ ἐπιστολὴ ἐκείνη εἰ καὶ πρὸς ὥραν ἐλύπησεν ὑμᾶς, ⁹ νῦν χαίρω, οὐχ ὅτι ἐλυπήθητε ἀλλ᾽ ὅτι ἐλυπήθητε εἰς μετάνοιαν· ἐλυπήθητε γὰρ κατὰ θεόν, ἵνα ἐν μηδενὶ ζημιωθῆτε ἐξ ἡμῶν. ¹⁰ ἡ γὰρ κατὰ θεὸν λύπη μετάνοιαν εἰς σωτηρίαν ἀμεταμέλητον ἐργάζεται· ἡ δὲ τοῦ κόσμου λύπη θάνατον κατεργάζεται. ¹¹ ἰδοὺ γὰρ αὐτὸ τοῦτο τὸ κατὰ θεὸν λυπηθῆναι πόσην κατειργάσατο ὑμῖν σπουδήν, ἀλλὰ ἀπολογίαν, ἀλλὰ ἀγανάκτησιν, ἀλλὰ φόβον, ἀλλὰ ἐπιπόθησιν, ἀλλὰ ζῆλον, ἀλλὰ ἐκδίκησιν. ἐν παντὶ συνεστήσατε ἑαυτοὺς ἁγνοὺς εἶναι τῷ πράγματι. ¹² ἄρα εἰ καὶ ἔγραψα ὑμῖν, οὐχ ἕνεκεν τοῦ ἀδικήσαντος οὐδὲ ἕνεκεν τοῦ ἀδικηθέντος ἀλλ᾽ ἕνεκεν τοῦ φανερωθῆναι τὴν σπουδὴν ὑμῶν τὴν ὑπὲρ ἡμῶν πρὸς ὑμᾶς ἐνώπιον τοῦ θεοῦ. ¹³ διὰ τοῦτο παρακεκλήμεθα. Ἐπὶ δὲ τῇ παρακλήσει ἡμῶν περισσοτέρως μᾶλλον ἐχάρημεν ἐπὶ τῇ χαρᾷ Τίτου, ὅτι ἀναπέπαυται τὸ πνεῦμα αὐτοῦ ἀπὸ πάντων ὑμῶν· ¹⁴ ὅτι εἴ τι αὐτῷ ὑπὲρ ὑμῶν κεκαύχημαι, οὐ κατῃσχύνθην, ἀλλ᾽ ὡς πάντα ἐν ἀληθείᾳ ἐλαλήσαμεν ὑμῖν, οὕτως καὶ ἡ καύχησις ἡμῶν ἡ ἐπὶ Τίτου ἀλήθεια ἐγενήθη. ¹⁶ καὶ τὰ σπλάγχνα αὐτοῦ περισσοτέρως εἰς ὑμᾶς ἐστιν ἀναμιμνησκομένου τὴν πάντων ὑμῶν ὑπακοήν, ὡς μετὰ φόβου καὶ τρόμου ἐδέξασθε αὐτόν. ¹⁶χαίρω ὅτι ἐν παντὶ θαρρῶ ἐν ὑμῖν.

²Open your hearts to us; we have wronged no one, we have corrupted no one, we have taken advantage of no one. ³I do not say this to condemn you, for I said before that you are in our hearts, to die together and to live together. ⁴I have great confidence in you; I have great pride in you; I am filled with comfort. With all our affliction, I am overjoyed. ⁵For even when we came into Macedonia, our bodies had no rest but we were afflicted at every turn—fighting without and fear within. ⁶But God, who comforts the downcast, comforted us by the coming of Titus, ⁷ and not only by his coming but also by the comfort with which he was comforted in you, as he told us of your longing, your mourning, your zeal for me, so that I rejoiced still more. ⁸For even if I made you sorry with my letter, I do not regret it (though I did regret it), for I see that that letter grieved you, though only for a while. ⁹As it is, I rejoice, not because you were grieved, but because you were grieved into repenting; for you felt a godly grief, so that you suffered no loss through us. ¹⁰For godly grief produces a repentance that leads to salvation and brings no regret, but worldly grief produces death. ¹¹For see what earnestness this godly grief has produced in you, what eagerness to clear yourselves, what indignation, what alarm, what longing, what zeal, what punishment! At every point you have proved yourselves guiltless in the matter. ¹²So although I wrote to you, it was not on account of the one who did the wrong, nor on account of the one who suffered the wrong, but in order that your zeal for us might be revealed to you in the sight of God. ¹³Therefore we are comforted. And besides our own comfort we rejoiced still more at the joy of Titus, because his mind has been set at rest by you all. ¹⁴For if I have expressed to him some pride in you, I was not put to shame; but just as everything we said to you was true, so our boasting before Titus has proved true.

¹⁵And his heart goes out all the more to you, as he remembers the obedience of you all, and the fear and trembling with which you received him. ¹⁶ I rejoice, because I have perfect confidence in you.

After the long aside of 6:14-7:1, Paul resumes where he left off at 6:13b: "Widen up (*platynthēte*) you also" (6:13b);[1] "Open up to (*khōrēsate*) us." (7:2)[2] The verb *khōrēsate* is the opposite of *stenokhōreisthe* (be restricted)—from the same root *khōrō*—that occurred twice in 6:12, and corresponds in meaning to the verb *platynthēte*. Though reviewing earlier concerns, chapter 7 pushes ahead toward chapters 8 and 9 where Paul will be pressuring the Corinthians into the collection for the saints in Jerusalem; he will do this by appealing to the example of the Macedonians. The link between the three chapters (7, 8, and 9) is secured through the mention of Macedonia and Titus, who were last heard of together in 2:13. Now, after a long silence, they are brought together again in 7:5-6, and will be frequently mentioned in chapters 7-9.

The verse 7:2 is ingeniously conceived in that the three verbs used therein encompass the entire Corinthian correspondence. The verse brings to the fore topics discussed earlier in order to elaborate on them further: "we have wronged (*ēdikēsamen*; from the verb *adikō*, behave in an unrighteous manner) no one, we have corrupted (*ephtheiramen*; from the verb *phtheirō*) no one, we have taken advantage of (*epleonektēsamen*; from the verb *pleonektō*) no one." On the other hand, all three verbs are connected, as we shall see, in their aim to steer the Corinthians

---

[1] RSV has "widen up your hearts also."
[2] RSV has" open up your hearts."

away from the two most prominent dangers: the Gentile mores and Paul's opponents.

The verb *adikō* occurred earlier twice (1 Cor 6:7, 8) in a context where Paul dealt with the Roman courts (6:1-11). Before concluding with an invitation to relinquish Gentile mores (v.11), we hear a list of such under the heading of *pornoi* (immoral, adulterers; vv.9-10). Two similar lists, also under the heading of the same term appeared at the end of the previous passage (5:10 [*pornois*] and 11 [*pornos*]) that dealt with the case of the *porneia* (v.1) of the man who was consorting with his father's wife. Later in 2 Corinthians 7:12, the same verb *adikō* occurs twice in conjunction with that same person, and more specifically with Paul's decision regarding him, which was the topic of 2:5-11. The verb *phtheirō* occurred earlier in relation to Paul's opponents' nefarious influence in Corinth (1 Cor 3:17), and will be used later regarding this same topic (2 Cor 11:3). Finally the verb *pleonektō* is linked to the subject of Paul's apostleship both earlier in 2:11, and later in 12:17, 18.

Paul proceeds with a *captatio benevolentiae* using the terminology of 4:10-12 (7:3) and 3:12 (7:4a)[3] as well as that of the beginning of the letter (7:4).[4] Then he immediately brings Macedonia into the picture and depicts his experience there as an affliction in the arena (v.5) just as was the case in Asia (1:3-11).[5]

---

[3] In the original we hear in both cases the Greek *parrhēsia* (boldness): "Since we have such a hope, we are very bold (*pollē parrhēsia khrōmetha*: we are using much boldness" (3:12); "I have great confidence (*pollē parrhēsia*; much boldness) in (regarding) you." (7:4a)

[4] Compare "I am filled with comfort. With all our affliction, I am overjoyed" (7:4b) with 1:3-7.

[5] See also 4:7-12 that I showed to be referring to the same affliction: the phrase *en panti thlibomenoi* occurs in both 4:8 (We are afflicted in every way) and 7:5 (we were afflicted at every turn).

However—and this is the most impressive feature of his *captatio benevolentiae*—whereas in Asia it is God who comforted him for the sake of the Corinthians, in Macedonia the divine comfort reached him *through them* in the good news Titus brought to him about them (7:6-7).[6] The reason for his comfort is that they acquiesced to his request that they forgive the immoral man in spite of his having caused them pain (vv.8-13a).[7] They passed the test of sorrow just as he that of affliction. Furthermore, not only is Paul appreciative to them in that they did not let him down before Titus (7:13b-14), but also, even more importantly, that Titus' "heart (*splankhna*; entrails) goes out all the more to you" (v.15), thus making of him, after Paul's eventual demise, another "father figure" that will lead them on the gospel path (v.14a). This is the ultimate reason for Paul's joy and confidence (v.15).[8] That Paul was preparing for the future is evident in the phraseology of verse 15b (obedience in fear and trembling) which recalls that of Philippians: "Therefore, my beloved, as you have always *obeyed*, so now, not only as in my presence but *much more in my absence* (*apousia*), work out your own salvation with fear and trembling." (2:12) Such a thought is on Paul's mind here in 2 Corinthians as can be seen in his concluding phrase, "I

---

[6] Compare with a similar situation where the good news brought by Timothy comforted Paul: "But now that Timothy has come to us from you, and has brought us the good news of your faith and love and reported that you always remember us kindly and long to see us, as we long to see you—for this reason, brethren, in all our distress and *affliction* we have been *comforted* about you through your faith; for now we live, if you stand fast in the Lord." (1 Thess 3:6-8)

[7] Verse 12 (So although I wrote to you, it was not on account of the one who did the wrong, nor on account of the one who suffered the wrong, but in order that your zeal for us might be revealed to you in the sight of God) corroborates my understanding of 2:5-11 that the actual test was for the Corinthians and not for Paul or for the sinner.

[8] This rejoins what Paul does at the end of Philippians (4) and Colossians (4) as well as 1 Corinthians (16) where he paves the path for the leaders among his followers after his death. See *C-Phil* 183-5; *C-Col* 100-5; *C-1Cor* 307-11.

have perfect confidence (*tharrō*; I am emboldened) in you (*hen hymin*; regarding you)" (7:16b), that reappears later as "(I am) bold (*tharrō*) toward you (*eis hymas*) when I am away (*apōn* [from the same root as *apousia*]; absent)" (10:1).[9] Moreover, by linking Titus to the gospel teaching that is to be obeyed with strictness Paul is positing him as the equal of Timothy (1 Cor 4:14-21), the co-sender of this letter (2 Cor 1:1). Notice also how Titus has been presented as a carrier of a Pauline letter or at least the carrier of the Corinthians' response to that letter (7:6-8).

Commentators often argue about how many letters Paul wrote to the Corinthians, given that he mentions a supposedly "extra-canonical" correspondence written to them in his two canonical epistles (1 Cor 5:9; 16:3; 2 Cor 2:3, 4, 9; 7:8). However, as indicated in my discussion of 1 Corinthians 5:6-13, the aorist "I wrote" (*egrapsa*) refers to what he has just written in the letter at hand.[10] In the same vein, one should take what he says in 2 Corinthians 7:8 as a reference to what he wrote earlier in this same letter.[11] The phrase "that letter" (*hē epistolē ekeinē*) is just a literary device referring to what he had written much earlier (ch.2) concerning the subject he is bringing up again here. This is confirmed by the very high incidence of the root *lyp*— ([cause] pain, sorrow, grief) which is virtually restricted to those two chapters in the entire Corinthian correspondence:[12]

---

[9] Furthermore, he proceeds to write in v.2 "I beg of you that when I am present (*parōn*; from the same as root as *parousia* [presence] in Phil 2:12) I may not have to show boldness (*tharrēsai*)."

[10] *C-1Cor* 105-6.

[11] See my discussion of the phrase *en tē epistolē* (in the letter) in *C-1Cor* 105.

[12] The only exception being 2 Cor 9:7: "Each one must do as he has made up his mind, not reluctantly (*ek lypēs*; out of pain, sorrow) or under compulsion, for God loves a cheerful giver."

> For I made up my mind not to make you another painful visit. For if I *cause you pain*, who is there to make me glad but the one whom I have *pained*? And I wrote as I did, so that when I came I might not *suffer pain* from those who should have made me rejoice, for I felt sure of all of you, that my joy would be the joy of you all. For I wrote you out of much affliction and anguish of heart and with many tears, not to *cause you pain* but to let you know the abundant love that I have for you. But if any one has *caused pain*, he has caused it not to me, but in some measure—not to put it too severely—to you all. For such a one this punishment by the majority is enough; so you should rather turn to forgive and comfort him, or he may be overwhelmed by excessive *sorrow*. So I beg you to reaffirm your love for him. (2:1-8)

> But God, who comforts the downcast, comforted us by the coming of Titus, and not only by his coming but also by the comfort with which he was comforted in you, as he told us of your longing, your mourning, your zeal for me, so that I rejoiced still more. For even if I *made you sorry* with my letter, I do not regret it (though I did regret it), for I see that that letter *grieved* you, though only for a while. As it is, I rejoice, not because you *were grieved*, but because you *were grieved* into repenting; for you felt a godly *grief*, so that you suffered no loss through us. For godly *grief* produces a repentance that leads to salvation and brings no regret, but worldly *grief* produces death. For see what earnestness this godly *grief* has produced in you, what eagerness to clear yourselves, what indignation, what alarm, what longing, what zeal, what punishment! At every point you have proved yourselves guiltless in the matter. (7:6-11)

This reading is further confirmed by the close correspondence in the use of the root *phaner—* (reveal, show) that occurs in conjunction with Paul's *writing* to the Corinthians concerning the immoral man (2 Cor 7:12). Earlier in 2:14 we have the first instance of this same root also regarding the same topic.[13] What is more striking though is that, a few verses later, we hear of the Corinthians' not only being themselves "our letter" (3:2) but also being "shown (*phaneroumenoi*) as that letter" (v.3). In chapter 3 that "letter" was written on hope (v.12) while here, after a few chapters, Paul is referring to his joy (7:16) at seeing the fruitfulness of his teaching in that the Corinthians, despite their grief, have "shown" (*phanerōthēnai*) a zeal (*spoudēn*) to do Paul's—God's—bidding (7:12). The introduction of *spoudēn* twice in a row (vv.11, 12) for the first time in the Corinthian correspondence prepares for its use in the following chapter where RSV renders it as "earnestness (8:7 and 8) and "earnest" (v.16), which reflects that they still have to "excel" in their labor of love (v.7) to encompass not only one of theirs, but also Paul's Jewish counterparts in Jerusalem (chs. 8-9). As usual, the Apostle's *captatio benevolentiae* is costly for his hearers; his aim for them as "God's children" is nothing less than perfection in the imitation of their Father's goodness toward all (Eph 5:1-2; Mt 5:43-48).

---

[13] "But thanks be to God, who in Christ always leads us in triumph, and through us spreads (*phanerounti*) the fragrance of the knowledge of him everywhere."

Chapter 8

Vv. 1-4 *¹Γνωρίζομεν δὲ ὑμῖν, ἀδελφοί, τὴν χάριν τοῦ θεοῦ τὴν δεδομένην ἐν ταῖς ἐκκλησίαις τῆς Μακεδονίας, ² ὅτι ἐν πολλῇ δοκιμῇ θλίψεως ἡ περισσεία τῆς χαρᾶς αὐτῶν καὶ ἡ κατὰ βάθους πτωχεία αὐτῶν ἐπερίσσευσεν εἰς τὸ πλοῦτος τῆς ἁπλότητος αὐτῶν· ³ ὅτι κατὰ δύναμιν, μαρτυρῶ, καὶ παρὰ δύναμιν, αὐθαίρετοι ⁴ μετὰ πολλῆς παρακλήσεως δεόμενοι ἡμῶν τὴν χάριν καὶ τὴν κοινωνίαν τῆς διακονίας τῆς εἰς τοὺς ἁγίους, ⁵ καὶ οὐ καθὼς ἠλπίσαμεν ἀλλὰ ἑαυτοὺς ἔδωκαν πρῶτον τῷ κυρίῳ καὶ ἡμῖν διὰ θελήματος θεοῦ*

> *¹We want you to know, brethren, about the grace of God which has been shown in the churches of Macedonia, ²for in a severe test of affliction, their abundance of joy and their extreme poverty have overflowed in a wealth of liberality on their part. ³For they gave according to their means, as I can testify, and beyond their means, of their own free will, ⁴begging us earnestly for the favor of taking part in the relief of the saints—⁵and this, not as we expected, but first they gave themselves to the Lord and to us by the will of God.*

Chapters 8 and 9 deal with the "ministry to the saints" (9:1; see also 8:4) which is the collection that Paul promised at the Jerusalem meeting where those same "saints" were referred to as "poor" (Gal 2:10). That Paul is referring to the people of Jerusalem is borne out in what he writes elsewhere concerning the same topic: "At present, however, I am going to Jerusalem with aid for the saints. For Macedonia and Achaia have been pleased to make some contribution for the poor among the saints at Jerusalem." (Rom 15:25-26) The connection is further reflected in that the *spoudēs* (earnestness) of the Macedonians which the Corinthians are to emulate (2 Cor 8:8)[1] is of the same root as the verb used in Galatians: "only they would have us remember the poor, which very thing I *was eager (espoudasa)* to do." (2:10)[2]

In order to preempt any feeling of self-righteousness on the part of the Corinthians, Paul immediately refers to the collection required of them and the Macedonians as being the result of God's gift to both: "We want you to know, brethren, about the grace (*kharin*; gift) of God which has been shown in the churches of Macedonia." (2 Cor 8:1) A few verses later their sharing in the ministry to the saints is outright equated with divine grace: "For they gave according to their means, as I can testify, and beyond their means, of their own free will, begging us earnestly for the favor (*kharin*; grace) of taking part in the relief (*diakonias*; ministry) of the saints." (vv.3-4) Nonetheless, this does not mean that their contribution is void of any taxing effort on their part: "for in a severe test (*dokimē*) of affliction (*thlipseōs*), their abundance of joy and their extreme poverty have overflowed in a wealth of liberality on their part." (v.2) Looking more closely at the wording of this verse, one will immediately notice the writer's ingenuity in preparing the Corinthians to take up the challenge earnestly as well as without hesitation. He does so by bringing into the picture a series of terms he used in his request that the Corinthians forgive the adulterer. Paul referred to their forgiveness as "grace" (2:7-10),[3] which is precisely how he introduces the collection of the offering to the saints (8:4). Paul also spoke of such forgiveness as a test (*dokimēn*; 2:9), and

---

[1] See also v.7 (Now as you excel in everything—in faith, in utterance, in knowledge, in all earnestness (*spoudē*), and in your love for us—see that you excel in this gracious work also).

[2] In 2 Cor 7:11 RSV translates *spoudēn* as "eagerness."

[3] See earlier my comments on that passage.

he describes the collection likewise (8:2). The close link between these two instances is evident in that the first occurrence of "test" after 2:9 is in 8:2. The ministry of the collection is once again referred to as "test" in 9:13.[4] Moreover, in 8:2 the test is qualified as being one of "affliction," which is an oblique reminder to what Paul wrote in 1:3-7 where he invites the Corinthians to share in his afflictions in order to bestow divine comfort on others as well as enjoy it themselves. This is precisely what he did in his request that they forgive the sinful brother (2:7-10), and he equated their graceful action with "comforting" the sinner (v.7). Finally, this comfort in affliction is later mentioned in conjunction with Paul being "overjoyed": "I have great confidence in you; I have great pride in you; I am filled with comfort. With all our affliction, I am overjoyed (*hyperissevomai tē khara*; I am filled of joy in abundance)." (7:4) This is precisely the same phraseology used to describe the liberality of the Macedonians, which the Corinthians are to emulate: "for in a severe test of affliction, their abundance of joy (*perisseia tēs kharas*) and their extreme poverty have overflowed (*eperissevsen*) in a wealth of liberality on their part." (8:2)

Chapter 8 begins with Paul smoothing the pressure he is putting on the Corinthians regarding the upcoming test by reminding them that they had, hopefully, already passed a similar test, and that both tests consisted of sharing God's grace with those who need it. By the same token, and in spite of any new "test of affliction," be it even their "poverty," they ought to be ready to pass the muster in the upcoming test of willingly sharing, in liberality, their table fellowship with inimical outsiders.

---

[4] Except for 13:3 where the test (RSV, proof) applies to Paul, those are the only three instances of "test" in 2 Cor.

As he does in Philippians, where he offers Timothy, himself, and even Christ as examples to follow in the matter of being a "slave" to God, here also, beyond the Macedonians, and after having given himself as a prototype in the service of "common table fellowship" (chs.3-6), Paul presents the Corinthians with the challenge of Titus (8:6) and then of Christ himself (v.9). In all three cases, Paul's clear intent is to up the pressure on the Corinthians. Not only was the Macedonians' response "overflowing with joy" (v.2) and "of their own free will" (v.3), but it was also beyond even the expectation (hope; *ēlpisamen*) of Paul himself (v.5a). More important, however, is the reason behind their attitude: before "giving" toward the collection, *"first they gave themselves to the Lord* and to us by the will of God" (v.5b). In other words, it is the commitment to the Pauline gospel, which was sealed at Jerusalem and included Paul's "eagerness (*spoudē*)" not to forget the poor of Judea (Gal 2:10), that was the ultimate motive behind any response to its dictates. That which lies at the core of the "ministry" (*diakonia*) carried out by Paul is not negotiable! The failure of others, even other leaders (vv.11-14), is not an excuse for one's own shortcoming.

Vv. 6-7 ⁶ εἰς τὸ παρακαλέσαι ἡμᾶς Τίτον, ἵνα καθὼς προενήρξατο οὕτως καὶ ἐπιτελέσῃ εἰς ὑμᾶς καὶ τὴν χάριν ταύτην. ⁷ Ἀλλ᾽ ὥσπερ ἐν παντὶ περισσεύετε, πίστει καὶ λόγῳ καὶ γνώσει καὶ πάσῃ σπουδῇ καὶ τῇ ἐξ ἡμῶν ἐν ὑμῖν ἀγάπῃ, ἵνα καὶ ἐν ταύτῃ τῇ χάριτι περισσεύητε.

> ⁶*Accordingly we have urged Titus that as he had already made a beginning, he should also complete among you this gracious work.* ⁷*Now as you excel in everything—in faith, in utterance, in knowledge, in all earnestness, and in your love for us—see that you excel in this gracious work also.*

Although his service to the gospel is described in conjunction with his mission among the Corinthians, Titus is summarily introduced at this junction (2 Cor 8:6). His obedience to the call will be qualified with the same term used to express the attitude of the Macedonians: "For they gave according to their means, as I can testify, and beyond their means, *of their own free will* (*avthairetoi*)" (v.3); "For he [Titus] not only accepted our appeal, but being himself very earnest he is going to you *of his own accord* (*avthairetos*)." (v.17) This sameness of attitude is borne out by the fact that these are the only instances of the root *avthairet—* in the New Testament. Thus, Paul is portraying the Gentile Macedonians, in their response to the appeal for the collection for Jerusalem, as on par with that of Titus, the Gentile, in his earnestness for the same cause. In so doing, Paul is steering the Corinthians away from a kind of "fleshly"—human style—emulation with the Macedonians and toward obedience to the message of Titus, Paul's emissary who was showcased in the Apostle's showdown with the Jerusalemite leaders (Gal 2:1-3). Actually, since the Corinthians have already begun doing Paul's bidding (2 Cor 8:6b) for a weekly collection (1 Cor 16:1-2), all they have to do now is to proceed on that path until its completion (2 Cor 8:6c). However, in order that their efforts not be a cause for hubris, Paul phrases his statement to reflect that the entire matter is merely the fruit of God's grace(fullness) toward them through Paul and his disciple Titus: "Accordingly *we have urged* (*parakalesai*) Titus that as *he* had already *made a beginning, he* should also *complete* among you this *gracious work* (*kharin*; grace)." (v.6) Notice, on the other hand, how not only Titus' effort is presented as "grace" but also Paul's urging him is cast as *parakalesai*, whose other meaning is "comfort."[5] Furthermore, in order not be misunderstood, the Corinthians' "effort" required by the Apostle is bracketed between the reference to that "grace": "Now as you excel in everything—in faith, in utterance, in knowledge, in all earnestness, and in your love for us—see that you excel in this gracious work (*khariti*) also." (v.7) The Pauline view that everything is the fruit of divine grace, and not the result of human effort, is at the heart of his teaching. Its most compelling rendition is found in Philippians:

> I thank my God in all my remembrance of you, always in every prayer of mine for you all making my prayer with joy, thankful for your partnership in the gospel from the first day until now. And I am sure that he who began a good work in you will bring it to completion at the day of Jesus Christ. It is right for me to feel thus about you all, because I hold you in my heart, for you are all partakers with me of grace, both in my imprisonment and in the defense and confirmation of the gospel. For God is my witness, how I yearn for you all with the affection of Christ Jesus. And it is my prayer that your love may abound more and more, with knowledge and all discernment, so that you may approve what is excellent, and may be pure and blameless for the day of Christ, filled with the fruits of righteousness which come through Jesus Christ, to the glory and praise of God. (Phil 1:3-11)

> Therefore, my beloved, as you have always obeyed, so now, not only as in my presence but much more in my absence, work out your own salvation with fear and trembling; for God is at work in you, both to will and to work for his good pleasure. Do all things without grumbling or questioning, that you may be blameless and innocent, children of God without blemish in the midst of a

---

[5] See earlier my comments on 2:8 where Paul uses the same verb to "beg" the Corinthians to do the "graceful action" (*kharisasthai*) of "comforting" (*parakalesai*) the sinful man (v.7).

crooked and perverse generation, among whom you shine as lights in the world, holding fast the word of life, so that in the day of Christ I may be proud that I did not run in vain or labor in vain. (Phil 2:12-16)

Revisiting 2 Corinthians 8:7, a keen ear will pick up the craftsmanship in its phraseology. At the beginning of the Corinthian correspondence, Paul wrote:

> I give thanks to God always for you because of the grace (*khariti*) of God which was given you in Christ Jesus, that in every way (*en panti*; in everything) you *were enriched* in him with all *speech* (*logō*; word) and all *knowledge* (*gnōsei*)—even as the testimony to Christ was confirmed among you— (1 Cor 1:4-4)

One hears the same tune in 2 Corinthians 8:7: "Now as you *excel* in everything (*en panti*)—in faith, in *utterance* (*logō*; word), in *knowledge* (*gnōsei*), in all *earnestness* (*spoudē*), and in your love for us—see that you *excel* in this *gracious work* (*khariti*) also." The only other instance of *en panti* in conjunction with the Corinthians, in between these two occurrences, is found in 7:11:

> For see what *earnestness* (*spoudē*) this godly grief has produced in you, what eagerness to clear yourselves, what indignation, what alarm, what longing, what zeal, what punishment! At every point (*en panti*) you have proved yourselves guiltless in the matter. So although I wrote to you, it was not on account of the one who did the wrong, nor on account of the one who suffered the wrong, but in order that your *zeal* (*spoudēn*) for us might be revealed to you in the sight of God. (7:11-12)

Thus, the Apostle's intention behind his statement in 8:7 is to invite the Corinthians to do what is required by the "grace of God" that was communicated to them through Paul's "testimony" among them. Having been enriched "in everything" through that grace, they are to "excel" in what they had been granted freely. Since they already showed earnestness in this matter by having acted "gracefully" toward the immoral brother (7:11-12; see 2:7), Paul is prodding them to proceed further and show the same gracefulness toward their as well as his hostile opponents in Jerusalem. Furthermore, this is to be done out of "your love for us" (8:7).

Vv. 8-15 *⁸ Οὐ κατ' ἐπιταγὴν λέγω ἀλλὰ διὰ τῆς ἑτέρων σπουδῆς καὶ τὸ τῆς ὑμετέρας ἀγάπης γνήσιον δοκιμάζων· ⁹ γινώσκετε γὰρ τὴν χάριν τοῦ κυρίου ἡμῶν Ἰησοῦ Χριστοῦ, ὅτι δι' ὑμᾶς ἐπτώχευσεν πλούσιος ὤν, ἵνα ὑμεῖς τῇ ἐκείνου πτωχείᾳ πλουτήσητε. ¹⁰ καὶ γνώμην ἐν τούτῳ δίδωμι· τοῦτο γὰρ ὑμῖν συμφέρει, οἵτινες οὐ μόνον τὸ ποιῆσαι ἀλλὰ καὶ τὸ θέλειν προενήρξασθε ἀπὸ πέρυσι· ¹¹ νυνὶ δὲ καὶ τὸ ποιῆσαι ἐπιτελέσατε, ὅπως καθάπερ ἡ προθυμία τοῦ θέλειν, οὕτως καὶ τὸ ἐπιτελέσαι ἐκ τοῦ ἔχειν. ¹² εἰ γὰρ ἡ προθυμία πρόκειται, καθὸ ἐὰν ἔχῃ εὐπρόσδεκτος, οὐ καθὸ οὐκ ἔχει. ¹³ οὐ γὰρ ἵνα ἄλλοις ἄνεσις, ὑμῖν θλῖψις, ἀλλ' ἐξ ἰσότητος· ¹⁴ ἐν τῷ νῦν καιρῷ τὸ ὑμῶν περίσσευμα εἰς τὸ ἐκείνων ὑστέρημα, ἵνα καὶ τὸ ἐκείνων περίσσευμα γένηται εἰς τὸ ὑμῶν ὑστέρημα, ὅπως γένηται ἰσότης, ¹⁵ καθὼς γέγραπται· ὁ τὸ πολὺ οὐκ ἐπλεόνασεν, καὶ ὁ τὸ ὀλίγον οὐκ ἠλαττόνησεν.*

⁸I say this not as a command, but to prove by the earnestness of others that your love also is genuine. ⁹For you know the grace of our Lord Jesus Christ, that though he was rich, yet for your sake he became poor, so that by his poverty you might become rich. ¹⁰And in this matter I give my advice: it is best for you now to complete what a year ago you began not only to do but to desire, ¹¹so that your readiness in desiring it may be matched by your completing it out of what you have. ¹²For if the readiness is there, it is acceptable according to what a man has, not according to what he has not. ¹³I do not mean that others should be eased and you burdened, ¹⁴but that as a matter of equality your abundance at the present time should supply their want, so *that their abundance may supply your want, that there may be equality. *¹⁵*As it is written, "He who gathered much had nothing over, and he who gathered little had no lack."*

Love of a junior toward a senior is tantamount to obeying the senior's directive. Yet, instead of phrasing his will as a command (*epitagēn*), Paul writes that he is testing them, which is the meaning of the original *dokimazōn,* translated as "prove" in RSV. The idea is that, should they pass the test, Paul will have proven to the Macedonians that the Corinthians' "love" for him is genuine (v.8). Still, Paul's test is not as easy as it looks, since the one the Corinthians are to emulate is their "lord," Jesus Christ. A Roman paterfamilias is, by definition, "rich" in estate and possessions; Jesus Christ, their Lord and master, "for your sake became poor, so that by his poverty you might become rich" (v.9). In Corinth, Paul is tantamount to Jesus Christ.[6] This is corroborated in what he wrote in chapter 6: "but as servants of God we commend ourselves in every way … as poor, yet making many rich; as having nothing, and yet possessing everything" (vv.4a, 10b). The equality of value between the Lord and his Apostle is further evidenced in the following verse where Paul speaks of his "advice" (*gnōmēn*; 8:9).

Earlier in discussing the touchy issue of marriage versus celibacy (1 Cor 7), Paul differentiated between the divine command (*epitagēn*) and his "opinion" (*gnōmēn*) (v.25);[7] however, he emphatically presented his opinion as being delivered with the authority of the divine spirit: "But in my judgment (*gnōmēn*) she is happier if she remains as she is. And I think that I have the Spirit of God." (v.40) In 2 Corinthians

---

[6] See earlier my comments on 2 Cor 1:3-11.
[7] Notice the correspondence in terminology between 1 Cor 7:25 and 2 Cor 8:9-10.

8:10-11 he is doing the same thing; his aim is have them match the desire they have already expressed with the actual effort toward the collection. Their aim, however, should not be to surpass the Macedonians by depleting themselves: "For if the readiness is there, it is acceptable according to what a man has, not according to what he has not." (v.12) Rather, the aim should be to relieve the poor of Jerusalem so that both are on an equal level (vv.13-14). In order to make his request more potent Paul quotes scripture itself (v.15). As usual, to save as much parchment space as possible, the short quotation is an invitation for the hearers to recall the full passage: "And the people of Israel did so; they gathered, some more, some less. But when they measured it with an omer, he that gathered much had nothing over, and he that gathered little had no lack; each gathered according to what he could eat." (Ex 16:17-18) It becomes clear then that the main point in the previous verses is "equality": "I do not mean that others should be eased and you burdened, but that as a matter of equality (*isotētos*) your abundance at the present time should supply their want, so that their abundance may supply your want, that there may be equality (*isotēs*)." (2 Cor 8:13-14)[8]

Vv. 16-24 ¹⁶ Χάρις δὲ τῷ θεῷ τῷ δόντι τὴν αὐτὴν σπουδὴν ὑπὲρ ὑμῶν ἐν τῇ καρδίᾳ Τίτου, ¹⁷ ὅτι τὴν μὲν παράκλησιν ἐδέξατο, σπουδαιότερος δὲ ὑπάρχων αὐθαίρετος ἐξῆλθεν πρὸς ὑμᾶς. ¹⁸ συνεπέμψαμεν δὲ μετ' αὐτοῦ τὸν ἀδελφὸν οὗ ὁ ἔπαινος ἐν τῷ εὐαγγελίῳ διὰ πασῶν τῶν ἐκκλησιῶν, ¹⁹ οὐ μόνον δέ, ἀλλὰ καὶ χειροτονηθεὶς ὑπὸ τῶν ἐκκλησιῶν συνέκδημος ἡμῶν σὺν τῇ χάριτι ταύτῃ τῇ διακονουμένῃ ὑφ' ἡμῶν πρὸς τὴν [αὐτοῦ] τοῦ κυρίου δόξαν καὶ προθυμίαν ἡμῶν, ²⁰στελλόμενοι τοῦτο, μή τις ἡμᾶς μωμήσηται ἐν τῇ

---

[8] The express intentionality of the reference to "equality" is borne out in that, with the exception of Col 4:1, these are the only two instances occurrences of *isotēs* in the New Testament.

ἁδρότητι ταύτῃ τῇ διακονουμένῃ ὑφ' ἡμῶν· ²¹ προνοοῦμεν γὰρ καλὰ οὐ μόνον ἐνώπιον κυρίου ἀλλὰ καὶ ἐνώπιον ἀνθρώπων. ²²συνεπέμψαμεν δὲ αὐτοῖς τὸν ἀδελφὸν ἡμῶν ὃν ἐδοκιμάσαμεν ἐν πολλοῖς πολλάκις σπουδαῖον ὄντα, νυνὶ δὲ πολὺ σπουδαιότερον πεποιθήσει πολλῇ τῇ εἰς ὑμᾶς. ²³ εἴτε ὑπὲρ Τίτου, κοινωνὸς ἐμὸς καὶ εἰς ὑμᾶς συνεργός· εἴτε ἀδελφοὶ ἡμῶν, ἀπόστολοι ἐκκλησιῶν, δόξα Χριστοῦ. ²⁴ τὴν οὖν ἔνδειξιν τῆς ἀγάπης ὑμῶν καὶ ἡμῶν καυχήσεως ὑπὲρ ὑμῶν εἰς αὐτοὺς ἐνδεικνύμενοι εἰς πρόσωπον τῶν ἐκκλησιῶν.

¹⁶But thanks be to God who puts the same earnest care for you into the heart of Titus. ¹⁷For he not only accepted our appeal, but being himself very earnest he is going to you of his own accord. ¹⁸With him we are sending the brother who is famous among all the churches for his preaching of the gospel; ¹⁹and not only that, but he has been appointed by the churches to travel with us in this gracious work which we are carrying on, for the glory of the Lord and to show our good will. ²⁰We intend that no one should blame us about this liberal gift which we are administering, ²¹for we aim at what is honorable not only in the Lord's sight but also in the sight of men. ²²And with them we are sending our brother whom we have often tested and found earnest in many matters, but who is now more earnest than ever because of his great confidence in you. ²³As for Titus, he is my partner and fellow worker in your service; and as for our brethren, they are messengers of the churches, the glory of Christ. ²⁴So give proof, before the churches, of your love and of our boasting about you to these men.

Paul then proceeds to impress upon his hearers that common table fellowship between Gentile and Jew, in spite of any animosity on the part of the Jewish authorities, is an essential feature of the gospel message that was agreed upon at the Jerusalem summit (Gal 2:1-10). He does so by writing that this "earnest care" (*spoudēn*) originates with God himself (2 Cor

8:16) and is the duty of all Paul's adjutants (vv.16-24). He even underscores literally this reality by qualifying both Titus (v.17) and another "tested brother" (v.22) as *spoudaioteros*[9] which is the comparative form of *spoudaios*, meaning "more earnest" (v.22) and thus "very earnest" (v.17). In so doing the Apostle is inviting the Corinthians to always "excel" further in their "eagerness" (*spoudē*) in that "ministry." The pressure is further heightened in that not only Titus is introduced as accepting Paul's appeal "of his own accord," but the Macedonians (v.4) are also given as an example for the Corinthians to emulate.

In addition to Titus, Paul gives the example of two more "brethren" who are referred to as "messengers of the churches" (*apostoloi ekklēsiōn*, church apostles; v.23), the first being also more specifically introduced as being "appointed (*kheirotonētheis*; appointed by the laying on of hands) by the churches" (v.19). In discussing the case of Epaphroditus (Phil 2:25-30) whom Paul honors with the highest title of "(your) apostle" (*apostolon*, messenger; v.25), I have shown that the name stood for anyone who would not only join in, but also continue the work of Paul and Timothy after their demise.[10] The same applies to the series of names of helpers in Colossians 4:7-17 and 1 Corinthians 16:10-20.[11] The general connotation of each of the names finds corroboration in that, in our case here, Paul refers to two "brothers" without naming them, yet are "well-known" among all the Pauline churches. Bringing in "three" brothers into the picture is Paul's way to assure the Corinthians that the mission of the collection to ensure full table fellowship *will* continue with or without the Corinthians' help. In other words, should they

---

[9] *spoudaioteros* (v.17) has a different ending *spoudaioteron* (v.22) in the accusative case (verb complement).
[10] See *C-Phil* 144-7.
[11] See my comments in *C-Col* 94-105 and *C-1Cor* 304-11.

not heed Titus' directives and "give proof, before the churches, of your love and of our boasting about you to these men" (2 Cor 8:24), it would be *their* loss to their own shame at the divine judgment, since the Apostle would not have a reason to boast about them, as he is hoping he would (2 Cor 7:4; see also 9:3), and as he would be able to do about others (Phil 2:16; 1 Thess 2:19). Put otherwise, Paul is challenging the Corinthians to be among "those who are being saved" and for whom "the aroma of Christ" spread through Paul's gospel" would be "a fragrance from life to life," and not be among "those who are perishing" and for whom the same aroma would be "a fragrance from death to death" (2 Cor 2:15-16).

Chapter 9

Vv. 1-15 ¹Περὶ μὲν γὰρ τῆς διακονίας τῆς εἰς τοὺς ἁγίους περισσόν μοί ἐστιν τὸ γράφειν ὑμῖν· ² οἶδα γὰρ τὴν προθυμίαν ὑμῶν ἣν ὑπὲρ ὑμῶν καυχῶμαι Μακεδόσιν, ὅτι Ἀχαΐα παρεσκεύασται ἀπὸ πέρυσι, καὶ τὸ ὑμῶν ζῆλος ἠρέθισεν τοὺς πλείονας. ³ ἔπεμψα δὲ τοὺς ἀδελφούς, ἵνα μὴ τὸ καύχημα ἡμῶν τὸ ὑπὲρ ὑμῶν κενωθῇ ἐν τῷ μέρει τούτῳ, ἵνα καθὼς ἔλεγον παρεσκευασμένοι ἦτε, ⁴ μή πως ἐὰν ἔλθωσιν σὺν ἐμοὶ Μακεδόνες καὶ εὕρωσιν ὑμᾶς ἀπαρασκευάστους καταισχυνθῶμεν ἡμεῖς, ἵνα μὴ λέγω ὑμεῖς, ἐν τῇ ὑποστάσει ταύτῃ. ⁵ἀναγκαῖον οὖν ἡγησάμην παρακαλέσαι τοὺς ἀδελφούς, ἵνα προέλθωσιν εἰς ὑμᾶς καὶ προκαταρτίσωσιν τὴν προεπηγγελμένην εὐλογίαν ὑμῶν, ταύτην ἑτοίμην εἶναι οὕτως ὡς εὐλογίαν καὶ μὴ ὡς πλεονεξίαν. ⁶ Τοῦτο δέ, ὁ σπείρων φειδομένως φειδομένως καὶ θερίσει, καὶ ὁ σπείρων ἐπ᾽ εὐλογίαις ἐπ᾽ εὐλογίαις καὶ θερίσει. ⁷ ἕκαστος καθὼς προῄρηται τῇ καρδίᾳ, μὴ ἐκ λύπης ἢ ἐξ ἀνάγκης· ἱλαρὸν γὰρ δότην ἀγαπᾷ ὁ θεός. ⁸ δυνατεῖ δὲ ὁ θεὸς πᾶσαν χάριν περισσεῦσαι εἰς ὑμᾶς, ἵνα ἐν παντὶ πάντοτε πᾶσαν αὐτάρκειαν ἔχοντες περισσεύητε εἰς πᾶν ἔργον ἀγαθόν, ⁹ καθὼς γέγραπται· ἐσκόρπισεν, ἔδωκεν τοῖς πένησιν, ἡ δικαιοσύνη αὐτοῦ μένει εἰς τὸν αἰῶνα. ¹⁰ ὁ δὲ ἐπιχορηγῶν σπόρον τῷ σπείροντι καὶ ἄρτον εἰς βρῶσιν χορηγήσει καὶ πληθυνεῖ τὸν σπόρον ὑμῶν καὶ αὐξήσει τὰ γενήματα τῆς δικαιοσύνης ὑμῶν. ¹¹ ἐν παντὶ πλουτιζόμενοι εἰς πᾶσαν ἁπλότητα, ἥτις κατεργάζεται δι᾽ ἡμῶν εὐχαριστίαν τῷ θεῷ· ¹² ὅτι ἡ διακονία τῆς λειτουργίας ταύτης οὐ μόνον ἐστὶν προσαναπληροῦσα τὰ ὑστερήματα τῶν ἁγίων, ἀλλὰ καὶ περισσεύουσα διὰ πολλῶν εὐχαριστιῶν τῷ θεῷ. ¹³ διὰ τῆς δοκιμῆς τῆς διακονίας ταύτης δοξάζοντες τὸν θεὸν ἐπὶ τῇ ὑποταγῇ τῆς ὁμολογίας ὑμῶν εἰς τὸ εὐαγγέλιον τοῦ Χριστοῦ καὶ ἁπλότητι τῆς κοινωνίας εἰς αὐτοὺς καὶ εἰς πάντας, ¹⁴ καὶ αὐτῶν δεήσει ὑπὲρ ὑμῶν ἐπιποθούντων ὑμᾶς διὰ τὴν ὑπερβάλλουσαν χάριν τοῦ θεοῦ ἐφ᾽ ὑμῖν. ¹⁵ Χάρις τῷ θεῷ ἐπὶ τῇ ἀνεκδιηγήτῳ αὐτοῦ δωρεᾷ.

¹Now it is superfluous for me to write to you about the offering for the saints, ²for I know your readiness, of which I boast about you to the people of Macedonia, saying that Achaia has been ready since last year; and your zeal has stirred up most of them. ³But I am sending the brethren so that our boasting about you may not prove vain in this case, so that you may be ready, as I said you would be; ⁴lest if some Macedonians come with me and find that you are not ready, we be humiliated—to say nothing of you—for being so confident. ⁵So I thought it necessary to urge the brethren to go on to you before me, and arrange in advance for this gift you have promised, so that it may be ready not as an exaction but as a willing gift. ⁶The point is this: he who sows sparingly will also reap sparingly, and he who sows bountifully will also reap bountifully. ⁷Each one must do as he has made up his mind, not reluctantly or under compulsion, for God loves a cheerful giver. ⁸And God is able to provide you with every blessing in abundance, so that you may always have enough of everything and may provide in abundance for every good work. ⁹As it is written, "He scatters abroad, he gives to the poor; his righteousness endures for ever." ¹⁰He who supplies seed to the sower and bread for food will supply and multiply your resources and increase the harvest of your righteousness. ¹¹You will be enriched in every way for great generosity, which through us will produce thanksgiving to God; ¹²for the rendering of this service not only supplies the wants of the saints but also overflows in many thanksgivings to God. ¹³Under the test of this service, you will glorify God by your obedience in acknowledging the gospel of Christ, and by the generosity of your contribution for them and for all others; ¹⁴while they long for you and pray for you, because of the surpassing grace of God in you. ¹⁵Thanks be to God for his inexpressible gift!

Chapter 9

Having put a theoretical and moral pressure on the Corinthians concerning "the ministry to the saints" in chapter 8, Paul puts factual pressure on them in chapter 9: he has been boasting to the Macedonians that the Corinthians had fulfilled their duty since the previous year (vv.2-3). Consequently, "if some Macedonians come with me and find that you are not ready, we be humiliated—to say nothing of you—for being so confident" (v.4). In order that such not happen, Paul is sending the brethren ahead of him to ensure that all is according to expectation and, moreover, that the offering is "a willing gift, not an exaction" (v.5; see also 8:11-12).

Paul then brings into the picture the classic metaphor of sowing and harvesting, which allows him to play on three different levels at the same time. First, he can appeal to the generosity of his addressees since "he who sows sparingly will also reap sparingly, and he who sows bountifully will also reap bountifully" (9:6). Secondly, according to scripture, cheerful giving is after God's heart (v.7; see Prov 22:8 LXX). Finally, with the mention of God Paul can again remind the Corinthians that all their doing is the result of divine grace (2 Cor 9:8); he does so by referring to three more scriptural passages in a very ingenious manner. He starts with an express quotation from Ps 112:9 which, however, is "redirected" (2 Cor 9:9). In the original, the description refers to the action of "the man who fears the Lord, who greatly delights in his commandments" (Ps 112:1). In the epistle's setting, the hearer perceives it as applying to God since he is the subject of the previous verse (2 Cor 9:8). The result is that the scripture quoted in v.9 is made to corroborate Paul's statement in v.8. The immediate reaction is to ask whether such "maneuver" is justifiable. When hearing the following v.10, "He who supplies seed to the sower and bread for food (*ho de epikhorēgōn sperma tō speironti kai arton eis brōsin*) will supply and multiply your resources and increase the harvest of your righteousness," a keen ear will detect a direct reference to Isaiah 55:10 followed by an oblique reference to Isaiah 45:8. The first part clearly points to "For as the rain and the snow come down from heaven, and return not thither but water the earth, making it bring forth and sprout, *giving seed to the sower and bread to the eater* (LXX *dō sperma tō speironti kai arton eis brōsin*), so shall my word be that goes forth from my mouth; it shall not return to me empty, but it shall accomplish that which I purpose, and prosper in the thing for which I sent it" (Is 55:10-11). What is stressed here is that the Lord's "word," which is carried to both Israel and the nations (42:6; 49:6) through Paul's gospel, is the promoter of both the seed and its fruitfulness, which is the point of 2 Corinthians 9:8 and what Paul is saying throughout this letter. However, v.10 ends with a reference to "the harvest (*genēmata*; produce) of *your righteousness*" as well as "*your resources* (*sporon* [from the same root as *sperma* and *speironti*]; what is sown)." It is as though the righteousness of God and that of the Corinthians are blended into one, which is the precise format that Paul used when he "redirected" Psalm 112:9 (2 Cor 8:9). The clue to understanding v.10 is to hear it against a previous passage from Isaiah: "Shower, O heavens, from above, and let the skies *rain down righteousness*; let the earth open, that salvation may sprout forth, and let it *cause righteousness to spring up also*; I the Lord have created it." (Is 45:8) The one work (creation) of the Lord consists in raining down righteousness from heaven *so that* righteousness may spring forth out of the earth, just as Paul writes elsewhere: "This was to show God's righteousness (*dikaiosynēs*), because in his divine forbearance he had passed over former sins; it was to prove at the present time that he himself is righteous (*dikaion*) and that he justifies (*dikaiounta*; makes righteous) him who has faith in Jesus." (Rom 3:25b-26)

The ultimate aim of all the preceding is that the Corinthians' generosity "through us will produce thanksgiving to God" (2 Cor 9:11). Such goes hand in hand with the fact that Paul viewed himself as the high priest of the Gentiles in the sanctuary of the Jerusalem above,[1] as is evident from the phraseology that is similar to what he writes in Philippians: "Even if I am to be poured as a libation upon the sacrificial offering (*tē thysia kai leitourgia*; the sacrifice and common service) of your faith, I am glad and rejoice with you all ... for he [Epaphroditus] nearly died for the work of Christ, risking his life to complete (*anaplērōsē*) that which is wanting in[2] (*to hysterēma*) your service (*leitourgias*) to me ... I am filled (*peplērōmai*), having received from Epaphroditus the gifts you sent, a fragrant offering (*osmēn evōdias*),[3] a sacrifice (*thysian*) acceptable and pleasing to God" (Phil 2:17, 30; 4:18);[4] "for the rendering (*diakonia*; ministry) of this service (*leitourgias*) not only supplies (*prosanaplērousa*) the wants (*ta hysterēmata*) of the saints..." (2 Cor 9:12a) In other words, it is Paul who will bring to completion the "service" (*leitourgia*) of the Corinthians in fulfilling his "ministry" (*diakonia*) to the gospel by bringing to the "saints" what he had promised at the Jerusalem meeting *in conjunction* with that gospel (Gal 2:7-10). Should his mission succeed, then the fullness of the blessing (2 Cor 9:5-6)[5] shall be reaped: "When

---

[1] See Rom 15:15-16; Phil 2:17; 4:18; Gal 4:26-28.
[2] Omitted in RSV.
[3] Compare with 2 Cor 2:15-16: "For we are the aroma (*evōdia*) of Christ to God among those who are being saved and among those who are perishing, to one a fragrance (*osmē*) from death to death, to the other a fragrance from life to life. Who is sufficient for these things?"
[4] See my comments on these verses in *C-Phil* 138-9, 145, 185.
[5] See Rom 15:28-29.

therefore I have completed this, and have delivered to them what has been raised, I shall go on by way of you to Spain; and I know that when I come to you I shall come in the fulness of the blessing of Christ." (Rom 15:28-29) Hence, the tradition of the collection will pervade all the Pauline churches and "the rendering of this service not only supplies the wants of the saints *but also overflows in many thanksgivings to God*" (2 Cor 9:12), that is to say, in many more such offerings sealing the oneness at the same table fellowship between Jew and Gentile. In turn, the success in "the test (*dokimēs*)[6] of this service (*diakonias*; ministry)"[7] will result in the Jerusalemites' truly glorifying God,[8] which was their original reaction to Paul's apostolic activity among the Gentiles (Gal 1:23-24). Thus, the Jewish leaders will recognize that Paul's Gentiles are not resistant to God's law, but rather were brought into obedience to God's will expressed in his law through their acknowledgment (*homologias*; confession) of the gospel of Christ as preached by Paul (2 Cor 9:13a). In this manner, the Gentiles' generosity in their contribution to fellowship (*koinōnias*) will engulf not only the Jewish leaders but "all," that is to say, Jews and Gentiles throughout the Roman empire (v.13b). A further consequence is that, having recognized the work of the divine grace (v.14b) surpassing any human word (v.15), those leaders, "high priests" as Paul is, will follow his way in including the Gentiles in their prayer to God (v.14a), thus de facto sealing the Pauline teaching that the Jerusalem above is mother to all those who are children after the manner of Isaac, the son of the divine promise (Gal 4:26-28).

---

[6] See earlier 2:9 and 8:2 and my comments concerning the latter.
[7] In loosely translating into "service" both *leitourgias* in v.12 and *diakonias* in v.13—which it translated as "rendering" in v.12—RSV disrupts Paul's argument.
[8] RSV misses the point; see KJV and JB.

Chapter 10

Vv. 1-6 *¹Αὐτὸς δὲ ἐγὼ Παῦλος παρακαλῶ ὑμᾶς διὰ τῆς πραΰτητος καὶ ἐπιεικείας τοῦ Χριστοῦ, ὃς κατὰ πρόσωπον μὲν ταπεινὸς ἐν ὑμῖν, ἀπὼν δὲ θαρρῶ εἰς ὑμᾶς· ² δέομαι δὲ τὸ μὴ παρὼν θαρρῆσαι τῇ πεποιθήσει ᾗ λογίζομαι τολμῆσαι ἐπί τινας τοὺς λογιζομένους ἡμᾶς ὡς κατὰ σάρκα περιπατοῦντας. ³ Ἐν σαρκὶ γὰρ περιπατοῦντες οὐ κατὰ σάρκα στρατευόμεθα, ⁴τὰ γὰρ ὅπλα τῆς στρατείας ἡμῶν οὐ σαρκικὰ ἀλλὰ δυνατὰ τῷ θεῷ πρὸς καθαίρεσιν ὀχυρωμάτων, λογισμοὺς καθαιροῦντες ⁵ καὶ πᾶν ὕψωμα ἐπαιρόμενον κατὰ τῆς γνώσεως τοῦ θεοῦ, καὶ αἰχμαλωτίζοντες πᾶν νόημα εἰς τὴν ὑπακοὴν τοῦ Χριστοῦ, ⁶ καὶ ἐν ἑτοίμῳ ἔχοντες ἐκδικῆσαι πᾶσαν παρακοήν, ὅταν πληρωθῇ ὑμῶν ἡ ὑπακοή.*

> *¹I, Paul, myself entreat you, by the meekness and gentleness of Christ—I who am humble when face to face with you, but bold to you when I am away!—² I beg of you that when I am present I may not have to show boldness with such confidence as I count on showing against some who suspect us of acting in worldly fashion. ³For though we live in the world we are not carrying on a worldly war, ⁴for the weapons of our warfare are not worldly but have divine power to destroy strongholds. ⁵We destroy arguments and every proud obstacle to the knowledge of God, and take every thought captive to obey Christ, ⁶being ready to punish every disobedience, when your obedience is complete.*

Having reached the end of the road, at least on hope, all that remains for Paul to do is engrave the seriousness of the matter in the minds of the Corinthians. They are to stay the course he delineated for them at all costs until the Lord comes. In order to give them a foretaste of the Lord's Day when all, including Paul himself, shall be judged (1 Cor 4:1-5), the Apostle reminds them of his own third and thus final coming which will be an appearance with power and judgment (2 Cor

13:1-4). The similarity of the text in which he is accused of duplicity in attitude when absent compared to when present (13:1-4) confirms that he had this thought in mind at the beginning of chapter 10:

> I, Paul, myself entreat you, by the meekness and gentleness of Christ—I who am humble when face to face with you, but bold to you when I am away (*apōn*; absent)!—I beg of you that when I am present I may not have to show boldness with such confidence as I count on showing against some who suspect us of acting in worldly fashion. For though we live in the world we are not carrying on a worldly war, for the weapons of our warfare are not worldly but have divine power to destroy strongholds. We destroy arguments and every proud obstacle to the knowledge of God, and take every thought captive to obey Christ, being ready to punish every disobedience, when your obedience is complete. (vv. 1-6)

> This is the third time I am coming to you. Any charge must be sustained by the evidence of two or three witnesses. I warned those who sinned before and all the others, and I warn them now while absent (*apōn*), as I did when present on my second visit, that if I come again I will not spare them—since you desire proof that Christ is speaking in me. He is not weak in dealing with you, but is powerful in you. For he was crucified in weakness, but lives by the power of God. For we are weak in him, but in dealing with you we shall live with him by the power of God. (13:1-4)

However, before undeniably wielding the "rod" in chapter 13, he starts here with the opposite, that is, the "spirit of gentleness (*praytētos*)" (1 Cor 4:21): "I, Paul, myself entreat you, by the meekness (*praytētos*) and gentleness (*epieikeias*) of Christ." (2 Cor 10:1; see also Gal 6:1-2). Still—the Corinthians better beware!— if his gentleness is bound by Christ, Paul is still the Apostle filled with God's spirit, unlike his "fleshly" addressees (1 Cor 2:10- 3:3). Consequently, though he walks (*peripatountes*), and thus lives, "in the flesh" (*en sarki*; 2 Cor 10:3b), as all humans are bound to do, nevertheless, he does not walk (*peripatountas*) or thus live, "according to (the will of) the flesh" (*kata sarka*; v.2b).[1] To the contrary, the warfare he is waging is not "according to the flesh" (*kata sarka*; v.3b) but against adverse "arguments" (*logismous*; v.4) and "thought" (*noēma*: v.5) purporting to be according to God's spirit and yet actually being a "proud (arrogant, exalted) obstacle (*hypsōma epairomenon*) against the (true) knowledge of God" (v.5) as communicated through the Pauline gospel.[2] Paul uses military terminology here, as he does elsewhere,[3] to reflect the power[4] of his stand. In particular, he appeals to the description of the siege of a city (v.4b), a warfare that has been perfected by the Romans: Paul would "destroy" (tear down; *kathairountes*) the opposing arguments (v.5a) just as he would "destroy" (tear down; *kathairesin*) strongholds (v.4b). Furthermore, a siege is usually followed by captivity (v.5b). However, following the lead of the Prophets before him when dealing with the exile, Paul views God's punishment of disobedience (v.6a) as having the aim of bringing those punished into obedience; in our case, into obedience to Christ (v.5b) as taught by Paul (1 Cor 4:15). That is why, if he is exacting (divine) vengeance[5] against disobedience (2 Cor 10:6a), it is with the hope that the Corinthians will reach complete and full obedience (v.6b). This is corroborated later when Paul writes,

---

[1] RSV renders the original "fleshly" as "worldly" and thus conceals the intended opposition to the "spirit," which is God's "power."

[2] The root *logismous*— (vv.3 and 5) harks back to *dialogismous* (1 Cor 3:20).

[3] See 1 Cor 9:7; Gal 1:6; 2:4; Eph 6:13-17; Phil 2:25; Col 2:15; 2 Tim 2:3, 4; Philem 2.

[4] My readers are reminded that, in scripture and especially the Pauline writings, "spirit" and "power" are the two sides of the same coin. See, e.g., Rom 1:4; 15:13, 19; 1 Cor 2:4; Eph 2:2; 1 Thess 1:5; 2 Tim 1:7-8.

[5] Which is precisely the exact meaning of the original *ekdikēsai* translated as "punish" in RSV.

"For even if I boast a little too much of our authority, which the Lord gave for building you up and not for destroying (*kathairesin*) you, I shall not be put to shame" (v.8). He comments further on this at the end of the letter: "I write this while I am away (*apōn*; absent)[6] from you, in order that when I come I may not have to be severe in my use of the authority which the Lord has given me for building up and not for tearing down (*kathairesin*)." (13:10)

But then, whose disobedience, deserving of his "condemning vengeance," is Paul referring to in 10:6a? Given that the description of the adversaries is cast in a terminology reflecting arrogance (vv.3-5) and that he compares both his status (v.7) and his "apostolic" activity (vv.12-16) with theirs, the most plausible assumption is that he is aiming at the other "apostles" who are meddling with "his" church in Corinth. This will be borne out when analyzing the rest of the chapter. Challenging his meddling colleagues, who are stirring up the Corinthians, while criticizing both, is a stratagem Paul uses frequently. In fact, he did so earlier in 1 Cor 3:20 as is evident in the use of the two cognate nouns *logismous* (arguments; 2 Cor 10:5) and *dialogismous* (thoughts; 1 Cor 3:20), the only two instances of the nominal root *logism—* in the Corinthian correspondence. Further evidence can be seen in the statement "Let him who boasts, boast of the Lord" (2 Cor 10:17). Although it occurs verbatim earlier (1 Cor 1:31b) within a context aiming at the arrogance of the Corinthians (vv.26-30), the "men" in the contrasting statement, "So let no one boast of men" (3:21a), are evidently the apostles as is clear from the remark that immediately follows: "For all things are yours, whether Paul or Apollos or Cephas…" (vv.21b-22a)

---

[6] Same term he used in 10:1.

Vv. 7-11 ⁷ Τὰ κατὰ πρόσωπον βλέπετε. εἴ τις πέποιθεν ἑαυτῷ Χριστοῦ εἶναι, τοῦτο λογιζέσθω πάλιν ἐφ' ἑαυτοῦ, ὅτι καθὼς αὐτὸς Χριστοῦ, οὕτως καὶ ἡμεῖς. ⁸ ἐάν [τε] γὰρ περισσότερόν τι καυχήσωμαι περὶ τῆς ἐξουσίας ἡμῶν ἧς ἔδωκεν ὁ κύριος εἰς οἰκοδομὴν καὶ οὐκ εἰς καθαίρεσιν ὑμῶν, οὐκ αἰσχυνθήσομαι. ⁹ ἵνα μὴ δόξω ὡς ἂν ἐκφοβεῖν ὑμᾶς διὰ τῶν ἐπιστολῶν· ¹⁰ ὅτι αἱ ἐπιστολαὶ μέν, φησίν, βαρεῖαι καὶ ἰσχυραί, ἡ δὲ παρουσία τοῦ σώματος ἀσθενὴς καὶ ὁ λόγος ἐξουθενημένος. ¹¹ τοῦτο λογιζέσθω ὁ τοιοῦτος, ὅτι οἷοί ἐσμεν τῷ λόγῳ δι' ἐπιστολῶν ἀπόντες, τοιοῦτοι καὶ παρόντες τῷ ἔργῳ.

⁷*Look at what is before your eyes. If any one is confident that he is Christ's, let him remind himself that as he is Christ's, so are we.* ⁸*For even if I boast a little too much of our authority, which the Lord gave for building you up and not for destroying you, I shall not be put to shame.* ⁹*I would not seem to be frightening you with letters.* ¹⁰*For they say, "His letters are weighty and strong, but his bodily presence is weak, and his speech of no account."* ¹¹*Let such people understand that what we say by letter when absent, we do when present.*

Paul then advises the Corinthians to heed (*blepete*)—watch out for; not be fooled by—(false) appearances (2 Cor 10:7a).⁷ This understanding of *blepete* is confirmed in the following occurrences:

Only *take care* (*blepete*) lest this liberty of yours somehow become a stumbling block to the weak. (1 Cor 8:9)

Consider (*blepete*; heed the example of) the people of Israel; are not those who eat the sacrifices partners in the altar? (10:18)

But if you bite and devour one another *take heed* (*blepete*) that you are not consumed by one another. (Gal 5:15)

---

⁷ The original for RSV's "Look at what is before your eyes" is *Ta kata prosōpon blepete*.

Look carefully (*blepete*) then how you walk, not as unwise men but as wise. (Eph 5:15)

Look out for (*blepete*) the dogs, *look out for* (*blepete*) the evilworkers, *look out for* (*blepete*) those who mutilate the flesh. (Phil 3:2)

See to it (*blepete*) that no one makes a prey of you by philosophy and empty deceit, according to human tradition, according to the elemental spirits of the universe, and not according to Christ. (Col 2:8)

Take care (*blepete*), brethren, lest there be in any of you an evil, unbelieving heart, leading you to fall away from the living God. (Heb 3:12)

See that (*blepete*) you do not refuse him who is speaking. (12:25a)

This understanding is further supported by the phrase *kata prosōpon* (to the face, face to face, in the other's presence, openly), which refers to those immediately present and fits the context as well (2 Cor 10:1). The connection between the two instances (vv.1-2 and 7) is established through the use of the same verb *logizomai*: "I beg of you that when I am present I may not have to show boldness with such confidence as I count (*logizomai*) on showing against some who suspect (*logizomenous*; count) us of acting in worldly fashion" (v.2); "If any one is confident that he is Christ's, let him remind (*logizesthō*; count [in]) himself that as he is Christ's, so are we." (v.7) In v.7 Paul is "destroying (tearing down) the arguments (*logismous*)" (v.4) of his opponents in the minds of the Corinthians. Verse 2 is clearly one of misinterpreting what is seen "face to face" (v.1), and no less under the influence of his opponents (vv.3-5). It is reasonable to assume that in v.7 Paul is asking the Corinthians not to fall into the trap set by the same people who are criticizing

Paul as fake in his "gentle" appearance "face to face" (*kata prosōpon*) in Corinth (v.1) since these same people are asking the Corinthians to accept them *at face value* (*ta kata prosōpon*) when they are presenting themselves as bona fide authoritative representatives of Christ (v.7b). Let the Corinthians heed the fact that he, Paul, is no less Christ's representative (v.7c) and, in Corinth, he is Christ's sole representative (1 Cor 9:2; 2 Cor 3:1-3). As such, he has indisputable authority (*exousias*) over them from the Lord himself (10:8), as he explained in detail in 1 Corinthians 9. However, the authority of the house manager (*oikonomos*) is in view of the charge assigned to him, which is to build his master's household, not tear it down (2 Cor 10:8). And if such entails "appearing" subdued and gentle (v.1) toward the other members of the household (Lk 12:42-48), then of this Paul boasts and is in no way ashamed (2 Cor 10:8), even if his opponents' description of him (v.10) takes the edge away from his letters so that they are only seemingly "frightening" (v.9). The opponents as well as the Corinthians will soon learn that the threatening "word" (*tō logō*) of the letters, the Pauline gospel, is none other than God's word and is about to take effect "in deed" (*tō ergō*)[8] (v.11). Paul prepares to overturn the accusation in v.10 by purposely resorting to vocabulary he used at the beginning of 1 Corinthians to describe those who were chosen by God to reflect his power, in conjunction with boasting:

> but God chose what is foolish in the world to shame the wise, God chose what is weak (*ta asthenē*) in the world to shame the strong (*ta iskhyra*), God chose what is low and despised (*ta exouthenēmena*) in the world, even things that are not, to bring to nothing things that are, so that no human being might boast in

---

[8] KJV renders v.11 thus: "Let such an one think this, that, such as we are *in word* by letters when we are absent, such *will we be* also *in deed* when we are present."

the presence of God ... "Let him who boasts, boast of the Lord." (1 Cor 1:27-29, 31b)

For they say, "His letters are weighty (*bareiai*) and strong (*ischyrai*), but his bodily presence is weak (*asthenēs*), and his speech of no account (*exouthenēmenos*)" ... "Let him who boasts, boast of the Lord." (2 Cor 10:10, 17)

The hearers could not miss the connection.

Vv. 12-18 *¹² Οὐ γὰρ τολμῶμεν ἐγκρῖναι ἢ συγκρῖναι ἑαυτούς τισιν τῶν ἑαυτοὺς συνιστανόντων, ἀλλὰ αὐτοὶ ἐν ἑαυτοῖς ἑαυτοὺς μετροῦντες καὶ συγκρίνοντες ἑαυτοὺς ἑαυτοῖς οὐ συνιᾶσιν. ¹³ ἡμεῖς δὲ οὐκ εἰς τὰ ἄμετρα καυχησόμεθα ἀλλὰ κατὰ τὸ μέτρον τοῦ κανόνος οὗ ἐμέρισεν ἡμῖν ὁ θεὸς μέτρου, ἐφικέσθαι ἄχρι καὶ ὑμῶν. ¹⁴ οὐ γὰρ ὡς μὴ ἐφικνούμενοι εἰς ὑμᾶς ὑπερεκτείνομεν ἑαυτούς, ἄχρι γὰρ καὶ ὑμῶν ἐφθάσαμεν ἐν τῷ εὐαγγελίῳ τοῦ Χριστοῦ, ¹⁵ οὐκ εἰς τὰ ἄμετρα καυχώμενοι ἐν ἀλλοτρίοις κόποις, ἐλπίδα δὲ ἔχοντες αὐξανομένης τῆς πίστεως ὑμῶν ἐν ὑμῖν μεγαλυνθῆναι κατὰ τὸν κανόνα ἡμῶν εἰς περισσείαν ¹⁶ εἰς τὰ ὑπερέκεινα ὑμῶν εὐαγγελίσασθαι, οὐκ ἐν ἀλλοτρίῳ κανόνι εἰς τὰ ἕτοιμα καυχήσασθαι. ¹⁷ Ὁ δὲ καυχώμενος ἐν κυρίῳ καυχάσθω· ¹⁸ οὐ γὰρ ὁ ἑαυτὸν συνιστάνων, ἐκεῖνός ἐστιν δόκιμος, ἀλλὰ ὃν ὁ κύριος συνίστησιν.*

¹²Not that we venture to class or compare ourselves with some of those who commend themselves. But when they measure themselves by one another, and compare themselves with one another, they are without understanding. ¹³But we will not boast beyond limit, but will keep to the limits God has apportioned us, to reach even to you. ¹⁴For we are not overextending ourselves, as though we did not reach you; we were the first to come all the way to you with the gospel of Christ. ¹⁵We do not boast beyond limit, in other men's labors; but our hope is that as your faith increases, our field among you may be greatly enlarged, ¹⁶so that we may preach the gospel in lands beyond you, without boasting of work already done in another's field. ¹⁷*"Let him who boasts, boast of the Lord." * ¹⁸*For it is not the man who commends himself that is accepted, but the man whom the Lord commends.*

Having defended himself against the false accusations, Paul moves to the offensive to show that his opponents have only fake power (vv.12-18). He starts with a statement (v.12) that is cast in terminology reminiscent of what he used earlier to show his superiority when comparing himself with others. Here again his addressees could not have possibly missed his intention to challenge them while defying the opponents. The verb "compare" which appears twice (*synkrinai* [v.12a] and *synkrinontes* [v.12b]) is found in the New Testament only once more (1 Cor 2:13) where Paul is reminding the Corinthians that he is the one who judges them, and not they him (vv.13-15).[9] In 2 Cor 10:12a he uses it in conjunction with the other apostles "who commend (*synistantōn*) themselves." This same verb *synistēmi* occurred profusely in chapters 3-7 where Paul repeatedly asserted that he would not, nor did he need to, commend himself (3:1; 5:12) since the record of his apostolic activity did that (4:2; 6:4). By prefacing *synkrinai* with *enkrinai* (RSV "class"; 10:12), a unique instance in the New Testament and whose meaning is "judge in order to assess someone within a certain class of people," Paul is clearly drawing attention to the fact that such an assessment is exclusively a divine prerogative (1 Cor 4:1-5). This explains his judgment that those who compare themselves to one another "are without understanding" (2 Cor 10:12b). As a parallel to "compare" (*synkrinontes*), Paul astutely throws in the verb "measure" (*metrountes*) in preparation for the use of the root *metr*— that pervades the following verses, thrice

---

[9] See my comments in *C-1Cor* 63-9.

in v.13 (*ta ametra, to metron,* and *metrou*) and once in v.15 (*ta ametra*).

In vv.13-16 it becomes clear to any hearer why it is actually foolish to even consider comparing apostles. As Paul explains here and elsewhere (Gal 2:7-8; Rom 15:20-21; 1 Cor 9:2; 2 Cor 3:2-3), every apostle is assigned a different area so that there would not be overlapping in duties, which would allow the gospel to reach "the ends of the earth" more readily: "So faith comes from what is heard, and what is heard comes by the preaching of Christ. But I ask, have they not heard? Indeed they have; for 'Their voice has gone out to all the earth, and their words to the ends of the world.'" (Rom 10:17-18) If Paul is hoping that the Corinthians endorse his gospel as quickly as possible, it is only so that he can cover other areas in his "field," which is "the nations" assigned to him (2 Cor 10:15b; see Gal 2:7-8) as is clear from Romans 15:19-20. Since the assignment of each to his given "field" originates in God (2 Cor 10:13), should one decide to boast, one should do so "in the Lord" (v.17) who alone decides whether an apostle has been found "accepted" (*dokimos*; approved, tested, having passed the test)"[10] and whose "commendation" in the matter of apostleship is the only valid one (v.18).

It is important to remember that Paul refers to his apostolic "field" as *kanōn* (rule, canon):

> But we will not boast beyond limit, but will keep to the limits *of the rule* (*kanonos*) God has apportioned us, to reach even to you. For we are not overextending ourselves, as though we did not reach you; we were the first to come all the way to you with the gospel of Christ. We do not boast beyond limit, in other men's

---

[10] See earlier my comments on *dokimē* in 8:2 and 9:13.

labors; but our hope is that as your faith increases, our field among you may be greatly enlarged (*en hymin megalynthēnai kata ton kanona hēmon eis perisseian*), so that we may preach the gospel in lands beyond you, without boasting of work already done in another's field (*kanoni*). "Let him who boasts, boast of the Lord." (vv.13-17)

The Pauline "rule" is actually God's "rule" since it is God himself who apportions the limits of such to each of the apostles. Given that the noun "canon" occurs only once more in the entire New Testament, in Galatians 6:16 where it unequivocally refers to Paul's gospel teaching, it ensues then that, for Paul, the flip side of the canon of the one gospel is the canon of the one apostle for one given church.[11] The corollary is that he is shutting any and all other apostles out of the Corinthian "field," which he is about to clearly underscore in the following chapter.

---

[11] See my article "Paul, the One Apostle of the One Gospel" in *The Journal of the Orthodox Center for the Advancement of Biblical Studies* (*JOCABS*) 2 (2009) 2-5.

Chapter 11

Vv. 1-15 ¹ Ὄφελον ἀνείχεσθέ μου μικρόν τι ἀφροσύνης· ἀλλὰ καὶ ἀνέχεσθέ μου. ² ζηλῶ γὰρ ὑμᾶς θεοῦ ζήλῳ, ἡρμοσάμην γὰρ ὑμᾶς ἑνὶ ἀνδρὶ παρθένον ἁγνὴν παραστῆσαι τῷ Χριστῷ· ³ φοβοῦμαι δὲ μή πως, ὡς ὁ ὄφις ἐξηπάτησεν Εὔαν ἐν τῇ πανουργίᾳ αὐτοῦ, φθαρῇ τὰ νοήματα ὑμῶν ἀπὸ τῆς ἁπλότητος [καὶ τῆς ἁγνότητος] τῆς εἰς τὸν Χριστόν. ⁴ εἰ μὲν γὰρ ὁ ἐρχόμενος ἄλλον Ἰησοῦν κηρύσσει ὃν οὐκ ἐκηρύξαμεν, ἢ πνεῦμα ἕτερον λαμβάνετε ὃ οὐκ ἐλάβετε, ἢ εὐαγγέλιον ἕτερον ὃ οὐκ ἐδέξασθε, καλῶς ἀνέχεσθε. ⁵ Λογίζομαι γὰρ μηδὲν ὑστερηκέναι τῶν ὑπερλίαν ἀποστόλων. ⁶ εἰ δὲ καὶ ἰδιώτης τῷ λόγῳ, ἀλλ' οὐ τῇ γνώσει, ἀλλ' ἐν παντὶ φανερώσαντες ἐν πᾶσιν εἰς ὑμᾶς. ⁷ Ἢ ἁμαρτίαν ἐποίησα ἐμαυτὸν ταπεινῶν ἵνα ὑμεῖς ὑψωθῆτε, ὅτι δωρεὰν τὸ τοῦ θεοῦ εὐαγγέλιον εὐηγγελισάμην ὑμῖν; ⁸ ἄλλας ἐκκλησίας ἐσύλησα λαβὼν ὀψώνιον πρὸς τὴν ὑμῶν διακονίαν, ⁹ καὶ παρὼν πρὸς ὑμᾶς καὶ ὑστερηθεὶς οὐ κατενάρκησα οὐθενός· τὸ γὰρ ὑστέρημά μου προσανεπλήρωσαν οἱ ἀδελφοὶ ἐλθόντες ἀπὸ Μακεδονίας, καὶ ἐν παντὶ ἀβαρῆ ἐμαυτὸν ὑμῖν ἐτήρησα καὶ τηρήσω. ¹⁰ ἔστιν ἀλήθεια Χριστοῦ ἐν ἐμοὶ ὅτι ἡ καύχησις αὕτη οὐ φραγήσεται εἰς ἐμὲ ἐν τοῖς κλίμασιν τῆς Ἀχαΐας. ¹¹ διὰ τί; ὅτι οὐκ ἀγαπῶ ὑμᾶς; ὁ θεὸς οἶδεν. ¹² Ὃ δὲ ποιῶ, καὶ ποιήσω, ἵνα ἐκκόψω τὴν ἀφορμὴν τῶν θελόντων ἀφορμήν, ἵνα ἐν ᾧ καυχῶνται εὑρεθῶσιν καθὼς καὶ ἡμεῖς. ¹³ οἱ γὰρ τοιοῦτοι ψευδαπόστολοι, ἐργάται δόλιοι, μετασχηματιζόμενοι εἰς ἀποστόλους Χριστοῦ. ¹⁴ καὶ οὐ θαῦμα· αὐτὸς γὰρ ὁ σατανᾶς μετασχηματίζεται εἰς ἄγγελον φωτός. ¹⁵ οὐ μέγα οὖν εἰ καὶ οἱ διάκονοι αὐτοῦ μετασχηματίζονται ὡς διάκονοι δικαιοσύνης· ὧν τὸ τέλος ἔσται κατὰ τὰ ἔργα αὐτῶν.

¹*I wish you would bear with me in a little foolishness. Do bear with me!* ²*I feel a divine jealousy for you, for I betrothed you to Christ to present you as a pure bride to her one husband.* ³*But I am afraid that as the serpent deceived Eve by his cunning, your thoughts will be led astray from a sincere and pure devotion to Christ.* ⁴*For if some one comes and preaches another Jesus than*

the one we preached, or if you receive a different spirit from the one you received, or if you accept a different gospel from the one you accepted, you submit to it readily enough. ⁵I think that I am not in the least inferior to these superlative apostles. ⁶Even if I am unskilled in speaking, I am not in knowledge; in every way we have made this plain to you in all things. ⁷Did I commit a sin in abasing myself so that you might be exalted, because I preached God's gospel without cost to you? ⁸I robbed other churches by accepting support from them in order to serve you. ⁹And when I was with you and was in want, I did not burden any one, for my needs were supplied by the brethren who came from Macedonia. So I refrained and will refrain from burdening you in any way. ¹⁰As the truth of Christ is in me, this boast of mine shall not be silenced in the regions of Achaia. ¹¹And why? Because I do not love you? God knows I do! ¹² And what I do I will continue to do, in order to undermine the claim of those who would like to claim that in their boasted mission they work on the same terms as we do. ¹³For such men are false apostles, deceitful workmen, disguising themselves as apostles of Christ. ¹⁴And no wonder, for even Satan disguises himself as an angel of light. ¹⁵So it is not strange if his servants also disguise themselves as servants of righteousness. Their end will correspond to their deeds.

Although Paul emphatically stated that he tried to behave reasonably (2 Cor 5:13), in 11:1 he is overplaying the card of foolish boasting (11:1), as the other leaders do, so that the Corinthians could hear and feel the absurdity of such a stand. However, before openly going that route (v.16), he attacks his opponents head-on in order to unveil their ill-intentioned cunning (vv.2-15) and to draw his addressees' full attention to his "mockery." After having asked the Corinthians "to bear with him with a little foolishness," he shares with them the real reason for his harshness against the other apostles: his intention is to protect the church of Corinth as a "pure bride" for Christ (v.3; see earlier 1 Cor 6:17-18; also Eph 5:25-27). One is not to conclude, as was done in classical theology, that the church, as Christ's bride, is by definition pure although its members are more or less sinful. To the contrary, the church (*ekklēsia*) is co-extensive with its members who remain "called" (*klētoi*) until judgment day when only "a few" will be "chosen" (*eklektoi*) (Mt 22:14). Indeed, the bride church will have to be "presented" (*parastēsai*; 2 Cor 11:2), that is, "stand trial."[1] Until then she has to be "cleansed by the washing of water with the [Pauline] word" in order to be "presented to himself [Christ, the bridegroom] in splendor, without spot or wrinkle or any such thing, that she might be holy and without blemish" (Eph 5:27). "Pure" (*hagnēn*; 2 Cor 11:2) occurs only one other time in the entire Corinthian correspondence and then in a setting that reflects "guiltlessness" facing divine judgment:

> As it is, I rejoice, not because you were grieved, but because you were grieved into *repenting* (*metanoian*); for you felt a godly grief, so that you suffered no loss through us. For godly grief produces a *repentance* (*metanoian*) *that leads to salvation* and brings no regret, but worldly grief produces death. For see what earnestness this godly grief has produced in you, what eagerness *to clear yourselves* (*apologian*; defense as in a court of law), what indignation, what alarm, what longing, what zeal, what *punishment* (*ekdikēsin*; just retaliation by the judge)! At every point you have proved yourselves guiltless (*hagnous*) in the matter. (7:9-11)[2]

Notice further how Paul works hard for that purpose, with no less than a *divine* "jealousy" (*zelon*; zeal; 11:2a) that would invite

---

[1] See *C-Rom* 226.
[2] See earlier my comments on those verses.

the same kind of zeal (*zēlon*; 7:11) on the part of the Corinthians so that they, the Corinthian church, be found "guiltless" on the day of the Lord (7:11; 11:2).

All this is on hope, and not within the realm of factuality. Paul is still "afraid" (*phoboumai*; 11:3) for the future of the Corinthians as he is for that of the Galatians: "I am afraid (*phoboumai*) I have labored over you in vain." (4:11) The closeness between these two instances is betrayed in that, in both cases, Paul's fear is triggered by the potential influence of his opponents (2 Cor 11:2-15; Gal 4:10[3]). In preparation for the depiction of the influence perpetrated by outsiders who are bringing their own slant to the true gospel that originates in God through Paul (2 Cor 11:4; see Gal 1:1, 11-12), he likens the Corinthian community to Eve who was "deceived" by the "cunning" (*panourgia*) of the serpent that twisted God's own "words" and gave them a different meaning than the originally intended.[4] This accusation fits perfectly Paul's depiction of his opponents: "For if some one comes and preaches *another* Jesus than the one we preached, or if you receive a *different* spirit from the one you received, or if you accept a *different* gospel from the one you accepted, you submit to it readily enough." (2 Cor 11:4) Moreover, a keen ear will have readily detected that "cunning" is used specifically in reference to the preaching of the gospel; it occurred earlier twice, once in conjunction with God's unveiling the "craftiness" (*panourgia*) of the falsely wise (1 Cor 3:19) and the other time in Paul's own defense of not practicing "cunning" in his apostolic activity (2 Cor 4:2). That Paul was aiming at his nemeses is further confirmed in the phrase "your thoughts will

---

[3] Gal 4:10 (You observe days, and months, and seasons, and years!) reflects Jewish cultic traditions that Paul's opponents were trying to impose on his followers.
[4] The reference to church as Eve in conjunction with Christ may also have been prepared for by the reference to Christ as the "last Adam" in 1 Cor 15:45b.

be led astray" (*phtharē to noēmata hymōn*; 11:3). He used the noun *noēmata* (thoughts, minds) twice earlier in conjunction with the other apostles (3:14; 4:4) and once with Satan (2:11) who soon will be introduced as their mentor (11:14). On the other hand, *phtharē* is the subjunctive aorist passive of the verb *phtheirō* (destroy; corrupt; make rot; bring to naught) that occurred once to speak of the opponents' meddling activity in Corinth and the corresponding divine punishment (If any one destroys [*phtheirei*] God's temple, God will destroy [*phtheirei*] him; 1 Cor 3:17) and another time in defense of Paul's mission among the Corinthians (we have corrupted [*ephtheiramen*] no one; 2 Cor 7:2).

In 11:4 it becomes clear that the Christ spoken of in v.3 is not an ethereal Christ that remains one and the same under all circumstances; rather it is the Christ offered in the gospel preached by Paul and not by anyone else.[5] This equation between "Christ" and the Pauline "gospel" is a Pauline trademark (1 Cor 4:15; Rom 2:16; 2 Tim 2:8). Let us try to pinpoint which aspect of his gospel Paul is specifically alluding to in 2 Corinthians 11:3-4. First, in v.3, Paul speaks of thoughts led astray from "sincere devotion (*haplotētos*) to Christ"[6] instead of simply "Christ." This Greek noun *haplotētos* was used thrice earlier in the two chapters dealing with the monetary collection at table fellowship (8:2; 9:11, 13); the only other instance is in conjunction with Paul's behavior *as apostle* (1:12). Secondly, "spirit" as well as *noēmata* is a central term in chapters 3 and 4 where Paul discussed in detail his *diakonia*, his "ministry" of the

---

[5] The link to Galatians, which I pointed out in conjunction with Paul's "fear" (2 Cor 11:3), is transparent in the phrase "different gospel" that occurs elsewhere only in Galatians 1:6.

[6] *hagnotētos* (purity, pure devotion) is an addition corresponding to *hagnēn* (pure) in v.2.

one table fellowship, an essential feature of his gospel he defended in Antioch (Gal 2:11-14) and in Jerusalem (vv.1-10). Consequently, the sudden expansion of Christ (2 Cor 11:3) into the triad Christ-spirit-gospel (v.4) is not as unexpected as it seems at first hearing. On the other hand, it is the final term "gospel," *his* preaching to the Corinthians (v.7 and 1 Cor 15:1-2) which they have already accepted (2 Cor 11:4), that Paul is emphasizing as is evident in the phraseology of the following verses:

1. Paul is in no way lesser than the other apostles (v.5).

2. The phrase "in every way" (*en panti*) as well as the nouns "word" and "knowledge," and the verb "*phanerōsantes*" (make plain; reveal) (v.6) occurred earlier in conjunction with Paul's preaching the gospel.[7]

3. The ironic comparison between Paul and his addressees (v.7a) is a trademark of the Corinthian correspondence.

4. The rare double absolute "God's gospel" (*to tou theou evangelion*) in v.7b[8] is found elsewhere in conjunction with the collection (Rom 15:16), on the one hand, and the ill-intentioned malice of the opponents (1 Thess 2:2), on the other hand. The other two instances in the Pauline corpus occur in Paul's description of the voluntary and unnecessary sacrificial attitude he took while

---

[7] See 1 Cor 1:12; 3:4-6, 22; 9:4-6; 15:5-11; 2 Cor 3:12-18.
[8] By absolute I mean the inclusion of the definite article before each noun in Greek.

preaching the gospel, in order not to burden his "children" (vv.8 and 9). The closeness in mindset between 2 Corinthians 11 and 1 Thessalonians 2 is sealed through the root *bar—* (be heavy; use one's authority) in both cases (2 Cor 11:9; 1 Thess 2:7, 9).[9]

5. The reference to the gospel preaching as "ministry" (*diakonian*; 2 Cor 11:8)[10] has been a staple of 2 Corinthians.

6. Burdening others to lessen the Corinthians' burden in matter of the collection (11:9-10) pervaded chapters 8 and 9.

7. Finally, Paul's boasting regarding his being the sole apostle not only to Corinth, but also to the entire province of Achaia (11:10) has been on his mind all along in the Corinthian correspondence and is reflected in his greeting address at the start of each letter: "To the church of God which is at Corinth, to those sanctified in Christ Jesus, called to be saints together with all those who *in every place* call on the name of our Lord Jesus Christ, both their Lord and ours" (1 Cor 1:2); "To the church of God which is at Corinth, with all the saints who are *in the whole of Achaia*." (2 Cor 1:1b) Notice also how Paul brings in the "truth (of [concerning] Christ)" (11:10), a term that has been tantamount to the gospel preaching earlier in the letter (4:2; 6:7; 7:14).

---

[9] See my comments in *1 Thess* 89-90.
[10] RSV translates the original *diakonian* into "serve."

The passage culminates with the highly caustic frontal attack on his opponents (11:12-15) in terms of "ministry" at table fellowship (*diakonia*): "So it is not strange if his [Satan's] servants (*diakonoi*; ministers) also disguise themselves as servants (*diakonoi*; ministers) of righteousness. Their end will correspond to their deeds." (11:15) This confirms that the previous passage (vv.2-11) is essentially referring to the centrality of the oneness of table fellowship, a thought on Paul's mind throughout chapters 1-10, especially in chapters 3-6, and 8-9. Yet the way he goes about it here is unrivaled. Paul is actually accusing his opponents of promoting table fellowship with God's quintessential adversary, which is similar to telling the Corinthians that not abiding in the kind of table fellowship he taught them is tantamount to "having fellowship with demons" (1 Cor 10:20-21). Put otherwise, when it comes to table fellowship, Satan and the demons *function* as "gods," with whom one shares the cup and the table *just as* one does with the Lord himself:

> The cup of blessing which we bless, is it not a participation (*koinōnia*; fellowship) in the blood of Christ? The bread which we break, is it not a participation (*koinōnia*; fellowship) in the body of Christ? ... Consider the people of Israel; are not those who eat the sacrifices partners (*koinōnoi*; fellows) in the altar? What do I imply then? That food offered to idols is anything, or that an idol is anything? No, I imply that what pagans sacrifice they offer to demons and not to God. I do not want you to be partners (*koinōnous*; fellows) with demons. You cannot drink the cup of the Lord and the cup of demons. You cannot partake of the table of the Lord and the table of demons. (vv.16, 18-21)

Indeed, Satan earlier has been dubbed as no less than "*the god* (*ho theos*) of this world" in conjunction with blinding the minds of those who do not put their trust in Paul's gospel (2 Cor 4:4). Moreover, Satan's "designs" (*noēmata*; minds, thoughts, 2:11) aim at keeping the brother who was excised from the common table fellowship within Satan's realm (see 1 Cor 5:5a). This Paul could not allow (2 Cor 2:5-11) given that the punishment's ultimate goal was the brother's salvation (1 Cor 5:5b). By endorsing the attitude of not allowing their Jewish followers to sit at the same table as their Gentile counterparts (Gal 2:11-14), the minds (*noēmata*) of Paul's opponents were "hardened" (2 Cor 3:14) and "blinded" (4:4) and they became, by the same token, "ministers" of Satan, the sower of division,[11] and thus the one behind two tables instead of the one fellowship around the one Christ (Gal 3:16, 26-29). As for Paul, he is "foolish" enough to force upon his churches the implementation of the one table fellowship even in the absence of Jews. How? By asking the Corinthians to think of their Jerusalemite brethren and raise the collection for them which he promised to do (Gal 2:10). Paul is not about to allow any "pseudo-apostles" (*psevdapostoloi*; false apostles, 2 Cor 11:13) to transform his *ekklēsiai* (churches) into alternate *synagōgai* (synagogues)!

Vv. 16-20 ¹⁶ Πάλιν λέγω, μή τίς με δόξῃ ἄφρονα εἶναι· εἰ δὲ μή γε, κἂν ὡς ἄφρονα δέξασθέ με, ἵνα κἀγὼ μικρόν τι καυχήσωμαι. ¹⁷ ὃ λαλῶ, οὐ κατὰ κύριον λαλῶ ἀλλ' ὡς ἐν ἀφροσύνῃ, ἐν ταύτῃ τῇ ὑποστάσει τῆς καυχήσεως. ¹⁸ ἐπεὶ πολλοὶ καυχῶνται κατὰ σάρκα, κἀγὼ καυχήσομαι. ¹⁹ ἡδέως γὰρ ἀνέχεσθε τῶν ἀφρόνων φρόνιμοι ὄντες· ²⁰ ἀνέχεσθε γὰρ εἴ τις ὑμᾶς καταδουλοῖ, εἴ τις κατεσθίει, εἴ τις λαμβάνει, εἴ τις ἐπαίρεται, εἴ τις εἰς πρόσωπον ὑμᾶς δέρει.

> ¹⁶ *I repeat, let no one think me foolish; but even if you do, accept me as a fool, so that I too may boast a little.* ¹⁷*(What I am saying I say not with the Lord's authority but as a fool, in this*

---

[11] This is the literal meaning of the Greek *diabolos* (devil), the LXX rendering of the Hebrew *śaṭan* (Job 1-2). Actually the Hebrew *śaṭan* had the function of prosecutor in the divine council, which is precisely the role he plays in Job 1:6-11.

boastful confidence; ¹⁸since many boast of worldly things, I too will boast.) ¹⁹For you gladly bear with fools, being wise yourselves! ²⁰For you bear it if a man makes slaves of you, or preys upon you, or takes advantage of you, or puts on airs, or strikes you in the face.

In order to convey the "foolishness" of the Corinthians, Paul resorts to playing the role of buffoon or court jester (v.16), thus forcing them to hear with their own ears what those "false apostles" sound like in reality, that is, "glorying in the flesh of others" (Gal 6:13b). Right from the beginning he makes his intention clear: he is doing what he is doing not "with the Lord's authority" (*kata kyrion*; according to the Lord, 2 Cor 11:17) but he is boasting "the way humans do" (*kata sarka*; according to the flesh, v.18).[12] The irony reflected in v.18 is obviously aimed at dragging the Corinthians themselves into the picture; by allowing themselves to be "fooled" by "fools" they prove to be "fools" themselves in spite of their "appearing" wise. The attentive hearer will notice that this irony is reminiscent of the earlier, "We are fools for Christ's sake, but you are wise in Christ" (1 Cor 4:10a). However the context of this verse (10a) deals not so much with the manner of behaving as it does with the content of the preaching (vv.14-21). The same can be detected here where Paul is deftly attacking the teaching of his opponents, and not so much their attitude. Indeed, earlier Paul used the two verbs "accept (*dexasthe*)" (2 Cor 11:16) and "bear (*anekhesthe*)" (vv.19 and 20) specifically in conjunction with the gospel: "… or if you accept a different gospel from the one you

---

[12] By translating *kata sarka* into "of worldly things," RSV obscures the intended opposition between the manner, and thus will, of the Lord and that of humans. Paul is mimicking the boasting of his opponents who are merely "flesh and blood" (Gal 1:16-17).

accepted (*edexasthe*),[13] you submit to (*anekhesthe*; bear) it readily enough." (v.4c) Further, the verb "makes slaves" (*katadouloi*; enslaves fully, v.20) is found elsewhere in the New Testament only in Galatians 2:4 in conjunction with "false brethren": "But because of false brethren (*psevdadelphous*) secretly brought in, who slipped in to spy out our freedom which we have in Christ Jesus, that they *might bring* us *into bondage* (*katadoulōsousin*)—to them we did not yield submission even for a moment, that *the truth of the gospel* might be preserved for you." (vv.4-5) The link with Galatians can also be seen in that, after having referred to the opponents as "false apostles" (*psevdapostoloi*; 2 Cor 11:13), we hear later in the chapter of "false brethren" (*psevdadelphois*; v.26), which is the only other instance of that noun in the New Testament.

The following four verbs (v.20) are astutely chosen to describe the aim as well as the strategy of the opponents. The first one "preys upon" (*katesthiei*; eats completely; swallows up; devours) parallels in meaning and thus underscores the effect of the preceding (makes slaves). The verb *katesthiei* occurs only once more in the Pauline corpus in Galatians 5:15, again in conjunction with Paul's gospel as opposed to his opponents' teaching (5:13-15):

> For you were called to freedom, brethren; only do not use your freedom as an opportunity for the flesh, but through love be servants of one another. For the whole law is fulfilled in one word, "You shall love your neighbor as yourself." But if you bite and devour (*katesthiete*) one another take heed that you are not consumed by one another.

---

[13] The original has "accepted" only once. KJV reads "or another gospel, which ye have not accepted, ye might well bear with *him*".

It is worth noting that Mark and his successors, Luke and Matthew, correctly understood Paul's intention when they used that same verb in the parable of the sower in conjunction with the seed that fell along the path: "And as he sowed, some seed fell along the path, and the birds came and devoured (*katephagen*[14]) it." (Mk 4:4; Lk 8:5; Mt 13:4) Jesus' explanation describes perfectly the work of Satan as presented by Paul: "And these are the ones along the path, where the word is sown; *when they hear, Satan immediately comes and takes away (*airei*) the word which is sown in them*"; (Mk 4:15) "The ones along the path are those who have heard; *then the devil comes and takes away (*airei*) the word from their hearts, that they may not believe and be saved*" (Lk 8:12); "When any one hears the word of the kingdom and does not understand it, *the evil one comes and snatches away what is sown in his heart*; this is what was sown along the path." (Mt 13:19) Notice how Mark, followed by Luke, use the verb *airei* (takes away) that is from the same root as the verb *epairetai* (puts on airs), which is the fourth in the series of verbs used by Paul (2 Cor 11:20).

"Makes slaves" (*katadoulei*) and "preys upon" (*katesthiei*) are used to underscore doubly the opponents' action and its result. The following three verbs, when taken together, describe the opponents' strategy. First they "receive" (*lambanei*), that is to say, welcome the Corinthians so that they, in turn, would "receive" the "(false) spirit" that is being offered (v.20b). Put otherwise, the opponents' strategy is to show interest with the sole intention to be loved, or as RSV renders it, "[if a man] *takes advantage* (*lambanei*) *of you.*" Here again, one cannot miss that Galatians looms in the background: "They make much of you, but for no good purpose; they want to shut you out, that you

---

[14] This is the aorist tense of the verb *katesthiei*.

may make much of them" (4:17); "... they desire to have you circumcised that they may glory in your flesh." (6:13b) The second step is *epairetai* (lifts [you] up; exalt [you]), which RSV incorrectly renders as "puts on airs."[15] When one realizes that the third verb *derei* (strikes in the face) is found only once more in the Pauline corpus where it refers to an action taken by a pugilist (1 Cor 9:26b)[16]—again within a context where Paul is distancing himself as apostle from the other "apostles"—then it makes sense to understand the last three verbs (2 Cor 11:20) as a sequence of actions aiming at one result: as though in a boxing ring, the opponents first "lure" (*lambanei*) the Corinthians to draw near to them, then "lift up their faces" (*epairetai*) in order to "punch" (*derei*) them in those faces.

Vv. 21-33 ²¹ κατὰ ἀτιμίαν λέγω, ὡς ὅτι ἡμεῖς ἠσθενήκαμεν. Ἐν ᾧ δ' ἄν τις τολμᾷ, ἐν ἀφροσύνῃ λέγω, τολμῶ κἀγώ. ²² Ἑβραῖοί εἰσιν; κἀγώ. Ἰσραηλῖταί εἰσιν; κἀγώ. σπέρμα Ἀβραάμ εἰσιν; κἀγώ. ²³ διάκονοι Χριστοῦ εἰσιν; παραφρονῶν λαλῶ, ὑπὲρ ἐγώ· ἐν κόποις περισσοτέρως, ἐν φυλακαῖς περισσοτέρως, ἐν πληγαῖς ὑπερβαλλόντως, ἐν θανάτοις πολλάκις. ²⁴ Ὑπὸ Ἰουδαίων πεντάκις τεσσεράκοντα παρὰ μίαν ἔλαβον, ²⁵ τρὶς ἐρραβδίσθην, ἅπαξ ἐλιθάσθην, τρὶς ἐναυάγησα, νυχθήμερον ἐν τῷ βυθῷ πεποίηκα· ²⁶ ὁδοιπορίαις πολλάκις, κινδύνοις ποταμῶν, κινδύνοις λῃστῶν, κινδύνοις ἐκ γένους, κινδύνοις ἐξ ἐθνῶν, κινδύνοις ἐν πόλει, κινδύνοις ἐν ἐρημίᾳ, κινδύνοις ἐν θαλάσσῃ, κινδύνοις ἐν ψευδαδέλφοις, ²⁷ κόπῳ καὶ μόχθῳ, ἐν ἀγρυπνίαις πολλάκις, ἐν λιμῷ καὶ δίψει, ἐν νηστείαις πολλάκις, ἐν ψύχει καὶ γυμνότητι· ²⁸ χωρὶς τῶν παρεκτὸς ἡ ἐπίστασίς μοι ἡ καθ' ἡμέραν, ἡ μέριμνα πασῶν τῶν ἐκκλησιῶν. ²⁹ τίς ἀσθενεῖ καὶ οὐκ ἀσθενῶ; τίς

---

[15] *epairetai* is to be taken as middle—and not passive—voice since the other four verbs are in the active voice and transitive, having "you" as the object complement. The middle voice reflects an action done to someone else but whose benefit the doer reaps, as when one does *to* another something *for* oneself.

[16] See my comments on that verse in *C-1Cor* 171.

σκανδαλίζεται καὶ οὐκ ἐγὼ πυροῦμαι; ³⁰ Εἰ καυχᾶσθαι δεῖ, τὰ τῆς ἀσθενείας μου καυχήσομαι. ³¹ ὁ θεὸς καὶ πατὴρ τοῦ κυρίου Ἰησοῦ οἶδεν, ὁ ὢν εὐλογητὸς εἰς τοὺς αἰῶνας, ὅτι οὐ ψεύδομαι. ³² ἐν Δαμασκῷ ὁ ἐθνάρχης Ἀρέτα τοῦ βασιλέως ἐφρούρει τὴν πόλιν Δαμασκηνῶν πιάσαι με, ³³ καὶ διὰ θυρίδος ἐν σαργάνῃ ἐχαλάσθην διὰ τοῦ τείχους καὶ ἐξέφυγον τὰς χεῖρας αὐτοῦ.

²¹To my shame, I must say, we were too weak for that! But whatever any one dares to boast of—I am speaking as a fool—I also dare to boast of that. ²²Are they Hebrews? So am I. Are they Israelites? So am I. Are they descendants of Abraham? So am I. ²³Are they servants of Christ? I am a better one—I am talking like a madman—with far greater labors, far more imprisonments, with countless beatings, and often near death. ²⁴Five times I have received at the hands of the Jews the forty lashes less one. ²⁵Three times I have been beaten with rods; once I was stoned. Three times I have been shipwrecked; a night and a day I have been adrift at sea; ²⁶on frequent journeys, in danger from rivers, danger from robbers, danger from my own people, danger from Gentiles, danger in the city, danger in the wilderness, danger at sea, danger from false brethren; ²⁷in toil and hardship, through many a sleepless night, in hunger and thirst, often without food, in cold and exposure. ²⁸And, apart from other things, there is the daily pressure upon me of my anxiety for all the churches. ²⁹Who is weak, and I am not weak? Who is made to fall, and I am not indignant? ³⁰If I must boast, I will boast of the things that show my weakness. ³¹The God and Father of the Lord Jesus, he who is blessed for ever, knows that I do not lie. ³²At Damascus, the governor under King Aretas guarded the city of Damascus in order to seize me ³³but I was let down in a basket through a window in the wall, and escaped his hands.

In v.21a Paul pushes the irony to the extreme by saying that, to his own shame, he was too weak to do what the others did. By mentioning his own weakness, Paul is preparing for chapter 13 where, in spite of his perceived weakness, he will show the Corinthians what true power is all about (vv.1-4). For the time being, though, he will proceed on the path he started on: dare to boast in spite of the foolishness of the enterprise (11:21b).

He begins by emphatically stating that as a Hebrew and an Israelite he is as much Abraham's progeny as the "others" are (v.22); in other words, he is, as much as they are, a "Jewish leader" who is "entrusted with the oracles of God" (Rom 3:2). Still, when it comes to being "ministers" (*diakonoi*; RSV servants) concerning Christ he surpasses them all (2 Cor 11:23a) in that his preaching brought the "rule" of those "oracles of God" (scriptures) into the realm of the Gentiles throughout the Roman empire where the "others" did not dare to tread.[17] The description of this activity (vv.23b-27) follows a literary structure similar to that used earlier in 6:4b-10 to speak of the same "ministry": "We put no obstacle in any one's way, so that no fault may be found with our ministry (*diakonia*), but as servants (*diakonoi*; ministers) of God we commend ourselves in every way." (vv.3-4a) After a foursome of elements (2 Cor 11:23b) reflecting the universality of the Gentile realm, he adds a fifth pertaining specifically to the Jews: "Five times I have received at the hands of the Jews the forty lashes less one." (v.24) Upon hearing the last of the *five* elements, which begins—in the Greek—with the words "Jews" and "five times" (*pentakis*) one cannot miss Paul's intention. In a literarily compact tour de force, he reminds his hearers of the thesis he developed in

---

[17] See earlier my detailed comments on "ministry" (*diakonia*) in chapters 3 and 4, and on "rule" (*kanōn*) in 10:13-16.

chapter 3: in spite of hindrances by the Jews and recalcitrance by the Gentiles, he succeeded in his churches to seat both at the same table, under one roof, in order to listen to the *one* scripture of God whose quintessential expression is found in the Torah, the five books of Moses.

The following four items, again reflecting universality, are in turn subdivided into two sets of three plus one, underscoring again the numeral four (v.25): the not-only-three-but-four pattern is found often in wisdom literature (e.g., Prov 30:15, 18, 21, 29). The subdivision into two sets can be seen in that the first two elements describe hazards on land whereas the last two, at sea. In the following verse (2 Cor 11:26) we hear of eight (four doubled for underscoring) kinds of "dangers"[18] in conjunction with Paul's *apostolic* "journeys."[19] That this term functions as an introduction is evident in the phrase "on journeys often" (*odoiporiais pollakis*)[20] that is a far cry from the similar structure of the following eight phrases each of which begins with the same word "dangers" (*kindoinois*; RSV danger). Listening more carefully to the eight dangers the hearer will notice that the fourth is linked to "Gentiles" (nations) while the eighth, to "false brethren," resulting in the impression that the dangers were caused by "Jews as well as Gentiles." Actually the intentionality of such can be detected in each of the two sets of four; the third (my own people) and fourth (Gentiles) elements, on the one hand, and the seventh ([Roman] sea) and eighth (false brethren), on the other hand, also amount to the Pauline "Jews as well as Gentiles."

---

[18] RSV uses the singular "danger" for the original plural *kindynois*. KJV has "perils."
[19] The other two occurrences of the root *odoipor*— in the New Testament (Jn 4:6; Acts 10:9) confirm my understanding.
[20] RSV has "in frequent journeys." The original *pollakis* is an adverb. KJV reads "*In journeyings often.*"

Chapter 11

The last set is magisterially composed to sound as a recapitulation, both formally and materially, of all the preceding. Formally, it is composed of eight elements structured into five parts: "in toil and hardship, through many a sleepless night (often [*pollakis*] in sleepless night), in hunger and thirst, often (*pollakis*) without food, in cold and exposure." (v.27) Materially, its first term "toil" (*kopō*) recalls that of the entire passage "labors" (*kopois*; v.23b), which is from the root *kop(i)*— that Paul uses profusely to refer to his *apostolic* effort; furthermore, the adverb "often" (*pollakis*) that anchors v.27 recalls the beginning of v.26. Then Paul wraps up the costs linked to his "ministry" with the most important aspect of that ministry, that is, the *daily* care for all his Gentile churches (v.28) as a father or a mother would care for his or her children (1 Cor 4:14; Gal 4:19; 1 Thess 2:7, 11): "Who is weak, and I am not weak? Who is made to fall, and I am not indignant?" (2 Cor 11:29).

The mention again of "weakness" prepares for chapter 12 where Paul will expand on boasting of his own weakness (11:30). For the time being, he just gives a small example of how he was belittled from the outset in Damascus, the city where his apostolic mission started (Gal 1:17). Paul's statement concerning his experience in Damascus (2 Cor 11:32-33) plays on two levels. The first level concerns King Aretas' kingdom of Arabia. When these verses are heard in conjunction with Galatians 1:17 (nor did I go up to Jerusalem to those who were apostles before me, but I went away into Arabia; and again I returned to Damascus), the impact on the hearer is the following: not only all the efforts to contain Paul within Damascus—a temporary conquest of Aretas—were futile, but also upon his escape he went to Arabia, Aretas' heartland, and preached the gospel there unhindered for no less than three years! In other words, just as in the case of the Romans, Paul ended up spreading his teaching throughout their empire. The indirect reference to the Roman empire can be detected in the term "governor" whose Greek original *ethnarkhos* (ethnarch) is made up of the root *ethn*— whence *ethnē* (nations, Gentiles) and the root *arkh*— whence *arkhe* (authority) and *arkhontes* (rulers), which is how Paul referred earlier to the Roman authorities (1 Cor 2:6, 8). Add to this that Aretas was a client of the Romans. The second level relates to the scriptural story of the conquest of Jericho as is evident from the phrasing of Paul's escape: "but I was let down in a basket through a window in the wall, and escaped his hands" (2 Cor 11:33); "Then she let them down by a rope through the window, for her house was built into the city wall, so that she dwelt in the wall." (Josh 2:15)[21] Just as Joshua was granted to settle in the land God promised to the forefathers, so also Paul was granted to plant the seed of the gospel not only in Damascus and Arabia, but also throughout the Roman empire. The reference to the Book of Joshua was prepared for by the otherwise unwarranted, "The God and Father of the Lord Jesus, he who is blessed for ever, knows that I do not lie" (2 Cor 11:31); the Greek *Iēsous* (Jesus) is the LXX rendering of the Hebrew *yehošuaʿ* (Joshua).

---

[21] The Greek for rope, *sarganē*, indicates a basket woven out of heavy rope.

Chapter 12

Vv. 1-6 ¹Καυχᾶσθαι δεῖ, οὐ συμφέρον μέν, ἐλεύσομαι δὲ εἰς ὀπτασίας καὶ ἀποκαλύψεις κυρίου. ² οἶδα ἄνθρωπον ἐν Χριστῷ πρὸ ἐτῶν δεκατεσσάρων, εἴτε ἐν σώματι οὐκ οἶδα, εἴτε ἐκτὸς τοῦ σώματος οὐκ οἶδα, ὁ θεὸς οἶδεν, ἁρπαγέντα τὸν τοιοῦτον ἕως τρίτου οὐρανοῦ. ³ καὶ οἶδα τὸν τοιοῦτον ἄνθρωπον, εἴτε ἐν σώματι εἴτε χωρὶς τοῦ σώματος οὐκ οἶδα, ὁ θεὸς οἶδεν, ⁴ὅτι ἡρπάγη εἰς τὸν παράδεισον καὶ ἤκουσεν ἄρρητα ῥήματα ἃ οὐκ ἐξὸν ἀνθρώπῳ λαλῆσαι. ⁵ὑπὲρ τοῦ τοιούτου καυχήσομαι, ὑπὲρ δὲ ἐμαυτοῦ οὐ καυχήσομαι εἰ μὴ ἐν ταῖς ἀσθενείαις. ⁶ Ἐὰν γὰρ θελήσω καυχήσασθαι, οὐκ ἔσομαι ἄφρων, ἀλήθειαν γὰρ ἐρῶ· φείδομαι δέ, μή τις εἰς ἐμὲ λογίσηται ὑπὲρ ὃ βλέπει με ἢ ἀκούει [τι] ἐξ ἐμοῦ

> ¹*I must boast; there is nothing to be gained by it, but I will go on to visions and revelations of the Lord.* ²*I know a man in Christ who fourteen years ago was caught up to the third heaven—whether in the body or out of the body I do not know, God knows.* ³*And I know that this man was caught up into Paradise—whether in the body or out of the body I do not know, God knows—*⁴*and he heard things that cannot be told, which man may not utter.* ⁵*On behalf of this man I will boast, but on my own behalf I will not boast, except of my weaknesses.* ⁶*Though if I wish to boast, I shall not be a fool, for I shall be speaking the truth. But I refrain from it, so that no one may think more of me than he sees in me or hears from me.*

Chapter 12:1-6 reprises 11:30-33 from another perspective. The aim of both passages is to say that Paul boasts solely of his weakness. In the first case (11:30), the boasting is putative (*If I must boast*), whereas in 12:1 Paul asserts that he "*must* boast"—and he does boast—in order to show the foolishness of doing so. Consequently, in the second case, the actual boasting is ironical and thus functional; that is why it is cast in an extreme fashion. Paul's intent is to underscore that pure boasting of one's assumed importance (11:22) is of no value if one is not doing what one is supposed to do. The sole scale to assess this is to weigh it against the "common good" (*sympheron*; 12:1), as is also the case concerning the different spiritual gifts, including that of apostleship (1 Cor 12:7).[1] Paul is about to demonstrate that "visions and revelations" even "of (from) the Lord" (2 Cor 12:1b) are in vain if they do not accomplish their purpose, which is to share their content with others unto their edification. That is why, if the one who is privy to visions and revelations hears "things that *cannot be told*, which man *may not utter*" (v.4), then what is their use? He would simply be like "a noisy gong or a clanging cymbal" (1 Cor 13:1), "no one understands him, but he utters mysteries in the Spirit" (14:2b), for "If even lifeless instruments, such as the flute or the harp, do not give distinct notes, how will any one know what is played? And if the bugle gives an indistinct sound, who will get ready for battle?" (vv:7-8) All a person privy to such visions and revelations would be doing is merely uttering "speech that is not intelligible" and "speaking into the air" (v.9) without any "upbuilding (*oikodomēn*) and encouragement and consolation" (v.3). In actuality, he would be implementing *kathairesin* (tearing down, destroying) instead of *oikodomēn* (building up) (2 Cor 10:8; 13:10). In other words, he would be just like Paul *before* the "revelation of Jesus Christ" to him (Gal 1:12b): "For you have heard of my former life in Judaism, how I persecuted the church of God violently and tried to destroy it." (v.13; see also v.23). In that precisely lies the irony! The apostle is called from (the God who is in) heaven not in order to remain there "speaking the tongue of angels" (1 Cor 13:1a), but he is called to communicate, as a true "angel"

---

[1] See also my comments on 1 Cor 6:12; 10:23 (in *C-1Cor*); and 2 Cor 8:10, where we have the verb *sympherei*.

(*angelos*; messenger), the divine message through "five words with [his] mind, in order to instruct *others*" (14:19). Even if the hearer at first does not connect 2 Corinthians 12 and Galatians 1, he will do so one chapter later when he is hit with the only other instance of "fourteen years" in the entire Bible (Gal 2:1) immediately after the only other reference to Damascus (1:17) in the Pauline corpus besides that in 2 Corinthians 11:32. The hearer then will readily understand that in 12:1a-4 Paul is ironically referring to those "reputed to be pillars" (Gal 2:9). Unlike them (2 Cor 12:5a), he "will not boast, except of my weaknesses" (v.5b).

Vv. 7-10 ⁷ καὶ τῇ ὑπερβολῇ τῶν ἀποκαλύψεων. διὸ ἵνα μὴ ὑπεραίρωμαι, ἐδόθη μοι σκόλοψ τῇ σαρκί, ἄγγελος σατανᾶ, ἵνα με κολαφίζῃ, ἵνα μὴ ὑπεραίρωμαι. ⁸ ὑπὲρ τούτου τρὶς τὸν κύριον παρεκάλεσα ἵνα ἀποστῇ ἀπ' ἐμοῦ. ⁹ καὶ εἴρηκέν μοι· ἀρκεῖ σοι ἡ χάρις μου, ἡ γὰρ δύναμις ἐν ἀσθενείᾳ τελεῖται. ἥδιστα οὖν μᾶλλον καυχήσομαι ἐν ταῖς ἀσθενείαις μου, ἵνα ἐπισκηνώσῃ ἐπ' ἐμὲ ἡ δύναμις τοῦ Χριστοῦ. ¹⁰ διὸ εὐδοκῶ ἐν ἀσθενείαις, ἐν ὕβρεσιν, ἐν ἀνάγκαις, ἐν διωγμοῖς καὶ στενοχωρίαις, ὑπὲρ Χριστοῦ· ὅταν γὰρ ἀσθενῶ, τότε δυνατός εἰμι.

> ⁷*And to keep me from being too elated by the abundance of revelations, a thorn was given me in the flesh, a messenger of Satan, to harass me, to keep me from being too elated.* ⁸*Three times I besought the Lord about this, that it should leave me;* ⁹*but he said to me, "My grace is sufficient for you, for my power is made perfect in weakness." I will all the more gladly boast of my weaknesses, that the power of Christ may rest upon me.* ¹⁰*For the sake of Christ, then, I am content with weaknesses, insults, hardships, persecutions, and calamities; for when I am weak, then I am strong.*

Indeed Paul was not given much chance to be "too elated (*hyperairōmai*) by the abundance of revelations" (v.7a), let alone a chance to enjoy them, since "a thorn was given me in the flesh, a messenger of Satan, to harass me, to keep me from being too elated (*hyperairōmai*)" (v.7b). On the one hand, one can detect here an indirect blow against the opponents who were described earlier as someone who "puts on airs" (*epairetai*; elates others for his own benefit, 11:20). On the other hand and more importantly, the only other instance of the verb *hyperairōmai* in the New Testament describes the attitude of the "man of lawlessness" who commits the ultimate blasphemy in that he "opposes and exalts himself (*hyperairomenos*) against every so-called god or object of worship, so that he takes his seat in the temple of God, proclaiming himself to be God" (2 Thess 2:4). It is then no wonder that the thorn implanted by God in Paul's flesh is to remind him that, should he, Paul, fall in the trap of self-aggrandizement, he would become the "minister of Satan" (2 Cor 11:15) who is none else but the "angel (*angelon*; messenger) of light" (v.14). Consequently, the function of the "angel (*angelos*; messenger) of Satan" *assigned by God himself* is to stop Paul from becoming a "messenger and minister of Satan" instead of being the "apostle—and thus messenger—of God." The link with Galatians is again evident when, two chapters later in the scriptural canon, one hears: "But even if we, or *an angel from heaven*, should preach to you a gospel contrary to that which we preached to you, let him be accursed." (1:8)

So painful was the thorn that Paul prayed plentifully (three times) that it be taken away (2 Cor 12:8). However, should God have hearkened to Paul's request, then Paul would have run the risk of becoming "elated." So God kept up the pressure so that everyone, including Paul himself, would realize that "My grace is sufficient for you, for my power *is made perfect* (*teleitai*; reaches its scope) in weakness" (v.9a). Paul, fortunately, understood the lesson of God's "turning the deaf ear" to him: "I will all the more gladly boast of my weaknesses, that the power of Christ may rest (*episkēnōsē*; cover as a tent would) upon me." (v.9b). The verb *episkēnoō*, unique in the entire Bible, has been purposely coined by Paul to draw the hearers' attention to the two earlier instances of "tent" (*skēnos*; 5:1, 4), also unique in the New Testament.[2] The scriptural God does not abide in "glorious" stone buildings, but rather encounters his own in the "tent of meeting." Paul *as tentmaker* is God's Apostle: "… because he [Paul] was of the same trade he stayed with them [Aquila and Priscilla], and they worked, for by trade they were tentmakers." (Acts 18:3) Given that the only valid icon of the scriptural God, the (five books of the) Torah, is *aural* and not visual, Paul's "weakness" here is expressed in five elements: weaknesses, insults, hardships, persecutions, and calamities (2 Cor 12:10). Finally, given that the entire passage is dealing with Paul's apostolic activity in contradistinction to that of his colleagues, it is safe to surmise that the "thorn" is a metaphor for the continual "hindrance" by these colleagues to Paul's "ministry" among the Gentiles. Those colleagues are hindering Paul's final aim at establishing one table fellowship between Jews and Gentiles around the words of God's law, the "bread of life." Even though that hindrance is the handicraft of the "superlative apostles" (11:5; 12:11), it, just like the "thorn," is ultimately ascribed elsewhere to Satan:

> For you, brethren, became imitators of the churches of God in Christ Jesus which are in Judea; for you suffered the same things from your own countrymen as they did from the Jews, who killed both the Lord Jesus and the prophets, and drove us out, and displease God and oppose all men by hindering us from speaking

---

[2] Usually it is *skēnē* that is used.

to the Gentiles that they may be saved—so as always to fill up the measure of their sins. But God's wrath has come upon them at last! But since we were bereft of you, brethren, for a short time, in person not in heart, we endeavored the more eagerly and with great desire to see you face to face; because we wanted to come to you—I, Paul, again and again—but Satan hindered us. (1 Thess 2:14-18)

Vv. 11-21 ¹¹Γέγονα ἄφρων, ὑμεῖς με ἠναγκάσατε. ἐγὼ γὰρ ὤφειλον ὑφ' ὑμῶν συνίστασθαι· οὐδὲν γὰρ ὑστέρησα τῶν ὑπερλίαν ἀποστόλων εἰ καὶ οὐδέν εἰμι. ¹² τὰ μὲν σημεῖα τοῦ ἀποστόλου κατειργάσθη ἐν ὑμῖν ἐν πάσῃ ὑπομονῇ, σημείοις τε καὶ τέρασιν καὶ δυνάμεσιν. ¹³τί γάρ ἐστιν ὃ ἡσσώθητε ὑπὲρ τὰς λοιπὰς ἐκκλησίας, εἰ μὴ ὅτι αὐτὸς ἐγὼ οὐ κατενάρκησα ὑμῶν; χαρίσασθέ μοι τὴν ἀδικίαν ταύτην. ¹⁴ Ἰδοὺ τρίτον τοῦτο ἑτοίμως ἔχω ἐλθεῖν πρὸς ὑμᾶς, καὶ οὐ καταναρκήσω· οὐ γὰρ ζητῶ τὰ ὑμῶν ἀλλὰ ὑμᾶς. οὐ γὰρ ὀφείλει τὰ τέκνα τοῖς γονεῦσιν θησαυρίζειν ἀλλὰ οἱ γονεῖς τοῖς τέκνοις. ¹⁵ ἐγὼ δὲ ἥδιστα δαπανήσω καὶ ἐκδαπανηθήσομαι ὑπὲρ τῶν ψυχῶν ὑμῶν. εἰ περισσοτέρως ὑμᾶς ἀγαπῶ[ν], ἧσσον ἀγαπῶμαι; ¹⁶ Ἔστω δέ, ἐγὼ οὐ κατεβάρησα ὑμᾶς· ἀλλὰ ὑπάρχων πανοῦργος δόλῳ ὑμᾶς ἔλαβον. ¹⁷ μή τινα ὧν ἀπέσταλκα πρὸς ὑμᾶς, δι' αὐτοῦ ἐπλεονέκτησα ὑμᾶς; ¹⁸ παρεκάλεσα Τίτον καὶ συναπέστειλα τὸν ἀδελφόν· μήτι ἐπλεονέκτησεν ὑμᾶς Τίτος; οὐ τῷ αὐτῷ πνεύματι περιεπατήσαμεν; οὐ τοῖς αὐτοῖς ἴχνεσιν; ¹⁹Πάλαι δοκεῖτε ὅτι ὑμῖν ἀπολογούμεθα. κατέναντι θεοῦ ἐν Χριστῷ λαλοῦμεν· τὰ δὲ πάντα, ἀγαπητοί, ὑπὲρ τῆς ὑμῶν οἰκοδομῆς. ²⁰ φοβοῦμαι γὰρ μή πως ἐλθὼν οὐχ οἵους θέλω εὕρω ὑμᾶς κἀγὼ εὑρεθῶ ὑμῖν οἷον οὐ θέλετε· μή πως ἔρις, ζῆλος, θυμοί, ἐριθεῖαι, καταλαλιαί, ψιθυρισμοί, φυσιώσεις, ἀκαταστασίαι· ²¹μὴ πάλιν ἐλθόντος μου ταπεινώσῃ με ὁ θεός μου πρὸς ὑμᾶς καὶ πενθήσω πολλοὺς τῶν προημαρτηκότων καὶ μὴ μετανοησάντων ἐπὶ τῇ ἀκαθαρσίᾳ καὶ πορνείᾳ καὶ ἀσελγείᾳ ᾗ ἔπραξαν.

¹¹*I have been a fool! You forced me to it, for I ought to have been commended by you. For I was not at all inferior to these*

superlative apostles, even though I am nothing. ¹²*The signs of a true apostle were performed among you in all patience, with signs and wonders and mighty works.* ¹³*For in what were you less favored than the rest of the churches, except that I myself did not burden you? Forgive me this wrong!* ¹⁴*Here for the third time I am ready to come to you. And I will not be a burden, for I seek not what is yours but you; for children ought not to lay up for their parents, but parents for their children.* ¹⁵*I will most gladly spend and be spent for your souls. If I love you the more, am I to be loved the less?* ¹⁶*But granting that I myself did not burden you, I was crafty, you say, and got the better of you by guile.* ¹⁷*Did I take advantage of you through any of those whom I sent to you?* ¹⁸*I urged Titus to go, and sent the brother with him. Did Titus take advantage of you? Did we not act in the same spirit? Did we not take the same steps?* ¹⁹*Have you been thinking all along that we have been defending ourselves before you? It is in the sight of God that we have been speaking in Christ, and all for your upbuilding, beloved.* ²⁰*For I fear that perhaps I may come and find you not what I wish, and that you may find me not what you wish; that perhaps there may be quarreling, jealousy, anger, selfishness, slander, gossip, conceit, and disorder.* ²¹*I fear that when I come again my God may humble me before you, and I may have to mourn over many of those who sinned before and have not repented of the impurity, immorality, and licentiousness which they have practiced.*

If Paul went the path of foolishness, it is because he was forced to by the Corinthians themselves who should have known better since, even if his worth were nothing, *he*—and not the superlative apostles—is still *their* apostle (2 Cor 12:11; see also 3:1-3 and 1 Cor 9:1-2). The "signs" of his apostleship were "fully implemented" (*kateirgasthē*; performed) among them as "signs, wonders and mighty works" (2 Cor 12:12). These three elements reflect the fullness of divine intervention. Yet, Paul deftly throws in "in all patience" as a caveat so that the Corinthians not assume that "all is well." In the following verses he is going to make them feel the pressure of the *still* coming judgment through his own impending "face to face" visit (10:1b). He begins by resorting again to consummate irony (12:13), only to introduce his coming to them for "the third time" (v.14a), which hints at final judgment as will become clear a few verses later: "This is the third time I am coming to you ... I warned those who sinned before and all the others, and I warn them now while absent, as I did when present on my second visit, that if I come again I will not spare them." (13:1a, 2) However, as he did earlier (1 Cor 4:14-21), Paul is giving them an extra chance, as a father would give to his children, with the hope that they understand that the reason behind all his actions is his love for them (2 Cor 12:14b-15; see also 11:11). Yet, he still fears his intention would be misunderstood as being craftiness on his part (12:16). Such is clearly a literary device used as an exhortation in conjunction with the gospel message. The phraseology of guile and taking advantage, together with burdening others with one's weight (of seniority), and the metaphor of parental care toward one's children, is found also in 1Thessalonians:

> Here for the third time I am ready to come to you. And I will not be a burden (*katanarkēsō*), for I seek not what is yours but you; for children ought not to lay up for their parents, but parents for their children. I will most gladly spend and be spent for your souls. If I love you the more, am I to be loved the less? But granting that I myself did not burden you (*katebarēsa*), I was crafty, you say, and got the better of you by guile (*dolō*). Did I take advantage (*epleonektēsa*) of you through any of those whom I sent to you? I urged (*parekalesa*: appealed to) Titus to go, and sent the brother

with him. Did Titus take advantage (*epleonektēsen*) of you? (2 Cor 12:14-18)

> For our appeal (*paraklēsis*) does not spring from error or uncleanness, nor is it made with guile (*dolō*); but just as we have been approved by God to be entrusted with the gospel, so we speak, not to please men, but to please God who tests our hearts. For we never used either words of flattery, as you know, or a cloak for greed (*pleoneksias*; taking advantage), as God is witness; nor did we seek glory from men, whether from you or from others, though we might have made demands (*en barei einai*; shown our weight) as apostles of Christ. But we were gentle among you, like a nurse taking care of her children. So, being affectionately desirous of you, we were ready to share with you not only the gospel of God but also our own selves, because you had become very dear to us. For you remember our labor and toil, brethren; we worked night and day, that we might not burden (*epibarēsai*) any of you, while we preached to you the gospel of God. You are witnesses, and God also, how holy and righteous and blameless was our behavior to you believers; for you know how, like a father with his children, we exhorted (*parakalountes*; appealed to) each one of you and encouraged you and charged you to lead a life worthy of God, who calls you into his own kingdom and glory. (1 Thess 2:3-12)

Still, in spite of being a literary device, when heard within the context of this letter 2 Corinthians 12:16 sounds clearly as another attack against the opponents who are meddling in the affairs of the church of Corinth with the aim of troubling (Gal 1:7; 5:10) the Corinthians and stirring them up against Paul. Besides having defended himself regarding craftiness (*panourgos*) in guile (*dolō*) early in the letter (we refuse to practice cunning [*panourgia*; craftiness] or to tamper [*dolountes*] with God's word; 2 Cor 4:2), Paul has just accused the "superlative apostles" (11:5) of following the example of their master Satan (11:1-10) in his cunning (*panourgia*; v.3). However, what he is doing here is going a step further. Knowing that he is bound to die at some point, he is "anointing" his helpers as the true leaders in Corinth after him (12:17-18) as he did in 1 Corinthians 16.[3] At this juncture, Paul expresses the same fear (*phoboumai*; I fear, 2 Cor 12:20)[4] as he did in 11:3 (*phoboumai*; I am afraid) in conjunction with the possibility that the Corinthians would succumb to the cunning of the "adversary." That is why he ups the pressure here by saying openly that he is not at all defending himself before them (12:19a), for why should a father do so before his children (14b)? Rather what he is doing, and has been doing all along, is for their "upbuilding" (v.19) in order to save them from being "torn down" (13:10; see also 10:8), as they will be, should he, at his coming, find them proceeding in their destructive ways (12:20). Here Paul expands the four aforementioned items, "quarreling" (*eris*), "jealousy" (*zēlos*)[5], "conceit" (*phisiōseis*),[6] and "disorder" (*akatastasiai*),[7] into a list of eight (quarreling, jealousy, anger, selfishness, slander, gossip, conceit, and disorder). Such doubling is a sign of underscoring: in this case, stressing that the Corinthians are committing doubly all "possible" sins that one can commit.[8] The following three terms, "impurity, immorality, and licentiousness," are precisely those that head the series "works of the flesh" in Gal 5:19; practitioners of such "shall not inherit the kingdom of God" (v.21). The close link between the two passages is evident in that (1) Paul uses the verb *prassō* (practice, do) to speak of the action

---

[3] See also Phil 2:19-30; Col 4:7-14.
[4] I did not include the "I fear" in v.21 because it does not appear in the original. RSV added it to make the reading smoother.
[5] See 1 Cor 3:3 (jealousy [*zēlos*] and strife [*eris*]) as well as 1:11 (quarreling [*erides*, plural of *eris*]).
[6] See 1 Cor 4:6 and 8:1.
[7] See 1 Cor 14:33.
[8] The numeral four reflects universality.

related to those sins, and (2) it is only in these two instances that we find the couple "I warn, I warned"[9] (2 Cor 13:2; Gal 5:21) in the entire New Testament. In the hope that he is right in assuming that the Corinthians still consider themselves his children, Paul administers the ultimate blow—the *coup de grâce*. Should they persist in sinning without repenting, it is not they, but actually their father who will be demeaned by God for not having accomplished the mission to which he was assigned. Instead of proving to be his "glory, crown, and joy" (Phil 4:1; 1 Thess 2:19-20; see also 2 Cor 9:2), they will be the cause of his "shaming" by God for all to see! And if so, they will have to bear *their* shame for having done so to their father who both brought them to life and brought them true life.

---

[9] For "warned" Gal has the aorist *proeipon* whereas 2 Cor has the perfect *proeirēka*.

Chapter 13

Vv. 1-10 ¹Τρίτον τοῦτο ἔρχομαι πρὸς ὑμᾶς· ἐπὶ στόματος δύο μαρτύρων καὶ τριῶν σταθήσεται πᾶν ῥῆμα. ² προείρηκα καὶ προλέγω, ὡς παρὼν τὸ δεύτερον καὶ ἀπὼν νῦν, τοῖς προημαρτηκόσιν καὶ τοῖς λοιποῖς πᾶσιν, ὅτι ἐὰν ἔλθω εἰς τὸ πάλιν οὐ φείσομαι, ³ ἐπεὶ δοκιμὴν ζητεῖτε τοῦ ἐν ἐμοὶ λαλοῦντος Χριστοῦ, ὃς εἰς ὑμᾶς οὐκ ἀσθενεῖ ἀλλὰ δυνατεῖ ἐν ὑμῖν. ⁴ καὶ γὰρ ἐσταυρώθη ἐξ ἀσθενείας, ἀλλὰ ζῇ ἐκ δυνάμεως θεοῦ. καὶ γὰρ ἡμεῖς ἀσθενοῦμεν ἐν αὐτῷ, ἀλλὰ ζήσομεν σὺν αὐτῷ ἐκ δυνάμεως θεοῦ εἰς ὑμᾶς. ⁵ Ἑαυτοὺς πειράζετε εἰ ἐστὲ ἐν τῇ πίστει, ἑαυτοὺς δοκιμάζετε· ἢ οὐκ ἐπιγινώσκετε ἑαυτοὺς ὅτι Ἰησοῦς Χριστὸς ἐν ὑμῖν; εἰ μήτι ἀδόκιμοί ἐστε. ⁶ ἐλπίζω δὲ ὅτι γνώσεσθε ὅτι ἡμεῖς οὐκ ἐσμὲν ἀδόκιμοι. ⁷ εὐχόμεθα δὲ πρὸς τὸν θεὸν μὴ ποιῆσαι ὑμᾶς κακὸν μηδέν, οὐχ ἵνα ἡμεῖς δόκιμοι φανῶμεν, ἀλλ᾿ ἵνα ὑμεῖς τὸ καλὸν ποιῆτε, ἡμεῖς δὲ ὡς ἀδόκιμοι ὦμεν. ⁸ οὐ γὰρ δυνάμεθά τι κατὰ τῆς ἀληθείας ἀλλὰ ὑπὲρ τῆς ἀληθείας. ⁹ χαίρομεν γὰρ ὅταν ἡμεῖς ἀσθενῶμεν, ὑμεῖς δὲ δυνατοὶ ἦτε· τοῦτο καὶ εὐχόμεθα, τὴν ὑμῶν κατάρτισιν. ¹⁰ Διὰ τοῦτο ταῦτα ἀπὼν γράφω, ἵνα παρὼν μὴ ἀποτόμως χρήσωμαι κατὰ τὴν ἐξουσίαν ἣν ὁ κύριος ἔδωκέν μοι εἰς οἰκοδομὴν καὶ οὐκ εἰς καθαίρεσιν.

¹This is the third time I am coming to you. Any charge must be sustained by the evidence of two or three witnesses. ²I warned those who sinned before and all the others, and I warn them now while absent, as I did when present on my second visit, that if I come again I will not spare them—³since you desire proof that Christ is speaking in me. He is not weak in dealing with you, but is powerful in you. ⁴For he was crucified in weakness, but lives by the power of God. For we are weak in him, but in dealing with you we shall live with him by the power of God. ⁵Examine yourselves, to see whether you are holding to your faith. Test yourselves. Do you not realize that Jesus Christ is in you?—unless indeed you fail to meet the test! ⁶I hope you will find out that we have not failed. ⁷But we pray God that you may not do wrong—not that we may appear to have met the test, but that you may do what is right, though we may seem to have failed. ⁸For we cannot do anything against the truth, but only for the truth. ⁹For we are glad when we are weak and you are strong. What we pray for is your improvement. ¹⁰I write this while I am away from you, in order that when I come I may not have to be severe in my use of the authority which the Lord has given me for building up and not for tearing down.

The "third time" entails the idea of judgment day. This is corroborated by what Paul writes in 13:1b, which is a quotation from Deuteronomy 19:15 dealing with the validity of a charge in a court of law. Thus, he is announcing that his coming for the third time to the Corinthians will be to settle their differences as though they would be standing in the divine court. The seriousness of his threat is evident in that this time he is not going to "spare" (2 Cor 13:2) them as he did twice before.

> But I call God to witness against me—it was to spare (*pheidomai*) you that I refrained from coming to Corinth. (1:23)

> Though if I wish to boast, I shall not be a fool, for I shall be speaking the truth. But I refrain (*pheidomai*) from it, so that no one may think more of me than he sees in me or hears from me. (12:6)

> I told you before, and foretell you, as if I were present, the second time; and being absent now I write to them which heretofore have sinned, and to all other, that, if I come again, I will not spare (*ou pheisomai*). (13:2)[1]

---

[1] I opted for KJV in this case because RSV hides the accurate meaning of the original: "I warned those who sinned before and all the others, and I warn them now while

From the last instance, it is clear that the second "visit" *in absentia* is the letter itself in which he is warning them a second time. The threat becomes all the more potent when one realizes that the double warning will be used five chapters later in Galatians 5:21 in conjunction with inheriting the kingdom of God. In other words, Paul's third "coming" would be tantamount to the "coming" of the Lord to judge all; should he find the Corinthians failing, his verdict would be to condemn them to a full anathema as he did the "angel from heaven" as well as himself (1:8-9). That is why, earlier, he described his visit in negative terms (For I fear that perhaps I may come and find you not what I wish, and that you may find me not what you wish; 12:20a) and, a few verses later, he will unequivocally state: "I write this while I am away from you, in order that when I come I may not have to be severe (*apotomōs*; cutting, rigorous, decisive [as a judge would be]) in my use of the authority which the Lord has given me for building up and not for tearing down." (13:10)

Such a threat necessitates a last warning for the Corinthians to "test" themselves beforehand. Such warning one can readily hear in the repeated use of the root *dokim*— (test, proof, examine) no less than six times over five verses in addition to the one instance of the synonym *peiraz*— (examine):

> since you desire proof (*dokimēn*) that Christ is speaking in me. He is not weak in dealing with you, but is powerful in you (*en hymin*; among you). For he was crucified in weakness, but lives by the power of God. For we are weak in him, but in dealing with you we shall live with him by the power of God. Examine (*peirazete*) yourselves, to see whether you are holding to your faith. Test

---

absent, as I did when present on my second visit, that if I come again I will not spare them."

(*dokimazete*) yourselves. Do you not realize that Jesus Christ is in you (*en hymin*; among you)?—unless indeed you fail to meet the test (*adokimoi*)! I hope you will find out that we have not failed (*adokimoi*). But we pray God that you may not do wrong—not that we may appear to have met the test (*dokimoi*), but that you may do what is right, though we may seem to have failed (*adokimoi*). (vv.3-7)

Through Paul's gospel teaching, the Lord first *appeared* "weak" in the *apparent* "weakness" of his apostle who was entrusted, as a house manager (*oikonomos*), with the absolute authority. He could build up or tear down. Paul's assigned mission is to build up rather than to tear down (v.10). However, this time around, the "weak" Christ, who all along has been speaking through Paul (v.3a), is coming with "power" (v.3b) as the Lord who has been raised to live by the power of God (v.4a), again through the "words" of his apostle consigned in this letter (v.4b). As usual, Paul uses his "parental" authority for the good of his children *despite themselves*. In other words, he is challenging them thus: dare to prove our assessment of your behavior (12:21) wrong before the judging Lord by repenting *now* (13:7); dare to prove that you are the strong and we, the weak (v.9a); should you do so, you will have shown that "we cannot do anything against the truth, but only for the truth" (v.8) and, by the same token, that we are vindicated in that we "did not yield submission even for a moment, that the truth of the gospel might be preserved for you" (Gal 2:5). Such "parental" approach explains the fitting conclusion: "I write this while I am away from you, in order that when I come I may not have to be severe in my use of the authority which the Lord has given me for building up and not for tearing down." (2 Cor 13:10) That Paul is aiming at the Corinthians' "improvement" (*katartisin*; v.9b) is confirmed in that the same request (*katartizesthe*; mend your ways) is found two verses later (v.11) as part of the final farewell (vv.11-12).²

Vv. 11-14 ¹¹Λοιπόν, ἀδελφοί, χαίρετε, καταρτίζεσθε, παρακαλεῖσθε, τὸ αὐτὸ φρονεῖτε, εἰρηνεύετε, καὶ ὁ θεὸς τῆς ἀγάπης καὶ εἰρήνης ἔσται μεθ' ὑμῶν. ¹² Ἀσπάσασθε ἀλλήλους ἐν ἁγίῳ φιλήματι. Ἀσπάζονται ὑμᾶς οἱ ἅγιοι πάντες. ¹³ Ἡ χάρις τοῦ κυρίου Ἰησοῦ Χριστοῦ καὶ ἡ ἀγάπη τοῦ θεοῦ καὶ ἡ κοινωνία τοῦ ἁγίου πνεύματος μετὰ πάντων ὑμῶν.

> ¹¹*Finally, brethren, farewell. Mend your ways, heed my appeal, agree with one another, live in peace, and the God of love and peace will be with you.* ¹²*Greet one another with a holy kiss.* ¹³*All the saints greet you.* ¹⁴*The grace of the Lord Jesus Christ and the love of God and the fellowship of the Holy Spirit be with you all.*³

The final note (*loipon*; finally) is cast as a *torah* (five imperatives) that encompasses the content of both letters (1 and 2 Cor). The first imperative *khairete* is oddly rendered in both KJV and RSV as "farewell." In all its other occurrences in the Pauline corpus both KJV and RSV translate it into "rejoice" (Phil 2:18; 3:1; 4:4 [twice]; 1 Thess 5:16), which is also how JB understands it in our case (2 Cor 13:11). So Paul is inviting his hearers to remember the ultimate joy that is awaiting them in God's kingdom (1:24; 2:3). Therefore, they are to act in a manner that ensures their inheritance of that joy. In other words, they are to "mend their erroneous ways" (*katartizesthe*) through repentance (12:21). They would do that by heeding the third imperative, *parakaleisthe*: be *comforted* by heeding Paul's

---

² What makes the link even more forceful is that these are the only two instances of the root *katart—* in this letter.

³ RSV splits the Greek v.12 into two verses (12 and 13), which accounts for RSV's verse numbering up to 14 instead of 13.

exhortation, which is the double meaning of that verb.[4] Notice how this verb stands at the center of the *torah*: one is to heed the apostolic teaching. The fourth imperative is an invitation to be "at one" (*to avto phroneite*; think *the same* thing) which is the main point of 1 Corinthians, starting with 1:10 where, incidentally, one hears the only other instance of the root *katart*— in the Corinthian correspondence as well as the verb *parakalō* in an appeal to "sameness of mind": "I appeal to (*parakalō*) you, brethren, by the name of our Lord Jesus Christ, that all of you agree (*to avto legēte*; say the same thing) and that there be no dissensions among you, but that you be united (*katērtismenoi*; corrected, mended) in(to) *the same* (*tō avtō*) mind and *the same* (*tē avtē*) judgment." In so doing, the Corinthians will "live in peace" (*eirēnevete*). Peace, along with joy, is an essential facet of the coming Kingdom.[5] So the final *torah* is constructed as a chiasm ABCB'A': the first and the last are pointers to the Kingdom; the second and fourth are related to unity at the cost of correcting one's egotism; the sane behavior (B and B') that safeguards the inheritance of the Kingdom (A and A') is ensured inasmuch as the Corinthians abide by Paul's teaching (C). The importance of the oneness of mind in B and B' is further confirmed in that God is introduced as "the God of love and peace" (2 Cor 13:11b), a unique instance in the New Testament. It was coined for that specific purpose in the same way as the phrase "the Father of mercies and God of all comfort" (1:3b) was specifically coined to fit the immediate context (vv.3-

---

[4] See my comments earlier on the verb *parakalō* and the noun *paraklēsis* in my comments on 2 Cor 1:3-7.

[5] See my comments on 1 Cor 1:3 and also Rom 1:7; Gal 1:3; Phil 1:2; Col 1:2; 1 Thess 1:1; Philem 3, in my commentaries on those letters.

7). The thought of oneness is further corroborated in 13:12 concerning the "kiss" of brotherhood among "all" (RSV v.13).[6]

The special ending of the letter (v.14) fits as a reminder compendium of the entire Corinthian correspondence whose ultimate concern is the unity of all around God's gospel as expounded by Paul. Everything originates in the unwarranted divine love for all (v.14b; see especially Rom 5:1-11; 8:35-39). In order to underscore that this love is unwarranted, it was communicated as "grace" (free gift) through Jesus Christ (2 Cor 13:14a; see again Rom 5:1-11; 8:35-39). However, the tangible expression of that "grace-ful love," and thus the ultimate test as to whether it was received as it was intended, is the oneness of table fellowship (*koinōnia*; 2 Cor 13:14c) in any locality where the untamable "spirit" of God, which scattered to the four winds the rubble of Jerusalem and its temple (Isaiah; Jeremiah; Ezekiel), is made present through Paul's apostolic voice (2 Cor 4):

> Therefore remember that at one time you Gentiles in the flesh, called the uncircumcision by what is called the circumcision, which is made in the flesh by hands—remember that you were at that time separated from Christ, alienated from the commonwealth of Israel, and strangers to the covenants of promise, having no hope and without God in the world. But now in Christ Jesus you who once were far off have been brought near in the blood of Christ. For he is our peace, who has made us both one, and has broken down the dividing wall of hostility, by abolishing in his flesh the law of commandments and ordinances, that he might create in himself one new man in place of the two, so making peace, and might reconcile us both to God in one body through the cross, thereby bringing the hostility to an end. And he

---

[6] Concerning the "brotherly kiss" see my detailed comments on 1 Cor 16:20-22 in *C-1Cor*.

came and preached peace to you who were far off and peace to those who were near; *for through him [Christ] we both have access in one Spirit to the Father.* (Eph 2:11-18)

Further Reading

Commentaries and Studies

John Chrysostom, Homilies on 1 Corinthians in P. Schaff, ed., *The Nicene and Post-Nicene Fathers*. Grand Rapids, 1st Series, xii 1979: 271-420.

Garland, D. E. *2 Corinthians*. New American Commentary 29. Nashville, TN: Broadman & Holman, 1999.

Gooder, P. R. *Only the Third Heaven? 2 Corinthians 12.1-10 and Heavenly Ascent*. Library of NT Studies. London—New York : T&T Clark, 2006.

Goodwin, M. J. *Paul, Apostle of the Living God. Kerygma and Conversion in 2 Corinthians*. Harrisburg, PA: Trinity Press International, 2001.

Hall, D. R. *The Unity of the Corinthian Correspondence*. JSNT Supplement Series 251. London—New York: T&T Clark International, 2004.

Harris, M. J. *The Second Epistle to the Corinthians. A Commentary on the Greek Text*. New International Greek Testament Commentary. Grand Rapids—Cambridge UK: Eerdmans, 2005.

Hughes, R. K. *2 Corinthians. Power in Weakness*. Preaching the Word. Wheaton, IL : Crossway, 2006.

Keener, C. S. *1-2 Corinthians*. New Cambridge Bible Commentary. Cambridge, UK—New York: Cambridge University Press, 2005.

Lambrecht, J. *Second Corinthians*. Sacra Pagina, 8. Collegeville, MN: Liturgical Press, 2006.

Long, F. J. *Ancient Rhetoric and Paul's Apology. The Compositional Unity of 2 Corinthians*. SNTS Monograph Series 131. Cambridge, UK—New York: Cambridge University Press, 2004.

Matera, F. J. *II Corinthians. A Commentary.* New Testament Library. Louisville, KY—London: Westminster John Knox, 2003.

Roetzel, C. J. *2 Corinthians.* Abingdon New Testament Commentaries. Nashville, TN: Abingdon, 2007.

Thrall, M. E. *A Critical and Exegetical Commentary on the Second Epistle to the Corinthians.* International Critical Commentary. London—New York: T&T Clark International, 2004.

Vegge I. *2 Corinthians—a Letter about Reconciliation. A Psychological, Epistolographical and Rhetorical Analysis.* WUNT. Tübingen: Mohr Siebeck, 2008.

Wan, S.-K. *Power in Weakness. Conflict and Rhetoric in Paul's Second Letter to the Corinthians.* New Testament in Context. Harrisburg, PA: Trinity Press International, 2000.

Wright, N. T. *Paul for Everyone. 2 Corinthians.* Louisville, KY: Westminster John Knox, 2004.

Articles

Baker, W. R. "Did the Glory of Moses' Face Fade? A Reexamination of καταργέω in 2 Corinthians 3:7-18." *Bulletin for Biblical Research* 10 (2000) 1-15.

Bash, A. "A Psychodynamic Approach to the Interpretation of 2 Corinthians 10-13." *Journal for the Study of the New Testament* 83 (2001) 51-67.

Boers, H. "2 Corinthians 5:14-6:2: A Fragment of Pauline Christology." *Catholic Biblical Quarterly* 64 (2002) 527-547.

Brink. L. "A General's Exhortation to His Troops: Paul's Military Rhetoric in 2 Cor 10:1-11." *Biblische Zeitschrift* 49 (2005) 191-201.

Campbell, D. A. "An Anchor of Pauline Chronology: Paul's Flight from 'the Ethnarch of King Aretas' (2 Corinthians 11:32-33)." *Journal of Biblical Literature* 121 (2002) 279-302.

Duff, P. B. "Glory in the Ministry of Death. Gentile Condemnation and Letters of Recommendation in 2 Cor. 3:6-18." *Novum Testamentum* 46 (2004) 313-337.

Gignilliat, M. "A Servant Follower of the Servant: Paul's Eschatological Reading of Isaiah 44-66 in 2 Corinthians 5:14-6:10." *Horizons in Biblical Theology* 26 (2004) 98-124.

Gignilliat, M. "2 Corinthians 6:2: Paul's Eschatological 'Now' and Hermeneutical Invitation." *Westminster Theological Journal* 67 (2005) 147-161.

Glancy, J. A. "Boasting of Beatings (2 Corinthians 11:23-25)." *Journal of Biblical Literature* 123 (2004) 99-135.

Grelot, P. "Comment traduire 2 Cor 5,21?" *Revue Biblique* 113 (2006) 94-99.

Hester, D. A. "The Unity of 2 Corinthians: a test case for a rediscovered and re-invented rhetoric." *Neotestamentica* 33 (1999) 411-432.

Hock, A. "Christ Is the Parade: A Comparative Study of the Triumphal Procession in 2 Cor 2,14 and Col 2,15." *Biblica* 88 (2007) 110-119.

Jones, I. J. "Rhetorical Criticism and the Unity of 2 Corinthians: One 'Epilogue,' or More?" *New Testament Studies* 54 (2008) 496-524.

Joubert, S. "Religious reciprocity in 2 Corinthians 9:6-15: Generosity and gratitude as legitimate responses to the χάρις τοῦ θεοῦ." *Neotestamentica* 33 (1999) 7-90.

Kwon, Y.-G. " 'Αρραβών as Plegde in Second Corinthians." *New Testament Studies* 54 (2008) 525-541.

Lambrecht, J. "The Fool's Speech and Its Context: Paul's Particular Way of Arguing in 2 Cor 10-13." *Biblica* 82 (2001) 305-324.

Lambrecht, J. "Paul's Foolish Discourse. A reply to A. Pitta." *Ephemerides Theologicae Lovanienses* 83 (2007) 407-411.

Lambrecht, J. "A Matter of Method (II). 2 Cor 4,13 and the Recent Studies of Schenk and Campbell." *Ephemerides Theologicae Lovanienses* 86 (2010) 441-448.

Loubser, J. A. "Paul and the politics of apocalyptic mysticism: an exploration of 2 Cor 11:30-12:10." *Neotestamentica* 34 (2000) 191-206.

McDermott, J. M. "II Cor.3: the Old and New Covenants." *Gregorianum* 87 (2006) 25-63.

Roetzel, C. J. "The Language of War (2 Cor. 10:1-6) and the Language of Weakness (2 Cor. 11:21b-13:10)." *Biblical Interpretation* 17 (2009) 77-99.

Welborn, L. L. "Paul's Appeal to the Emotions in 2 Corinthians 1.1-2.13; 7.5-16." *Journal for the Study of the New Testament* 82 (2001) 21-60.

www.ingramcontent.com/pod-product-compliance
Lightning Source LLC
Chambersburg PA
CBHW031141160426
43193CB00008B/208